The Politics
of Story
in Victorian
Social Fiction

The Politics
of Story
in Victorian
Social Fiction

Rosemarie Bodenheimer

Cornell University Press

ITHACA AND LONDON

CORNELL UNIVERSITY PRESS GRATEFULLY ACKNOWLEDGES
A GRANT FROM THE ANDREW W. MELLON FOUNDATION THAT
AIDED IN BRINGING THIS BOOK TO PUBLICATION.

First published 1988 by Cornell University Press.

International Standard Book Number 0-8014-2099-7
Library of Congress Catalog Card Number 87-17313

Printed in the United States of America

*Librarians: Library of Congress cataloging information
appears on the last page of the book.*

*The paper in this book is acid-free and meets the guidelines for
permanence and durability of the Committee on Production Guidelines
for Book Longevity of the Council on Library Resources.*

In memory of my mother,
Brigitte Marianne Bodenheimer

Contents

Acknowledgments

Two gifts of time have made it possible to complete this book. I am grateful to the American Council of Learned Societies for a fellowship that allowed me to begin the project in 1981–82 and to Boston College for a Faculty Fellowship that gave me the freedom to write a draft through to the end.

I am indebted as well to the colleagues and friends who have contributed directly to this study. Special thanks are due to Catherine Gallagher, who generously gave me draft chapters of her yet unpublished *Industrial Reformation of English Fiction* during the early stages of my work. More than twenty years of Anne Ferry's unfailing support and friendship lie behind these pages; as always her reading pointed me directly toward the questions I had yet to answer. Harriet Ritvo also read the entire manuscript and made invaluable suggestions for strengthening it. Dayton Haskin and Christopher Wilson gave me good advice and encouragement about sections they read. Peter Weiler provided me with historical bibliographies and enlarged the scope of the project through our collaboration in courses on British social history and fiction. I am grateful in a more general way to Judith Wilt and Carolyn Williams for bringing me into discussion with other Victorian scholars, and to my family for the pleasure in writing which has been my inheritance.

The Gaskell section of Chapter 1 draws on an article that

originally appeared in *Nineteenth-Century Fiction*, © 1979 by The
Regents of the University of California. It is reprinted from vol.
34 , no. 3 (December 1979), pp. 281–301 , by permission of the
Regents, which is gratefully acknowledged.

Above all I thank my husband and colleague, Andrew Von
Hendy. His many generous readings, his wide knowledge, and
his editorial gifts have helped me to clarify the argument of
every part; his faith has sustained the whole.

R. B.

The Politics
of Story
in Victorian
Social Fiction

Introduction

This book is about the responses to social change expressed in the arrangements and directions of mid-Victorian novels. The "politics of story" of my title reflects the assumption on which the book is grounded: that it is in the shape and movement of narrative rather than in its proclaimed social ideology that we may find the "politics" of a novel in its deepest, most interesting, most problematical expression. Since a novel traces out a model of motion and transformation in time—or conflicting models within a single text—it can be understood as political in at least two initial ways. First, its plots define and delimit imagined possibilities for social thought, action, and change. Second, a narrative may be called "politic" because it evokes both social wishes and social fears and then negotiates among them, establishing fictional paths through highly charged ideological territories. If the paths prove to be circular, blocked, or discontinuous, they only mark out the terrain in greater clarity and detail.[1]

---

1. For a theoretical exposition of such a critical position, see Fredric Jameson, *The Political Unconscious: Narrative as a Socially Symbolic Act* (Ithaca, 1981). Jameson's development of Marxist critical theory assumes that "the aesthetic act is itself ideological, and the production of aesthetic or narrative form is to be seen as an ideological act in its own right, with the function of inventing imaginary or formal 'solutions' to unresolvable social contradictions" (p. 79). This book, though it is not grounded on Jameson's theory, is sympathetic to his enterprise.

4   THE POLITICS OF STORY IN VICTORIAN SOCIAL FICTION

When I began this book, I wanted to know what kinds of stories Victorian novelists invented and adapted when they wrote about contemporary social changes, and whether any recognizable kinds of plots and rhetorical strategies come regularly into play when particular issues are addressed. And I wanted to see how groups of stories trace out models of social change, reform, transformation, cycle, or stasis. While any Victorian novel could be profitably subjected to such questions, my scope is limited to the subgenre that has come to be known as the industrial or social-problem novel: work distinguished by its focus on specific social problems raised during the process of industrialization.[2] These novels set themselves in a dramatic way to the task of giving fictional shape to social questions that were experienced as new, unpredictable, without closure. Their story lines offer a particularly well-focused arena of inquiry because they must bring order and meaning to situations characterized exactly by their lack of established historical meaning, or by acute conflicts about the meanings assigned to them in public discourse.

The narratives I consider are full of description and dialogue about the factory system, industrial and rural poverty, working-class politics, and the plight of women; they link themselves directly with the condition-of-England debates that preoccupied so many public-minded Victorians during that critical period. Yet those public matters are necessarily reimagined as they are

2. The English social novel was first defined by the French critic Louis Cazamian in 1903 in *The Social Novel in England, 1830–1850*, trans. Martin Fido (London, 1973). Kathleen Tillotson identified the social-problem novel as a subgenre practiced by Disraeli, Kingsley, and Gaskell in *Novels of the Eighteen-Forties* (Oxford, 1954). Core groups of novels in the subgenre were also established in two essays published in 1958: Arnold Kettle, "The Early Victorian Social-Problem Novel," rpt. in *From Dickens to Hardy*, ed. Boris Ford (London, 1963), and Raymond Williams, "The Industrial Novels," in *Culture and Society, 1780–1950* (New York, 1958). For books that return to Cazamian to draw a wider range of minor fictions into the subgenre, see Ivan Melada, *The Captain of Industry in English Fiction, 1821–1871* (Albuquerque, 1970); Ivanka Kovačević, *Fact into Fiction: English Literature and the Industrial Scene, 1750–1850* (Leicester, 1975); and Joseph Kestner, *Protest and Reform: The British Social Narrative by Women, 1827–1867* (Madison, 1985). My own choices of texts for discussion have been made from within the subgenre as defined by these works, and are not meant to constitute an argument about its scope.

shaped to the forms and conventions of fiction, and the stories that contain them may reveal a good deal more than the controversies do about the tensions and contradictions in Victorian visions of social order. To invent a story that comes to rest in some kind of resolution, a novelist is forced to set both formulated and unexamined assumptions into action. The shape of experience that results tells us about the limits of that writer's imagination and about the pressures that allow or obstruct the depiction of significant social change. If we group novels that imagine similar patterns of action, it also becomes possible to distinguish common stories that attest to shared channels and impasses in social thought.

The center of my interest lies, then, in just those fictional stories and strategies that have often been understood by social and cultural critics as deflections from the delineation of social crisis or as evasions of its implications. My working assumption has been that Victorian social-problem novels are valuable in our time not primarily because they contain material that is continuous with nonfictional documentations of industrialization and its effects but because they allow us access to the minds of observant, sensitive, and articulate members of the middle class as they confronted troubling and unanswerable questions. For us the novels may be less about factory conditions or the status of trade unions than about the patterns of contradiction and paradox which characterize the formal fantasies of people living through a period of unprecedented social change. Once articulated, the content of those patterns points to a middle-class crisis of self-definition: insofar as the social-problem novels can be treated as a group, they display conflict about the nature and diversity of a newly empowered and newly fragmented middle class as they attempt to reimagine the roles that it should play in the maintenance of social order.

By discussing the novels in this way, I mean both to extend the critical history peculiar to the social-problem novels and to alter the predispositions and assumptions that have characterized earlier approaches to them. The most significant line of commentary was initiated by Raymond Williams in 1958, when he identified and named a core group of industrial novels in a discussion that set the terms for much of the subsequent work by critics with social orientations.[3] Sifting through that tradition, with all that it has done to trace social ideologies in fiction, the reader emerges with two recurrent themes, each an implicit accusation of failure. First, the middle-class Victorian novelists failed despite their sympathy to imagine or see the lives of working-class characters, or to recognize the industrial labor force as a rising class developing solidarity and political autonomy. The fear of social revolution resulted, the argument goes, in working-class portraits that alternate between recoil and sentimentality. Second, the novelists failed to find fictional solutions that would contain and acknowledge the social observation and criticism embodied in the expository sections of their narratives. This critique often takes form as a complaint that large public issues are abandoned in favor of personal or private plot resolutions, or that fictional solutions are imagined only outside of the industrial order itself.

Such observations do describe what happens in the narratives. But they derive from certain assumptions: that social-problem novels were intended, or should have been intended, as portraits of a rising working class; and that a private plot line cannot contain public issues. Both of those assumptions make the relationship between fiction and social life too literal. The emphasis on distortions in the portrayal of working-class life may overlook other social concerns that shape the structure of the fiction in ways to which a working-class character contributes. Like all other characters in fiction, a worker cannot be said to point to a "real" working class; the portrait is made from a mixture of social knowledge, social wish, documentary material,

3. Williams, *Culture and Society*, pp. 87–109. Works in this tradition that I have found most useful and stimulating are Patrick Brantlinger, *The Spirit of Reform: British Literature and Politics, 1832–1867* (Cambridge, Mass., 1977); P. J. Keating, *The Working Classes in Victorian Fiction* (London, 1971); Igor Webb, *From Custom to Capital: The English Novel and the Industrial Revolution* (Ithaca, 1981); and John Lucas, "Mrs. Gaskell and Brotherhood," in *Tradition and Tolerance in Nineteenth-Century Fiction*, ed. David Howard, John Lucas, and John Goode (London, 1966). See also David Craig, *The Real Foundations: Literature and Social Change* (London, 1973), and Sheila M. Smith, *The Other Nation: The Poor in English Novels of the 1840's and 1850's* (Oxford, 1980).

and literary convention, invoked or overturned. The character is significant as it is imagined in relation to other characters representing class configurations, as an indicator of the writer's model of social order and government. Similarly, a "private" plot may be a writer's most revealing account of a public problem: it traces out a model of imaginable action within an implicit construct of social life, creating a fantasy about the manner and direction of social change in time.

In *The Industrial Reformation of English Fiction*, Catherine Gallagher has taken essential steps to reshape discussion of social-problem novels.[4] Gallagher presents the novels as structures in which insoluble problems of social theory raised in the public debates about industrialization are formalized and made visible. Rather than revealing middle-class fears or demonstrating the gaps between social criticism and fictive resolution, the discontinuities in the fiction are, as she shows, inherent in the debate itself; even the measurement of public against private spheres is a strategy the novels share with arguments prevalent in nonfictional discourse. Gallagher's work reopens the case for social-problem novels by directing attention away from their overt social or political affiliations and toward the ideological determinants of their fictional forms and the challenges those determinants pose to realistic representation itself. Her methodology releases the novels from the tests of "realism" against which they have been measured according to the programs of their various earlier critics: while stressing the novels' continuities with nonfictional discourse, she makes it clear that their historical value does not depend on ways in which they either capture or distort the realities of one class experience or another.

More firmly than any of the critics who have described the social-problem subgenre, I have taken the position that the fictional "real" is both contained and created in the structural arrangements of its fantasy.[5] Consequently I have grouped the

4. Catherine Gallagher, *The Industrial Reformation of English Fiction: Social Discourse and Narrative Form, 1832–1867* (Chicago, 1985).

5. For a brief and useful theoretical development of the relationship between the text and the "Real," see Jameson, *Political Unconscious*, pp. 80–82.

novels I discuss according to recurring patterns of narrative, setting them primarily in relation to one another rather than in contexts provided by nonfictional discourses. As the groupings emerged, fantasies of reform or reconciliation proved, not surprisingly, to be located in three major narrative structures: in the characters and stories of women, in rhetorical appeals to nature, and in models of history which transcend politics. A second kind of grouping became evident as well: novels by middle-class women writers featuring the social development of middle-class heroines in narratives that engage one another in critical argument. Female characters in these novels are not simply asocial reconciling figures or pastoral equivalents, as they tend to be in works by men; rather their stories are about processes of education and action which bring them directly into the social fray even as they provide the novel's center for a separated vision of the social order. Thus, while both men and women writers participated in the development of the social-problem subgenre, women writers also made a distinct contribution of texts in which struggles with concepts of class and gender are intimately intertwined.[6]

Those different ways of grouping explain the major divisions of this book. Part One, "Women's Fates and Factory Questions," is a study of romantic plots centering on middle-class heroines in industrial novels written by middle-class women. Providing the story lines and the main arenas of activity in the narratives, these private plots are the fictional conduits for imagining the nature of social government and the possible directions of social change. They fall into two story patterns, each of which is shaped in response to a separate set of class tensions in the industrial order. One pattern, featuring an actively interventionist heroine, explores the implications of paternalism as a model of government in both the public and the domestic realms. In chapter 1 the mixtures of fantasy in that pattern are traced in two social-problem novels of Frances Trollope and in Charlotte

---

6. Ellen Moers makes the point that women writers created and sustained the factory novel, in *Literary Women* (New York, 1976), p. 23. The predominance of women writers in the social-problem subgenre is a major thesis of Kestner's *Protest and Reform*, which collects and comments on a wide range of novels.

Brontë's *Shirley*; Elizabeth Gaskell's *North and South* emerges as a dismantling of the paternalist assumptions that underlie the plots of her predecessors.

The second story pattern addresses the struggle for social power between the landed gentry and the newly ascendant industrial entrepreneurs of the north. Conventionally shaped as the education of a passive middle-class heroine with pretensions to social status, this plot develops the differences between moral and social power by attempting to define the concepts of gentility and vulgarity. Chapter 2 traces that story line from Elizabeth Stone's *William Langshawe, the Cotton Lord* through Geraldine Jewsbury's *Marian Withers* to its critical inversion in George Eliot's *Felix Holt the Radical*. In both chapters I am particularly interested in the way that middle-class heroines, because of their intermediary position in the hierarchy of class, serve as fictional vehicles with special resources for putting contradictory social ideas into motion.

Part Two, "Narrative History and the Social Record," turns away from romantic plot lines toward Romantic rhetoric. While the earlier chapters show female characters enacting their (often contradictory) ideals within the social context, the novels discussed here create pastoral realms and mythic histories that function as alternatives or correctives to courses of thought and action fixed in the social order. Fictional appeals to nature or to a value-laden past are particularly open to dismissal as escapist or nostalgic fantasy. But in the dialectic of narrative argument, they can function as genuine alternatives: not as better worlds elsewhere but as challenges to the assumptions of a dominant social theory. Chapter 3 groups three novels in which the creation of a pastoral "place" is a chief strategy of social argument—Charles Dickens's *Oliver Twist*, Charles Kingsley's *Alton Locke*, and Elizabeth Gaskell's *Ruth*—and looks at the special connection between the use of pastoral and the problem of social determinism. In the texture of these narratives, post-Wordworthian pastoral writing emerges as a complex arena of resistance to the environmentalist view of character rather than as a univocal gesture toward a utopian place.

The final chapter collects three major novels that grapple

through fictional forms with the idea of history itself: Benjamin Disraeli's *Sybil*, Dickens's *Hard Times*, and, once again, Eliot's *Felix Holt*. All of these writers set two kinds of temporality against each other, creating a continuum between a valued past and an imagined future which excludes the fragmented and forgetful politics of the present. In the process of working out fantasies of continuity they all betray an essential despair about "progress" in ways that are not merely nostalgic or backward-looking. And in their emphases on the moral power of narrative, they implicitly revise the status of social-problem fictions as instruments of social intervention: in these works the novel form itself becomes a recuperation and a repository of history.

Placing minor works and flawed narratives next to greater and more central ones, this grouping calls attention to common conceptual struggles in very disparate writers, as well as to ways in which the novels exerted formal pressures on one another. It is also meant to raise the question of critical assessment. Bad novels unfold particularly clear examples of social fantasy; better ones may rely on similar fantasies even as they criticize and complicate them. In Part One I outline story patterns as they develop from initial appearances in revealing but escapist forms to more complex renditions in later works that examine the fantasies of their predecessors with critical eyes. In the discussions of Part Two similar connections are suggested among novels that do not form such clear lines of progression or influence.

The question of quality is, of course, a difficult one. Many of the stories in social-problem novels work unwittingly against the social claims of their narrators. Such gaps are symptoms of conflict that are not necessarily signs of failure: Elizabeth Stone shares the symptom with Charles Dickens, but *Hard Times* is a good novel and *William Langshawe, the Cotton Lord* is not. Moreover, serious novels invent fantasy reconciliations and escapes as surely as bad ones do. But it is possible to discriminate among fantasies: there are those that erase and deny what they transform and those that articulate in the very act of fantasy the pressures of an ineradicable social predicament. A narrative that forgets what it has said, or that revises the terms in which it presents its subject, can be charged with failure: its fictional

inconsequence is a refusal to credit the stubbornness of the ✓
issues it has raised. A serious novel—no matter how unshapely
its narrative—maintains a continuous attention to the intracta-
bilities of its subject. Discriminations of this kind form part of
the commentary in the chapters that follow.

Some of the peculiarities in the ordering of this book require
further comment. The novels grouped in each chapter were
written in different decades or at significantly different points in
the social turmoil that waxed and waned during the years
between 1832 and 1867. Each book reflects its immediate period
in the way it shapes or amends the pattern it shares with the
others in its chapter. A case for the development of this
short-lived subgenre lies in the structure of each chapter: not a
clear case of change decade by decade,[7] but rather a look at the
way different story patterns within the subgenre work themselves out in successive books by different writers. Needless to
say, these patterns overlap, not only with one another but with
other novels that do not fall into the social-problem category.

I attend to some of the overlap by discussing certain novels in
more than one chapter. *Felix Holt the Radical*, which includes both
a critique of gentility and a complex evocation of a historical ideal,
warrants two separate readings, in chapters 2 and 4. Frances
Trollope's *Michael Armstrong* appears as a version of pastoral as
well as a heroine's tale. Other connections are made in passing,
while some are present without any elaboration: one might, for
example, set the discussion of *Shirley*'s historical frame in chapter
1 next to the versions of history that emerge in chapter 4, or
pursue the collapsed romance of female paternalism in Dickens's
Louisa Gradgrind. The recourse to suggestion also holds for
industrial novels that are not given a full reading. The most
significant of these novels are Elizabeth Gaskell's *Mary Barton* and
Charlotte Elizabeth Tonna's *Helen Fleetwood*—the only two industrial novels that center themselves in the experience of a
working-class family as it encounters the pressures of factory life

7. Accounts of change and development decade by decade are organizing
ideas in Brantlinger, *Spirit of Reform;* Gallagher, *Industrial Reformation;* and
Kestner, *Protest and Reform*.

in Manchester.[8] Their plots are nevertheless shaped in recognizable conventional modes: *Mary Barton* hovers around the discussion of social rise stories in chapter 2; and *Helen Fleetwood*, wrought in the patterns of Evangelical conversion stories, figures briefly here in the chapter on pastoral arguments.

Although I concentrate on social arguments and events primarily as they are reimagined in fiction, I do assume some familiarity with the movements that shaped the history of the period framed by the two reform bills, and especially with the turbulent campaigns of the 1830s and 1840s.[9] The hard-fought Reform Bill of 1832, which extended the franchise to a limited number of propertyholders and increased parliamentary representation of the commercial and manufacturing interests, figures prominently in *Sybil* and *Felix Holt*. The first controversial piece of legislation to emerge from the newly constituted parliament, the New Poor Law of 1834, is a direct target of attack in Trollope's *Jessie Phillips*, *Oliver Twist*, and *Sybil*. Its utilitarian principles of social control, its implicit punishment of poverty through confinement in union workhouses, and the national scope of its administration are, however, at issue on philosophical grounds in many of the novels, notably *Hard Times*.[10] The difficult history of trade unionism, marked by governmental repression and by the development of the large-scale strike as a collective strategy of labor, is replicated in its fictional history: more or less lurid depictions of union activities appear in *William Langshawe*, *Sybil*, *Alton Locke*, and *Hard Times*; only in *North and South* does the union come into its own as a legitimate organization.[11]

8. Excellent readings of *Helen Fleetwood* and *Mary Barton* appear in chaps. 2 and 3 of Gallagher, *Industrial Reformation*. I have commented on *Mary Barton* in "Private Griefs and Public Acts in *Mary Barton*," *Dickens Studies Annual* 9 (1981), 281–301.

9. An overview of political reform and protest movements in the 1830s and 1840s can be found in Asa Briggs, *The Age of Improvement, 1783–1867* (New York, 1979), pp. 236–343.

10. Important discussions of the 1834 Poor Law appear in J. L. Hammond and Barbara Hammond, *The Bleak Age* (1934; rpt. Baltimore, 1947); Karl Polanyi, *The Great Transformation* (1944; rpt. Boston, 1957); and Gertrude Himmelfarb. *The Idea of Poverty: England in the Early Industrial Age* (New York, 1984).

11. For brief accounts of trade unionism, see Briggs, *Age of Improvement*, pp. 286–304; and G. D. H. Cole, *British Working-Class Politics, 1832–1914* (London,

Other forms of working-class activity play more central roles in the fiction. The industrial action in *Shirley* is based on a famous incident in the history of Luddite machine-breaking early in the century.[12] *Sybil* and *Alton Locke* give extended, respectfully critical accounts of Chartism, the long and complex working-class campaign for political power through manhood suffrage which had its final flare and failure in April 1848.[13] The Factory Movement or Ten Hours Movement, a Tory-Radical alliance of aristocrats, churchmen, and enlightened factory owners on behalf of the factory population, sponsored a series of increasingly effective laws to regulate the hours and conditions of factory work;[14] it provided the documentary material for *Michael Armstrong* and the propaganda that provoked defenses of the factory system in *William Langshawe* and *Marian Withers*.

Most pervasive of all, however, are the fictional renderings of shifts in status and realignments of power among the ruling classes. The fading aristocrat, the gentleman or lady rooted in the power conferred by inherited property, and the rising business entrepreneur appear in some central configuration of each novel. Through them the systemic philosophy of laissez-faire political economy, the rationalism of utilitarian social reform, and the local protectionism of the paternalist are moved into conflict and shaped into plot. How they are mobilized and how they are separated, combined, and reconstituted as social fantasy will be the central concerns of this investigation.

1941). For unions in fiction, see Patrick Brantlinger, "The Case against Trade Unions in Early Victorian Fiction," *Victorian Studies* 13 (1969), 37–52.

12. The great account of Luddism appears in chap. 14 of E. P. Thompson, *The Making of the English Working Class* (New York, 1963). For a good discussion of Luddism in relation to *Shirley*, see Webb, *From Custom to Capital*, pp. 124–142.

13. Major studies of Chartism appear in *Chartist Studies*, ed. Asa Briggs (London, 1959); Dorothy Thompson, *The Chartists: Popular Politics in the Industrial Revolution* (New York, 1984); and Himmelfarb, *Idea of Poverty*, pp. 253–269.

14. See J. T. Ward, *The Factory Movement, 1830–1855* (London, 1962). For a useful summary of the Factory Acts and their consequences, see Wanda Fraiken Neff, *Victorian Working Women* (New York, 1966) pp. 64–76.

PART ONE

Women's Fates and Factory Questions

The difficulties of the passage from daughterhood to womanhood shape the stories of most Victorian heroines. When their fathers and lovers are factory owners, magistrates, or political reformers, the conflicts and choices of the daughters also provide the structure of the novels' commentaries on industry and politics. The chapters in Part One group novels in which the crisis of middle-class self-definition is most directly expressed through stories that place a young middle-class heroine at odds with the ruling social assumptions of her neighborhood, making her moral development and romantic settlement dependent on her engagement with conflicts of class. Both as consequences and as critics of their fathers' worlds, daughters do the fictional work of reform: they attempt to remedy the injustices of their fathers or to provide missing elements in their lovers' assumptions of social power. No matter how conventionally they come to resolution, these romantic plots often provide the novel's sole arena for the testing of active social change.

Two quite distinct patterns of narrative emerge from the group of heroines' tales. In the first, the social activity of the heroine is associated with an investigation of paternalist power structures and with the corresponding question of a woman's role in that model of social order. This story responds directly to the plight of the working class and presents its heroine as an intermediary, with attributes and sympathies that link her both to workers and to men in her own class. The second pattern, while it may display concern for the condition of the working class in passages of discussion, is really a story about the quite different class tension between the traditional landed gentry and the rising business entrepreneur. The heroine's role in this pattern is the more conventionally passive one of choosing—or existing—between two men who place the standards of gentility against the energies of enterprise. If a search for adequate models of social government animates the first story group, the second is charged with tensions collected about the prospect of social mobility and ascent.

As Ellen Moers has pointed out, the factory novel in England was initiated and sustained by women writers.[1] In all of the stories collected here, middle-class heroines are the creations of middle-class women writers; although Disraeli, Kingsley, and Dickens also locate special moral activity in female characters, they do not in the same way hang their plots on the development of their heroines. Kingsley's Eleanor Staunton and Disraeli's Sybil Gerard are idealized and symbolic figures of paternalist benevolence. Dickens's Louisa Gradgrind participates briefly in both the story patterns outlined here without being "of" them; in this and many other ways *Hard Times* draws on narrative patterns made familiar by earlier factory novels.[2] The special position of the woman writer who enters the field of discourse

1. Moers, *Literary Women*, p. 23.

2. *Alton Locke*, *Sybil*, and *Hard Times* are discussed in chaps. 3 and 4. And for a different way of connecting the fictional functions of heroines in Disraeli, Gaskell, and Eliot, see Ruth Bernard Yeazell, "Why Political Novels Have Heroines: *Sybil*, *Mary Barton*, and *Felix Holt*," *Novel* 18 (1985), 126–144. Yeazell offers finely focused readings of the specific ways courtship stories deflect anxiety about male class violence. Her argument that stories of pure and passive heroines serve to cover or contain representations of dangerous aggression does depend, however, on the tradition of separating "public" from "private" stories in the reading of industrial novels.

about industrialism is represented, in her novels, by the complex mediations of her heroine.

To say that the heroines of these novels are central vehicles for storymaking about troubling class issues is not, however, to assert that factory novels by women are "really" (or "only") forms in which the oppression or suppression of women may be expressed in the guise of attention to issues of class. That model of feminist discussion, raised by Moers,[3] is to my mind a partial assessment of the ambition and achievement of the writers who joined and altered the public debate through their novels. Even less adequate are discussions of women's factory novels as expressions of womanly sympathy and charity which provided a feminizing cover for the audacity of going into print at all.[4] I propose, rather, a way of thinking about middle-class heroines' tales in terms that emphasize their flexible capacity to embody necessarily contradictory ideas about class and government or gentility and work. Through these tales, women writers represent the range of interconnected social dilemmas that constitute their own ideological membership in the Victorian middle class.

Occupying a peculiar position between classes and political philosophies, the middle-class heroine allows fantasies of good social government or good social ascent to be put in motion. She is exempted by her sex from obedience to the "natural" laws of supply and demand that, according to classical political economists, regulated the marketplace and its human contracts. Her actions can therefore represent alternatives to that philosophy without directly attacking its precepts or interfering with its

---

3. Moers argues that feminist impulses were channeled into social writing on behalf of oppressed workers or slaves during "the epic age" of women's writing (*Literary Women*, pp. 13–41). Elaine Showalter agrees; in *A Literature of Their Own: British Women Novelists from Brontë to Lessing* (Princeton, 1977), she says: "Protest fiction represented another projection of female experience onto another group" (p. 28). A good example of this view in practice can be found in the richly metaphorical reading of *Shirley* in Sandra M. Gilbert and Susan Gubar, *The Madwoman in the Attic: The Woman Writer and the Nineteenth-Century Literary Imagination* (New Haven, 1979), pp. 372–398.
4. Donald D. Stone articulates that idea in the context of his discussion of Romantic willfulness, suggesting that social reform alleviated women's guilt about the willful act of writing: *The Romantic Impulse in Victorian Fiction* (Cambridge, Mass., 1980), pp. 135–144.

power. Her exemption arises, of course, from the complementary ideology that marked out the separate woman's sphere as a haven of harmony and morality untainted by the competitive ethos of the marketplace.[5] Yet some of these novels exploit the exemption in order to challenge images of domestic tranquillity, endowing their heroines with a power to act in the public realm unburdened by the political economy that enslaves the minds of their male associates. Such a heroine may offer an active and powerful alternative to laissez-faire models of government by providing a story of efficacious individual moral action. The extent to which a writer presents that activity as enclosed within a separate world of female consciousness is the test of her ideological limits, however, for it defines the extent to which she finally relies on a paternalist model of order.

The middle-class heroine is also in a structurally double relation to working-class characters, figuring the latent social power of both classes while robbing it of its destructive power. When she acts on behalf of workers, she expresses a ruling-class power to serve and dominate through paternalist interventions. Insofar as her life is framed and confined by father-governors, it is formally analogous to the lives of the working poor. Her actions and feelings may therefore "mean" both as exemplary middle-class responses to industrial suffering and as articulations or justifications of working-class politics. Since the activity of one or two heroines is far less threatening than the collective activity of workers, the heroine's rebellions may both grant the terms in which power structures are condemned from below and channel them into isolated figures who come to rest in marriages within the middle class.

Oscillations between sympathy for a revitalized paternalism and sympathy for its rebellious antithesis characterize the stories of Frances Trollope, Charlotte Brontë, and Elizabeth Gaskell. Their novels fall into a continuum marked by deliberate revisions of preceding works as well as by the changing temper of

5. I am indebted to studies that integrate questions about the woman's sphere with issues of class conflict: Judith Lowder Newton, *Women, Power, and Subversion: Social Strategies in British Fiction, 1778–1860* (Athens, Ga., 1981) and Gallagher, "The Family versus Society," in *Industrial Reformation*, pp. 113–126.

industrial relations between 1840 and 1855. The novels by Elizabeth Stone, Geraldine Jewsbury, and George Eliot lay out a comparable sequence of redefinition and revision within a story pattern that uses the female figure in a somewhat different alignment: as the link and the center of conflict that defines the problem of social mobility within parts of the middle class. Anxiety about underemployment, idleness, and education links the stories of workers and women; the newly ornamental lives of genteel women and the newly threatened employment patterns of the industrial working class raise overlapping clusters of fear. Because of that (often submerged) linkage, these novels raise with a special intensity the frequently fictionalized problem of what a heroine is to do with her life.

The question is treated, or evaded, in a story directed to the conflict between gentility and work. The heroine's choice between luxurious idleness and earnest work constitutes for her, and for her reader, an education in the value of social aspiration; at the same time her story may stand in for the evolution of the working class as a whole. These novels channel anxiety about the threat of social power accumulated through industry, as those in chapter 1 tame and remold the possibility of rebellious social action. The placement of protest or education in the stories of heroines can, then, serve a wide variety of purposes. Through them the novelist enters the public discourse about industrial change; through them she lays claim to the special vision afforded by the woman's "swing" position in the hierarchy of class and shapes a story that takes that vision to its limits.

1 The Romance of the Female Paternalist

The revival of social paternalism was a dominant feature of the Victorian effort to counteract the consequences of a competitive market economy. Paternalist ideology reasserted a belief that relations between employers and workers should be constituted in moral as well as economic terms and that society was properly seen as a hierarchical order in which the wealthy and powerful would protect the poor in return for their deference and duty.[1] While the ideal of such a social order was frequently evoked in images of local government exemplified by the kindly squire and the wise parson, the political activities of social paternalists in the 1830s and 1840s were in fact interventionist and essentially defensive. In the attempts of Factory Movement agitators to regulate the hours and conditions of children's and women's factory work, for example, the ideal of social protection from above provided the rhetorical armory for arguments that aimed to insert humanitarian regulations in a capitalist marketplace that was imagined to run according to autonomous rules of supply and demand.[2] The passion of early Victorian pater-

1. The many strands and contradictions in the Victorian concept of paternalism are clearly described by David Roberts in *Paternalism in Early Victorian England* (New Brunswick, N.J., 1979).
2. For a description of the expansion in paternalist rhetoric during the course of the Factory Movement, see Gallagher, *Industrial Reformation*, pp. 121–122.

nalism was engendered, then, under the omnipresent shadow of "the system."

Paternalism made its theoretical claim as the natural order of harmony in social relations—an order temporarily and mistakenly broken by the industrialization and capitalization of the marketplace. In practice, paternalism was a rescue operation within the terms of capitalist organization.[3] Precisely because the laws of supply and demand created human injustices, acts of paternalist intervention could be justified as mitigators of evils intrinsic to the system. Defining himself through the role of rescuer, the paternalist accepts a secondary and mediating status that his social philosophy denies.

In Frances Trollope's *Michael Armstrong* (1840) and *Jessie Phillips* (1844), Charlotte Brontë's *Shirley* (1849), and Elizabeth Gaskell's *North and South* (1855), that unarticulated division between the social model and the interventionist practice of paternalism is formally embodied in a story pattern that I have called "the romance of the female paternalist." In simplified outline, the pattern goes like this: A wealthy and intelligent young heroine is awakened to a crisis of class conflict in which the ruling men in her neighborhood, relying on laissez-faire arguments, are perpetrating crimes of injustice or neglect against the working class. Learning to see through their rhetoric, the heroine is horrified by its implications, and goes into action to rescue the oppressed or to reform the minds of the oppressors. Specially empowered because she knows more than anyone around her, she also acts publicly and boldly, driven by the moral force of chivalry in defense of the weak. Her attempts at rescue may succeed in one or two individual cases, although of course she cannot touch "the system"; her attempts to educate middle-class men may result in the tempering of their business practices. Her most resounding success comes, finally, in the form of symbolic romance: political action leads her to her mate,

3. In *Paternalism in Early Victorian England* Roberts notes the frequent intersection of paternalist principle with laissez-faire practice (p. 7), and his book demonstrates the range of ways in which capitalist and paternalist motives and strategies were interconnected.

and to a symbolic marriage that bends the issues of the narrative into a wish for revised models of social government.

Established as a romantic melodrama in the novels of Trollope, complicated and undermined by Brontë, and liberally revised by Gaskell, this story pattern places active paternalist intervention in the hands of middle-class heroines while assigning proprietorship of "the system" to male manufacturers. The heroine's activities create a moral counterpoint to the apparently agentless system, revealing in the process how the laws of the market are used to justify manufacturers' forms of social control. Yet the contradictions between the systemic view and the attribution of personal responsibility are never resolved. Instead, the action of women within the terms of a male-dominated world reduplicates the activity of paternalism as a secondary rescue operation surrounded by an impervious course of political and economic events. In such contexts the story of female paternalism is a romance because it is a fantasy of intervention without power; it wishes for protectionist forms of class relations free from the taint of male power or social dominance.

While the story of untainted intervention fuels the progress of the socially active heroine, the effect of her story is threatened by its placement within a related cross fire raised by the ideology of woman's sphere. According to that doctrine, women could affect public morality by influencing men within the home; but influence was said to work exactly and only because women were separated from the public world and preserved in domestic innocence. A woman's indirect power depended, then, on that isolation and on her willing submission to her subordinate role within the paternalist structure of the household.[4]

In the work of all three novelists treated here, the "separateness" of women's action in the public realm works simultaneously as a challenge and as a submission to the notion that men and women have naturally distinct spheres of influence and

4. In chap. 5 of *Industrial Reformation*, Gallagher's analysis of domestic ideology directly links this notion of the family as a regenerative social force with the ideology of social paternalism. Judith Newton connects the rise of domestic ideology with changes in the economic status of middle-class women in her Introduction to *Women, Power, and Subversion*, pp. 1–22.

substantially different modes of social action. On the one hand, the novelists attack the paradoxes of domestic ideology by creating heroines whose social effectiveness is dependent on their penetration and knowledge of the strategies of male power and by depicting their action in the world rather than in the home. Yet the wish to celebrate female action is countermanded by an equally powerful pull toward representing woman's consciousness and activity as private, secret, or separate from the flow of public affairs known to male characters.

This troubled territory is made formally visible in two ways. The female sphere may itself be divided, between activity and passivity, publicity and privacy. In Trollope and Brontë, the doubling of heroines does this work, by playing out the consequences of active female paternalism next to a story of passive aquiescence. Gaskell imagines the opposing pulls in more directly psychological terms, within the consciousness of her single heroine. The second sign of conflict may be read in the way women's action is isolated from or merged with the social world that inspires it. The more fully that world is imagined as patriarchal, the more female action is hidden behind the scenes, or sealed off in a powerless complicity of knowledge.

As their social and domestic arguments intertwine, the novels tend to create altered versions of the very social arrangements they set out to criticize. The "romance" of the female paternalist relocates and energizes the spirit of paternalism while casting it as a subordinate social activity. Protests against the passivity and privacy of the woman's sphere move toward a reestablished separation of male and female consciousness. These tendencies are, however, very differently managed by Trollope, Brontë, and Gaskell. Trollope's *Michael Armstrong* depicts a triumph of female paternalism that requires a complete separation from middle-class male structures of power. *Shirley* deflates Trollope's fantasies while raising the contradictions within paternalism in terms that encompass both industrial and domestic life. *North and South* emerges as a step in the argument that turns on the idea of paternalism itself. Linking itself to *Shirley*, Gaskell's narrative rejects the separation and subordination of women and workers which follows from the paternalist model of social order. As the story pattern works itself out in her hands, the romance of female paternalism is transformed into an acceptance of the cooperative potential inherent in the "monster system" itself.

Frances Trollope's Female Knights

Frances Trollope's social-problem novels trace out a fantasy of female paternalism in which the boldness of women's action is insulated by its ultimate separation from the public sphere. In *Michael Armstrong, the Factory Boy* (1840), Trollope attacks the abuses of child labor in the northern cotton mills; *Jessie Phillips: A Tale of the Present Day* (1844) takes on the administration of the New Poor Law of 1834 in a rural village setting. In both novels Trollope reveals a social sensibility that is simultaneously paternalist and antipatriarchal. The workers and the poor (for the most part women and children) are imagined within a paternalist mode: they are passive, deferential, and grateful for charitable intervention from members of the class that victimizes them. The men who run the factory system are monsters of capitalist greed whose crimes are both defined and bolstered by political economy; the village Poor Law guardians are well-meaning but mistaken administrators, caught flailing in the moment of historical change. In Trollope's vision, masters and squires have been corrupted or confused by large-scale systematizations of labor or law, while the working class retains a preindustrial innocence along with its traditional status as victim.

The two classes therefore inhabit worlds that run according to different social and economic assumptions. The connecting terms and the moving pieces of the plots are provided by the middle-class heroines whose stories occupy the center of Trollope's interest. These enterprising daughters are descendants of the heroes of romance: female knights errant who unmask the guilty secrets of the patriarchs, set out to rescue the victimized poor, and reap their rewards in the conventional form of marriage. Their stories allow Trollope to mobilize the contradictions of her social vision, for her heroines are at once social paternalists and critics of male control, both socially active and innocent of the taint of power. Their moral education is a process during which they come to see through the deceptive languages of the ruling men and take the freedom to act independently, in isolation, against the male world. Such social activities are, however, redefined and recontained in plot actions that leave the heroines safely ensconced in domestic alliances that reward their activity while defusing its social content.

Michael Armstrong is generally labeled a "Tory-paternalist" novel written in support of the Ten Hours' Movement. It contains blocks of description and theoretical discussion that might certify it for such a classification,[5] but its main—and its best—story concerns the struggle for independence of mind and action in its middle-class heroine, Mary Brotherton. The orphaned daughter and heiress of a rich millowner who has made a killing through child labor, Mary becomes the novel's major actor when she sets out on a course that teaches her the concealed truths of the factory system and cures her soul of its wealth-bound cynical bent. Her quest is designed to uncover horrors of child abuse in the factory system like those publicized by Factory Movement propagandists; along these lines Trollope's imagination runs to the extreme and the spectacular, revealing a rather gruesome delight in the sadistic potential of her subject. But she is very little engaged by the Ten Hours' Movement that the novel is supposed to advocate; for her, individual acts of rescue and escape are the imaginable fictional responses to the evils of the factory system.[6]

5. For descriptions of Trollope's fact-finding journey to Manchester and her use of other sources, see W. H. Chaloner, "Mrs. Trollope and the Early Factory System," *Victorian Studies* 4 (1960), 159–166; Helen Heinemann, *Mrs. Trollope: The Triumphant Feminine in the Nineteenth Century* (Athens, O., 1979), pp. 169–182; and Kestner, *Protest and Reform*, pp. 52–58. Both Heinemann and Kestner discuss Trollope's uses and alterations of John Brown's *Memoir of Robert Blincoe*.

6. Heinemann's wholehearted defense of *Michael Armstrong* includes the opinion that the novel demonstrates the insufficiency of private philanthropy as a response to the sufferings of factory workers (*Mrs. Trollope*, pp. 174, 179, 181–182). The plot does not support so definite a reading. Angus Easson comes somewhat closer when he criticizes Trollope's reliance on the Ten Hours'

The novel is organized as a series of adoptive rescues in which innocent factory children become pawns in a power struggle between factory owners and their enlightened critics. It opens with a parodic adoption: the evil mill owner Sir Matthew Dowling wrests his young employee Michael Armstrong from the arms of a loving mother and brother and pretends to bring Michael up among his own children as a reward for his "service" in saving an aristocratic neighbor from the predations of a local cow. From the travesty of charity that results, Mary Brotherton attempts to release Michael; her activities on his behalf lead her to two adoptions of her own when she saves Michael's lame brother Edward and a young pauper apprentice girl from the horrors of factory work. These elaborately staged schemes pit heroine and villain against each other for possession of the guilty knowledge of what the factory system does to young children. Sir Matthew's adoption of Michael is a theatrical ploy, intended to deflect public criticism of factory conditions by focusing attention on his fraudulent private benevolence. Much of the interest of volume I lies in Trollope's satirical portrait of Dowling's charity as a public relations stunt and a kinky form of personal entertainment for the idle rich. Her best inventive energy lies in the elaborate demonstration that powerful classes manipulate and sell conventional images of the idle and ungrateful worker exactly because they themselves have so much to hide.[7]

It is from this context that the moral development of Mary Brotherton takes its value. The idle and satirical heroine has never been inside a factory and has never thought about her father's workers until she hears Michael being beaten behind the scenes for bursting into tears during a Dowling home theatrical in which he has—with rather grisly irony—been cast as a rescued and grateful factory boy. She now determines on a counter-rescue, to release the child from "the horrible bondage of Sir

Bill as a solution, emphasizing her appeal to feeling for children and her avoidance of larger issues. Easson's discussion appears in *Elizabeth Gaskell* (London, 1979), pp. 62–66.

7. For a treatment of *Michael Armstrong* as a Tory critique of the industrial middle class, see Melada, *Captain of Industry*, pp. 90–95. Heinemann also gives a good account of Trollope's attack on "the rhetoric of middle-class self-justification" in *Mrs. Trollope*, pp. 182–183.

Matthew Dowling's charity."[8] She fails; the villain masterminds a stagy scheme to ship Michael off to something worse—Mr. Elgood Sharpton's Deep Valley mill for pauper apprentices. But the failure begins Mary's education in millowner propaganda and her determination to know the truth and act on it in defiance of capitalist secrecy and brainwashing. Because her heroism is defined in these terms, at least as much plot attention is paid to her schemes for outwitting a world full of calculating millowners and their henchmen as to the scenes of industrial suffering that her quest discovers.[9]

Mary's moves against capitalist lies develop in two simultaneous but mutually exclusive directions, one expressed in theoretical exposition, the other through the plot. Soon after her observations have raised questions that challenge her father's business doctrines, she discovers a corroborating social vision in a neighboring minister who is a Factory Movement advocate. The Reverend Bell sees working-class degradation as an inevitable result of the employment practices of the factory system; his lengthy analysis follows the standard Tory argument that the family is destroyed by child labor.[10] Once having turned Mary's direct observations into grand rhetorical images of the poisonous and faceless monster that destroys children as powerfully and efficiently as it spins thread (II, 205–207), Bell offers Ten Hours legislation to mitigate the effects of the system; his belief in the systemic power of the marketplace is the basis for his advocacy of interventionist protective legislation. The novel pays brief lip service to Bell's solution when a workers' rally for Ten Hours makes its appearance later in the narrative, but that event is quickly summarized and consigned to history. Fiction, meanwhile, has taken its separate course.

8. Frances Trollope, *Life and Adventures of Michael Armstrong, the Factory Boy*, 3 vols. (London, 1840), I, II. Further references to this novel will appear in the text.

9. Kestner calls Mary the first female repository of social conscience in the subgenre (*Protest and Reform*, p. 57). Heinemann identifies Mary's independence with Trollope's own refusal of "the harness of gentility" (*Mrs. Trollope*, pp. 183–184).

10. Gallagher gives an excellent summary of the history of this argument on pp. 122–125 of *Industrial Reformation*.

If Trollope were working in terms of Bell's analysis, it would hardly be necessary to give us Sir Matthew Dowling and Mr. Elgood Sharpton; the monster system itself would suffice. But the laws of her marketplace are those of melodrama, not of capital. She embodies the workings of Bell's agentless system in two human monsters, child beaters and killers animated by cruelty as well as avarice, personally responsible because they are personally evil. Mary does not become a Factory Movement spokeswoman; she takes up a disguise and turns herself into a female knight errant on a mission of rescue, organizing a private tour of factories with the goal of finding and saving Michael. The children she does save are exempted from the consequential world of Bell's analysis: middle-class in mind and heart, they are worthy of rescue precisely because they are immune to the effects of the factory system. (Michael is reserved for a heroic escape episode of his own, which I discuss in chapter 3). The romantic rescue plot is based on an implicit contradiction of the Reverend Bell's arguments, for it posits a world in which the dispositions of millowners and workers are determined by nature rather than by the conditions of capitalist enterprise. Moreover, as Mary's adventures roll along and culminate in her storming of the Deep Valley mill, "system" disappears almost entirely from the novel. It becomes increasingly difficult to find the line between the expression of social outrage and the preemption of factory material for purposes of Gothic horror;[11] Mary's rescue of the apprentice child Fanny Fletcher, set in wild northern landscapes that produce pageants of death and madness, turns into the story of innocence liberated from the castle of a monster. As befits that kind of tale, retreat to a good castle is the plot's next step: Mary retires to one on the Rhône, abandoning England and its factories altogether.

11. Yet this blurring of the line between sensationalist melodrama and the novel of social conscience may mark Trollope's work as an essential precursor in the genre. As Peter Brooks argues in his discussion of Eugene Sue's *Les Mystères de Paris:* "Before 'social realism' could become a watchword—and perhaps with greater effect than was ever achieved by more sober novels—the lurid and melodramatic fiction opens up the social concerns, makes them imaginatively available" (*Reading for the Plot: Design and Intention in Narrative* [New York, 1984], p. 168).

Trollope's advocacy of Mary's bold rescue mission is under-
lined in her portrait of the secondary heroine, appropriately
named Martha. Martha is the one good daughter of Sir Matthew
Dowling, and the single person who helps and teaches Michael
Armstrong during his stay at the Dowling mansion. Like Mary,
Martha has been indoctrinated with the idea that factory workers are idle, degenerate, and ungrateful; unlike her, she has to
contend with the living presence of a father whom she loves and
wishes fervently to believe. Faced with the evidence of Michael's
virtue and suffering, she is nevertheless unable to revise her
faith in her father's authority; instead she becomes paralyzed by
the contradiction. As a result, she can be used as a tool of the
system: her father forces her to persuade Mrs. Armstrong to
sign a release that will put Michael away at the Deep Valley mill.
While Mary's intellectual independence releases her into action,
Martha's pained conflict between daughterly duty and accurate
vision reduces her to weakness and illness. The narrator tells us
that Mary's "condition was a far happier one than that of Martha
Dowling; for in her there was no mixture of motives to paralyse
every thought and act," while the union of love and fear in
Martha "reduces the mind to a state of slavery the most abject,
leaving no strength whereby any healthful moral feeling can be
sustained" (II, 274). The subplot makes an acute analysis of the
contradictions at the heart of conventional sphere ideology:
Martha's case shows that domestic subservience to the male
capitalist is emotionally and morally incompatible with womanly
sympathy and charity.

Accordingly, Mary's Rhône retreat establishes a separated
domestic paradise that significantly revises the conventional
arrangements of the woman's sphere. Love and gratitude between persons untainted by capitalism create an ideal family
with a woman's social and economic power at its head. This
superior structure collapses paternalism into the woman's
sphere, balancing the generous nurturance of the female paternalist against the spellbound gratitude of younger, powerless
working-class characters. The domestic tranquillity that re-
emerges in the final volume "resolves" the contradictions raised

by Martha Dowling's story because it is liberated from the necessity of confronting any middle-class men at all.

In Trollope's imagination, Mary's power triumphs at the cost of an extreme fantasy of separation. Once established, however, the female sphere also restores the domestic ideal of womanhood which Mary had violated in her earlier adventures. Summing up the meaning of her quest, the rescuing heroine sounds very much like the angel in the house: "How can I be sufficiently grateful to Providence for having redeemed my existence from the state of uselessness in which I vegetated before I met Edward Armstrong and Fanny Fletcher? Not an hour passes by me without leaving behind it some trace of my having advanced in the precious labor of making these two beloved beings happier" (III, 187). In this revisionary account of her own history, Mary recasts her original dilemma as a middle-class woman's "state of uselessness" rather than as a troubled vision of class exploitation. Her heroism, initially depicted as action against guilty social truths, has been transformed into the task of "making beloved beings happier"; the issue of child labor is absorbed into the "precious labor" of domestic creation. The revision significantly forgets the novel's most powerful proposition: that the relatively unfixed position of the single middle-class woman gives her special access to a critical vision of class relations.

In fact the female sphere collapses all social distinctions into domestic self-sufficiency. By adopting Fanny and Edward, Mary has not only made herself a family but brought up her own husband: the ending hints at romantic love between the heiress-mother and the working-class "son." The coy indirection with which Trollope approaches her romantic finale betrays her sense that she is violating taboos that go deeper than class difference; her focus on Edward's anguished sense of social inferiority functions more as a cover for the incest wish than as a serious continuation of the class plot. In any case, the final merging of the female paternalist with her working-class protégé can be read as the logical extension of Trollope's position, which bonds the middle-class woman with the childlike working class in a condition of reciprocity that banishes the problematics of male dominance in both the social and the familial worlds.

In *Jessie Phillips* (1844) Trollope makes a more balanced attempt to wrest large-scale problems of social organization into personal melodramas featuring young women as social rescuers. The novel's subtitle announces that it is "A Tale of the Present Day," but the New Poor Law of 1834 is investigated within an idealized pastoral vision of village life in the parish of Deepbrook, where class deference structures function in thoroughly traditional ways. The narrator openly introduces this world as a mythical one, linking it with childhood memory or primal fantasy;[12] nevertheless, the animation of the myth is her main line of defense both against the national bureaucracy established by the New Poor Law and against the large-scale rural poverty that led to the formulation of the law. No unemployed or starving multitudes mar Trollope's picture of village decency and individuality. The case against the law is free to rest on the degradation and cruelty imposed by the workhouse test, the physical and moral conditions imposed by confinement in the Poor Law Union, and local injustices and misjudgments of character that follow from the centralization of decision making.[13] In particular, the plot of *Jessie Phillips* attends to the implications of the bastardy clause, which prevented mothers of illegitimate children from receiving financial support elicited by parish relief boards from named fathers.[14]

Trollope is at least equally interested in the effects of the Poor Law on the village fathers who are called on to be its administrators; she is eager to demonstrate that right-feeling citizens

12. Frances Trollope, *Jessie Phillips: A Tale of the Present Day* (London, 1844), p. 1. Further references to this edition will appear in the text.

13. I concur with Robert's praise of *Jessie Phillips* for its full and relatively unexaggerated account of the impact of the New Poor Law (see *Paternalism*, pp. 89–90). Heinemann gives a thorough discussion of the Poor Law issues as they are treated in the novel (*Mrs. Trollope*, pp. 211–218).

14. For discussions of the bastardy clause and Trollope's fictional uses of it, see Heinemann, *Mrs. Trollope*, pp. 214–216, and Kestner, *Protest and Reform*, pp. 104–107.

find themselves in the uncomfortable position of doubting the rightness of an English Law. Two extended debates among members of the Poor Law Board engage us in this dilemma, dramatizing the depths of confusion generated among thoughtful magistrates and professional men. Trollope's most consistent—and consistently Tory—argument makes the case against centralizing poor relief by showing that decisions should depend on the paternalist's intimate knowledge of his neighbors. The assistant commissioner assigned to organize the Deepbrook Union is criticized not because he exemplifies utilitarian methods of social control but because he is a gentleman of pleasure who knows nothing of the parish or its inhabitants.

Attempting to remedy the mistakes made by the confused male Poor Law guardians, a team of middle-class daughters comes to the rescue. Ellen Dalton, the eldest daughter of the village squire, effects the most easily successful charitable intervention. The respectable widow Greenhill faces the workhouse, refused outdoor relief during her son's imprisonment for debt because of the cruelty of a guardian from a distant parish and the inattention of his colleagues during the hearing. Ellen donates a personal legacy, restores the widow to her cottage, and puts her on a temporary allowance; her father gives his blessing to this private version of parish relief without having to rock the boat of his legal guardianship. The charitable intervention leads, through the widow Greenhill, to the clarification of a thwarted love affair and to Ellen's marital reward.

The Martha of this novel is, however, the more energetic and active of the team. Martha Maxwell, Ellen's friend and Trollope's favorite, involves herself in a zanier plot to counteract the prohibitions of the bastardy clause in the case of Jessie Phillips, the beautiful village seamstress who has been seduced by Ellen's rake brother, Frederick Dalton. In an attempt to cover up his illicit liaison with Jessie, Frederick pretends to court Martha. Undeceived about his motives, Martha cooks up a counterscheme: she gets Frederick to sign a promise of marriage, planning to use the document as a blackmail weapon that will force him either to marry Jessie and legitimize her child or to provide her with the financial support that would have been available under the older parish law. Martha's singlehanded attempts to outwit both the villain and the law end in failure; Frederick compounds his villainy by murdering Jessie's baby shortly after its birth, under conditions that point to Jessie as the culprit. Martha can do no more than believe in Jessie's innocence and help provide legal counsel at the infanticide trial that follows; her quick, unsentimental intelligence and her ability to see through male strategies of domination are, however, the qualities Trollope celebrates in the novel.

The opposition between the strong-feeling observant heroines and the bureaucratic actions of the legal system is deepened in the last section of the novel. Here the weight of the general assumption that Jessie has killed her baby, based on carefully contrived circumstantial evidence, is set against the girls' helpless, guiltily intuited knowledge that Frederick is the murderer. Jessie herself is brainwashed by her interrogators into the notion that she must have killed her child; only Martha and Ellen believe that she didn't do it. The narrative is so arranged that even the most sensible and sympathetic witnesses would have to conclude that Jessie is guilty; in this way the truth is located and isolated in the heads of the legally powerless heroines, while the story points to all the truths of character that law cannot touch, and to the helplessness of the poor in the face of social and legal reasoning.

In both of the novel's plots, the heroines are given the kind of social knowledge that, Trollope argues, effected the charitable transactions of villages under the old system of patriarchal benevolence. As in *Michael Armstrong,* the social truths that lie buried in the heroines' hearts are never made contiguous with the realm of public affairs. Rather they create a kind of secret alliance among writer, reader, and heroines, remaining an insulated node of privileged information that floats in apparent innocence within the society of the village fathers. The backstage influence of the middle-class heroines does work toward some melodramatic resolutions that beg all of the legal questions: at the last moment Jessie is declared not guilty by virtue of temporary insanity, while on the same day Frederick drowns himself, finally and uncharacteristically haunted by guilty fears brought on by the feverish private accusations of his sister. But Jessie dies at the moment of aquittal: convention decrees that she die as a fallen woman if not as a condemned murderess; and no one but the heroines knows of Frederick's crime. The female alliance, empowered and burdened by knowledge that could destroy the honor of Deepbrook's first family, is defused and then dismantled as each heroine goes to her marital reward.

Frances Trollope reimagines paternalism as a relationship between active middle-class daughters and passive working-class victims within a separated and antipatriarchal version of the woman's sphere. Her heroines act for the poor in ways that ensure gratitude and submission, providing the guidance and rescue sought by a working class adrift in a capitalist bureaucracy. Yet for all the ways this rescuing role activates and educates the heroines, it always ends in isolating them from their culture: social motion, learning, and truth are located, and then locked, in their consciousnesses. The dramatically staged female subversions finally fail to engage with the novels' emphatically male structures of power.

Trollope's melodramatic plots display a comparable mixture of protest and evasion in their channeling of social problems. Melodrama insists on subjecting the world to the rigors of personal moral judgments, and the melodrama in these novels doles out the kind of justice that the laws of the market and the court entirely fail to dispense. In doing so, however, they leave untouched the systemic problems they raise. By turning the relations between unequally powered social groups into games of villains and victims, the plots pull away from acknowledging stresses inherent in the organization of class relationships. The extremity of the cases and of the solutions is, in fact, a measure of Trollope's inability to conceive—or at least to portray—the possibility of change in arrangements of class or gender. Her paternalist communities and her more modern capitalist and bureaucratic principles lie side by side in explicit contradiction; that one might threaten or alter the other is not a persuasive part of her imaginative vision.

Charlotte Brontë and the Dynamics of Paternalism

Early in the narrative of *Shirley,* Charlotte Brontë explicitly rejects the strategies of factory novels such as *Michael Armstrong:*

> . . . though I describe imperfect characters . . . I have not undertaken to handle degraded or utterly infamous ones. Child-torturers, slave masters and drivers, I consign to the hands of jailers; the novelist may be excused from sullying his page with the record of their deeds.
>
> Instead, then, of harrowing up my reader's soul, and delighting his organ of Wonder, with effective descriptions of stripes and scourgings, I am happy to be able to inform him that neither Mr Moore nor his overlooker ever struck a child in their mill.[15]

Written after the Ten Hours' Movement had achieved the paternalist labor regulations established by the Factory Acts of 1847, this passage, like the novel as a whole, marks the gradual shift of public attention during the 1840s from the brutalities of child and female labor toward the threat of autonomous working-class politics. More to the point, however, it sharply defines Brontë's critique of the line of fictions in which she places herself as she takes her reader into Robert Moore's textile mill. Consigning such characters as Sir Matthew Dowling and Elgood Sharpton "to the hands of jailers," Brontë puts her finger on Trollope's penchant for erasing social problems by transforming them into criminal acts, and for turning industrial suffering into the raw material for Gothic horror.

Brontë turns in the opposite direction: she uses her factory novel to subject all human power relations to a searching critique. Her many-faceted investigation has a shape, though not much of a plot: its importance lies in its relentless focus on the dynamics of power and rebellion rather than in the reconciliatory form of story. Like Trollope, however, Brontë relies on the structure of paternalism as a model for class relations; and she shares with her

---

15. Charlotte Brontë, *Shirley* (Harmondsworth, 1974), p. 90. Further references to this edition will appear in the text.

predecessor the urge to work out the complex relations between paternalism and women's action.[16]

Shirley is built on the intertwined stories of unemployed rebellious workers and idle, suppressed middle-class women. Both groups suffer and protest the misused power of the men who dominate in the factory and the village. Nevertheless, it is misleading to read the novel in a way that foregrounds its power of social protest—either as a failed attempt to write a novel about Luddism or as an indictment of the constraints in women's lives which is unfortunately undermined by conventional marriage resolutions.[17] Those emphases are misleading because they obscure the fact that paternalism is an assumption central to Brontë's imagination of human relations. Active interventionist guidance is the missing keystone to stability in *Shirley*; restless, rebellious activity or wasting passivity among women and workers is a symptom of its absence. Underlying all of Brontë's narrative shifts from one side of a question to the other is a quest for ruling figures who will restore social and psychological order and provide a firm point of appeal. The male characters who hold power in the community and the family are, consequently, condemned not for their exercise of power but for their withdrawal from it.

The characteristic narrative gesture of *Shirley* is an oscillation

16. Kestner notes the "anticipation" of *Shirley* in Trollope's female league against male authority (*Protest and Reform*, p. 108).

17. Brontë's inability to understand or sympathize with the activities of the Luddites is a complaint first recorded by E. P. Thompson (*Making of the English Working Class*, p. 561). It is elaborated by Terry Eagleton in *Myths of Power: A Marxist Study of the Brontës* (London, 1975), pp. 45–50; and by Igor Webb in *From Custom to Capital*, pp. 124–142. More pervasive in *Shirley* criticism is the opinion that "the woman question" is central, the industrial theme subordinate. Recent arguments include Robert Bernard Martin's assertion that the political plot is present only to throw light on personal conflicts; see *The Accents of Persuasion* (London, 1966), p. 136. In *Charlotte Brontë: The Self Conceived* (New York, 1976), Helene Moglen describes *Shirley* as an attack on social misuses of power in which woman is the symbol of powerlessness (pp. 152–189). Webb sees, in contrast to Brontë's failure to depict working-class culture, a treatment of single women "unsurpassed in English fiction of the Industrial Revolution" (p. 142; see pp. 142–158 for the full discussion). In *Madwoman in the Attic*, Gilbert and Gubar focus on the suffering and rebellion of women, arguing that Brontë links exploitive capitalism with sexual discrimination but then succumbs to conventional marital endings. Donald D. Stone sees the protest as even more stifled and disappointing; see *Romantic Impulse*, pp. 120–126.

within the paternalist frame, between rebellion or despair legitimated by the failure of paternalism and appeal to the heroic powers of male dominance. This pattern is bound to create frustration in any reader who wishes to discover in Brontë a consistent line of social or political analysis. But it does provide a rich anatomy of the ideological problems that are raised by a model of human order which assumes a fruitful relationship between the compassionate discipline of the authoritarian and the psychological health of the dependent. In contrast to Trollope's idealized view of the easy gratitude and esteem between the generous patroness and a working class that is both passive and morally self-sufficient, Brontë assumes that characters and societies are forged and marred in the dynamic play of power. Where Trollope creates a stir of female paternalism that comes to rest in a separate domestic sphere, Brontë sees the public and private realms in equivalent terms: both are fraught with the tensions that bind people of unequal status or power.

For her, the twin dangers of tyranny and withdrawal are latent in every human relationship. The question she asks is not "Should it be so?" but "How must the powerful part be played and responded to, so as to create loyal and trustful social bonds?" And her analysis of those relations does not divide the world simply along the lines of class or gender. Instead, she considers the reciprocal nature of all transactions, the ways command and response create each other. The curious opening scene, for example, is a small model of the shifting power configurations that are to be the actual content of the novel: here the rowdy curates impose on the landlady, whose "Yorkshire soul revolted absolutely" from Malone's "manner of command" (42). After the meal Donne and Sweeting become in turn the "victims" of Malone, each meeting "these attacks in his own way" (43). When their superior, the Reverend Helstone, enters, all of the young curates are "transfixed" in uneasy deference (45), becoming the targets of his sarcastic diatribes.[18]

18. This odd opening scene has been read by others in more ordinarily thematic terms. Moglen treats it as an attack on the misused power of the church (*Charlotte Brontë*, pp. 159–160). Webb finds it a representation of male dominance that illustrates the failure of piety and harmony in communal life (*From*

Relationships dominated by women have as much potential for damage as do those among men. In another apparent divergence that sits right at the heart of her subject, Brontë sketches the characters of the Yorke children, showing their range of reactions to the harsh rule of their mother. Rose contains herself, but will rebel if driven too hard; Jessie defies her mother easily and sweetly; Matthew's temper is so dangerous that his parents conciliate him, "fast making a tyrant of their own flesh and blood" (167, 169). Both Hortense Moore (comically) and Mrs. Yorke (threateningly) brandish the image of sacrificial womanhood in Caroline's face, until it becomes necessary that even this gentle character rise to self-defense when Mrs. Yorke insults her (387–390). When Caroline's lost parentage is restored in the reunion with her mother, the loving relation between the women is a version of the game of bidding and compliance; for the first time in her life Caroline finds a love that carries with it a power to command (422–425).

Brontë's overriding concern with balances of power allows for little sense of progress, change, or reformation; only Robert Moore's chastened acceptance of paternalist responsibility provides a story of moral development. For the most part, the flow of articulated contradiction undermines the possibility of a coherent or unified line of plot. This problem of form has generally been understood as a failure of composition,[19] but there is another way to see it: as a stubborn refusal to accede to any of the romantic fantasies that emerge in the narrative as potential havens of harmony, or stories of resolution. The shapelessness of the plot is also important, however, because it is linked to a nonprogressive view of history—a view that Brontë takes care to suggest in the novel's opening chapters and in its temporal frame.

Custom to Capital, pp. 142–144). For Gilbert and Gubar the voracious curates introduce a dominant metaphor: the hunger of the oppressed (*Madwoman in the Attic*, pp. 373–374).

19. The problem of unity was the central issue in *Shirley* criticism for some time. Examples of the debate may be found in Asa Briggs, "Private and Social Themes in *Shirley*," *Brontë Society Transactions* 13 (1958), 203–214; Jacob Korg, "The Problem of Unity in *Shirley*," *Nineteenth-Century Fiction* 12 (1957), 125–136; and Arnold Shapiro, "Public Themes and Private Lives: Social Criticism in *Shirley*," *Papers on Language and Literature* 4 (1968), 74–84.

Shirley's historical frame is defined and delimited by the orders in council that restricted British trade with its foreign markets during the Napoleonic Wars. Its actions are set between February and December 1811, when, as the narrative puts it, "distress reached its climax" (62) in the cumulative effects of halted trade, the introduction of new machinery into the mills, and a bad harvest. The final chapter is discontinuous with the rest: breaking the temporal progression, it records the revocation of the orders in June 1812 and the subsequent marriages of the heroines in August. Calling explicit and ironical attention to its conventionalities of ending, this chapter uses the historical fact of release from economic restriction to liberate its characters from the spells of inaction that have held them in suspense throughout the story.[20] There is to be a new season of activity—though not, as the novel's final vision of industrial landscape makes clear, necessarily one of improvement.

The brief and carefully chosen historical moment asserts a belief in the seasonality of national and personal history: *Shirley* is concerned with the endurance of a dry spell. The choice is formalized in analogies with natural and biblical cycles of despair and renewal. The novel's opening paragraph announces that the narrator will forget the present "noon" of midcentury in order to "dream of dawn," its early years. But within the next two paragraphs, past and present are confused and conflated: "those days" were "days of scarcity," but despite the "abundant shower of curates" said to have fallen of late, the present is also "dusty, sun-burnt, hot, arid" (39–40). The quick division and recombination of times, apparently aimed at the failures of religious regeneration in the nineteenth century, might also suggest the continuity between Brontë's historical focus on Luddism and the contemporary activities—and suppressions—of Chartism.[21] But it is important to notice that she is interested in the historical event not as a distanced substitution for contemporary politics but as an instance of cycle and repetition.

20. Gilbert and Gubar describe *Shirley* as a novel about impotence, or the inability to take action (*Madwoman in the Attic*, p. 375).

21. In Eagleton's reading Chartism is "the unspoken subject of *Shirley*" (*Myths of Power*, p. 43).

Brontë "dreams" of the beginning of the century only to undermine both the wish for a preindustrial golden age and the myth of progress. Her ironic view of history is presented through religious prototypes that reinforce her emphasis on that cyclical view of human history.

Warning her reader against expecting "anything like a romance," she offers a fictional menu appropriate to "Good Friday in Passion Week: it shall be cold lentils and vinegar and oil; it shall be unleavened bread with bitter herbs and no roast lamb" (39). These menus designate no ordinary unromantic meals, but major ritual celebrations of oppression and suffering in both the Christian and the Jewish calendars—rituals that reiterate the promise of release in resurrection or escape into freedom. In the act of disavowing conventional fictional shapes, Brontë implies that we might instead read her story as a modern instance of suffering, endurance, or resistance to tyranny. The suffering of contemporary workers can then be distanced in language that links them with biblical forebears: "so the unemployed underwent their destiny—ate the bread and drank the waters of affliction" (62). As a substitute for the conventions of romance or melodrama, the cyclical model merely plots alternations between fat and lean years, controlled by economic conditions and political leaders beyond the range of the story.

The peculiar improvisatory shape of *Shirley* can, then, be read as an act of resistance to romance or historical melodrama, progressing in roughly defined phases through a study of the conditions and responses that create tyranny or freedom. The first phase introduces us to the primarily male world of industrial politics; the next, to the internal condition of Caroline Helstone, a dependent in that world. Then the focus shifts to the mix of tension and harmony in the friendship between Caroline and Shirley Keeldar. At the center of the narrative lie the climactic events that gather the whole social organism together in motion: the Whitsuntide feast that celebrates the order of established church and state, and its shadow event, the night-time attack on Moore's mill by a well-organized band of Luddites. The novel's final third, written after the deaths of

Emily and Ann Brontë,[22] modulates in tone and takes the more
private direction of examining the forces that keep loved
persons away from one another and the reconciliations that are
engendered by confrontations with mortality. Despite the virtual
abandonment of the industrial issue, this section goes on with
the analysis of trust and alienation, control and dependence,
that constitutes Brontë's approach to the nature and psychology
of government.

What are the terms in which Brontë discusses the exercise of
authority? To begin with, it should create the conditions for
reciprocal feeling. This theme, linking the positions of women
and workers, is first sounded by Caroline when she chides
Moore for his haughty treatment of the working class: "'I know
it would be better for you to be loved by your workpeople than
to be hated by them, and I am sure that kindness is more likely
to win their regard than pride. If you were proud and cold to me
and Hortense, should we love you? When you are cold to me, as
you *are* sometimes, can I venture to be affectionate in return?'"
(118). Caroline's idea of oppression, here couched in a veiled
declaration of love, is simple and lethal: it consists in being
ignored. The novel begins by applying the concept equally to
women and workers. Caroline wastes away in the parsonage not
because her uncle hates her, but because he does not take
women seriously. His inattention has killed his wife, Mary Cave:
"He thought, so long as a woman was silent, nothing ailed her,
and she wanted nothing" (82). Robert Moore's inattention to his
workers, called by no harsher name than "negligence" (61), is of
a similar order. And when Brontë summarizes the Luddite
attacks, she emphasises their isolation and futility:

> The throes of a sort of moral earthquake were felt heaving under
> the hills of the northern counties. But, as is usual in such cases,
> nobody took much notice. When a food-riot broke out in a
> manufacturing town, when a gig-mill was burnt to the ground, or
> a manufacturer's house was attacked, the furniture thrown into

22. Elizabeth Gaskell tells us that the deaths of Branwell, Emily, and Anne
Brontë occurred as Charlotte was finishing vol. 2. The first chapter written
afterward was "The Valley of the Shadow of Death." See Gaskell, *The Life of
Charlotte Brontë* (Harmondsworth, 1975), pp. 379–380.

the streets, and the family forced to flee for their lives, some local measures were or were not taken by the local magistracy; a ringleader was detected, or more frequently suffered to elude detection; newspaper paragraphs were written on the subject, and there the thing stopped. As to the sufferers, whose sole inheritance was labour, and who had lost that inheritance—who could not get work, and consequently could not get wages, and consequently could not get bread—they were left to suffer on; perhaps inevitably left. . . . [62]

The narrative movement of mind here, switching as it does from the sufferings of the workers to the sufferings of their middle-class victims and back again, typifies the novel's fluctuating perspective, but its sides share a common ground: the trouble is that neither the "moral earthquake" nor the flight of the family commands attention; there is, in the universe at large, a vacuum of response.

Paternalist inactivity is so defined as a double failure: social order is not maintained and suffering is not allayed. Brontë is quite clear about the power that fuels paternalist activity even in the local, old-fashioned form practiced by Hiram Yorke, whose name evokes an honored tradition of customary labor relations:

He was much beloved by the poor, because he was thoroughly kind and very fatherly to them. To his workmen he was considerate and cordial: when he dismissed them from an occupation, he would try to set them on to something else; or, if that was impossible, help them to remove with their families to a district where work might possibly be had. It must also be remarked that if, as sometimes chanced, any individual among his 'hands' showed signs of insubordination, Yorke—who, like many who abhor being controlled, knew how to control with vigor—had the secret of crushing rebellion in the germ, of eradicating it like a bad weed, so that it never spread or developed within the sphere of his authority. [79]

Sentimental benevolence plays little part in this concept of paternalism: in metaphors relishing the violent potential of Yorke's fatherliness, the narrative acknowledges the controller's need to maintain his power. The pungent and personal style of Yorkshire management appears to be an ideal against which the sins of the "imported" factory owner Robert Moore are to be measured and amended. As Brontë works out that story, an important doubleness invades her narrative, revealing the collision between her local paternalist idea and her submerged recognition that the class relations of paternalism were being transformed into the antagonisms of class war.[23]

Moore, the modern millowner, is criticized for a failure of paternalism that creates hatred among his workers, and then glorified for the militance with which he smothers the Luddite attack that ensues. In the scenes of industrial confrontation—the return of the empty wagons (chap. 2), the arrest of Moses Barraclough (chap. 8), and the attack on Hollow's Mill (chap. 19)—Moore, with all his nonpaternalist faults on his head, is simply glamorous. He is wrong to allow his workers' rage to foment, wrong to fail his honest and deferent employee William Farren; yet the emotional weight of these scenes falls admiringly on his soldierly qualities: his strenuous response to challenge, his cool secret preparation, his personal courage, his endangered isolation. It is impossible to read the confrontation scenes without being pulled toward exactly that zest for chivalric warfare which Brontë rejects in the portrait of Helstone. If Hiram Yorke has the gift of crushing rebellion in the bud, Moore is given the power to restore troubled social order through efficient violence.

These contradictions in the depiction of Moore make it necessary to read him doubly: as a laissez-faire millowner in need of paternalist reform and as a canny hero in a sophisticated modern industrial war. Brontë's accounts of Moore's working-class antagonists mirror the doubleness exactly. On the one hand, she maintains a conventional stance consistent with the paternalist model, from which she rejects working-class politics as the mistaken ambition of dissolute, self-seeking leaders followed by innocent, starving workers. She brings Moses Barraclough and Noah o'Tim's onstage only to satirize their pathetically inflated rhetoric, to conflate false politics with false religion, and to diminish the whole affair by inventing a silly

23. See Patrick Brantlinger, *Spirit of Reform*, pp. 124–127, for a discussion of the contradictions in Moore read as indicators of Brontë's celebration of middle-class industrialism.

romantic rivalry between Barraclough and the workman who betrays him to Moore.[24] On the other hand, the scenes of Luddite action are strangely powerful and impressive; the movement is granted a scope, power, and organization that are virtually absent in other fictions about industrial action. When the empty wagons roll into the millyard carrying their note of threat (63–66), when we hear the tramp of feet and the disciplined dialogue about whether to attack the parsonage (329–330) or the roll call by number that precedes the attackers' dispersal (337), we are witnessing the power of collective action. Cloaked in darkness, the working class is invisible in these scenes, yet its very invisibility is the source of its dramatic power and its political presence. Brontë does not turn the carefully escalated sequence of actions to the purpose of demonstrating how working-class passions go out of bounds into disorderly riot or blind vengeance. Instead, her assertion of the conventional pieties—the "bad leaders" theory of revolt—contends against her recognition of successful working-class leadership, organization, and discipline.[25] The incompatible images of the working class complement the incompatible images of Moore: they argue simultaneously that Moore's failures of leadership send workers into the ranks of fools and that Moore is a military hero in a well-developed war between the classes.

The attack scene itself is presented as a romance of militant

24. Later in the narrative the Luddite leaders are conventionally described as "strangers," "downdraughts," "bankrupts," and "drunkards" (*Shirley*, p. 370).

25. The complications in Brontë's picture of Luddism make it necessary to revise the simple accusation of failure. Eagleton, for example, describes the Luddites as protagonists distinguished by absence and invisibility (*Myths of Power*, p. 47); Webb focuses on Brontë's failure to see that Luddism was a demand for traditional rights and control of the labor process (*From Custom to Capital*, pp. 131–135). But Thompson describes Luddism as "arising at the crisis-point in the abrogation of paternalist legislation, and in the imposition of the political economy of *laissez-faire* upon, and against the will and conscience of, the working people" (*Making of the English Working Class*, p. 543). Since *Shirley* is about the abrogation of paternalism, Brontë may be said to have had a general if not a specific grasp of the conditions under which Luddism emerged. While she follows such middle-class myths as the association of Luddism with Methodism (Thompson, p. 585), she also displays, perhaps unwittingly, a respect for the political strategies of the Luddite underground that Thompson brings so dramatically to light.

defense which tries to conceal its true nature. Watched and heard through screens of foliage by the hidden, mesmerized eyes of Caroline and Shirley, the "terrible drama" (341) is created in the choral commentaries of the women as they try to make out its action in the darkness. Their dialogue is a critical as well as a descriptive chorus, demanding that we think about the scene generically, as a new kind of romance. Seeing Moore in danger, Caroline loses her usually rigid control and moves to join him in the millyard. Shirley prevents "a romantic rush on the stage" (335), insisting that Caroline would be an embarrassment and an intruder in that strictly male world of "real danger." When Caroline pleads that she will help Moore, Shirley mocks her for imagining that she is beholding "a tilt at a tournament" and asserts that "it is not for love or beauty, but for ledger and broadcloth, that he is going to break a spear" (333–334).

Shirley's appeal to the "realism" of commercial motivation only serves to romanticize Moore all the more. He is in a realm beyond the domestic reach of women, who are in fact "beholding" him perform; the chivalric metaphor has merely been turned toward a modern world of ledger and broadcloth. Shirley's sarcasm, meant to break Caroline's infatuation with Moore, has the odd effect of placing "the real" at a particularly romantic distance, one that is retained throughout the drama of battle. The carefully framed scene sends up a brief flare of yearning for the heroics of definitive, single-minded action—of a kind that is reserved exclusively for the world of men, markets, and militia.

The doubling of paternalism and class war is also visible in Brontë's juxtaposition of the Luddite attack with the public image of social order displayed in the Whitsuntide festivities: the two long-developed actions are the daylight and the nighttime faces of social polity. The children's parade exhibits public care for the poor in its orderly ranks of neatly dressed children. Yet even this innocent emblem of successful local paternalism displays its militant potential when it is transformed into an "army" led by the squirearchy against the opposing Methodist phalanx. The "conquest" of the Methodists in a contest of voices echoes Moore's night victory in the tones of comic naiveté, while the "parade" of Luddites imitates the social forms of discipline demonstrated in the ritual order of the Whitsuntide assembly. Apparently intended to emphasize the gap between paternalist social harmony and unruly Methodist Luddism, these central episodes succeed rather in figuring the impasse in Brontë's social thinking. For her, a dominant social order necessarily creates and conceals an underside of rebellion and a responding violence of suppression. Yet the violent conflict glorifies paternalist power by bringing out its highest chivalric qualities. Rather than rejecting Moore and his industrial warfare, Brontë accommodates him to a public model of militant paternalism in which Yorkshire village order and class struggle are indistinguishably intertwined.

The impasse in Brontë's conception of paternalist order as social violence may account for her failure to pursue the industrial plot in any significant way after the central attack scenes. The double readings necessitated by her text do, however, find a kind of mirror in the doubled image of responsible paternalism that we are offered in the final brotherly partnership of Robert and Louis Moore. The four-way relationships among Robert, Caroline, Louis, and Shirley "marry" the landed estate with the business enterprise,[26] but they do so only indirectly. The ideal paternalism that the novel has consistently sought and feared is made up not of landowner Shirley and millowner Robert but of the strictly male alliance of a newly empowered Louis and a newly chastened Robert. Together their stories suggest the ambivalence of Brontë's encounter with paternalism as a social idea: Louis's energized moral power and Robert's restrained industrial energy pull together and apart in the play of doubling that constitutes Brontë's now domesticated dynamic of male power.

Where does female paternalism figure in this complex terrain? The oscillations between defiance and submission in the portraits of Shirley Keeldar and Caroline Helstone follow di-

26. For Eagleton, Shirley herself represents the combination of contradictory political positions: "a hybrid of progressive capitalist and traditional landowner" and a defender of "Romantic conservatism against bourgeois rationalism" (*Myths of Power*, p. 51).

rectly from Brontë's view of paternalism as order and violence. In Shirley she imagines a would-be female paternalist; Caroline voices her critique of domestic ideology; the relation of the two women creates a separate female sphere romantically allied with nature and myth. In each case, however, Brontë's narrative qualifies, constricts, or undermines the fantasies of female knowledge and rescue that animate the story lines of Frances Trollope.

In Shirley, Brontë created a character through whom she could both celebrate the romance of the female paternalist and subject it to the test of social pressure. Shirley creates a fantasy of herself as "Captain Keeldar," landowner and millowner, that has a real base in her inheritance. As the industrial battle brews, she attempts to intervene with a rescue operation; her plan for large-scale poor relief is preventive medicine through which she hopes to restore peace through charity rather than violence. But her charming bravado is effective only so far as it helps her negotiate or allot resources within a subsidiary role. Moore's commitment to defend his mill in case of attack is a determinant of her social attitudes and actions; in spite of her moral reservations, her tenant has the power of decision because he is a man. The brief social calm that follows on the administration of relief does not prevent the Luddite attack; although the paternalist rescue is administered scientifically and sensibly, it fails to fend off the working-class political organization that Moore sees as an inevitable result of the war (289). In the end, Shirley's political effectiveness comes to little more than her ability to treat her cottagers as a good old-fashioned Yorkshire person should.

The ironic separation between Shirley's romantic social attitudes and the secondary status of her actions is consistently maintained. When she prepares for the charitable venture, Brontë points out her financial incompetence and her social deference to Helstone's leadership of her planning council. Shirley defends her right to hold political opinions at the very moment in the plot when she is most excluded from the elaborate plan to defend the mill; even the poor cottager Farren knows more about what's afoot on the eve of the attack than she does. The women's midnight escapade to witness the attack, an important and radical secret to Shirley, is entirely peripheral to the course of public events. Even in the lavish provision of supplies to the victims of the attack, Shirley's largess as "lord of the manor" is belated and overdone; the critical moves have already been taken by the men. All of this, along with the scene in which Shirley prevents Caroline from rushing to Moore's side, establishes a strictly limiting perspective on the romance of female social rescue.

In fact, Shirley's verbal bravado leads to no action inimical to female propriety until she commits the very conventional fictional rebellion of marrying a man of whom her guardian disapproves. The self-consciousness of her play-acting at masculinity is itself a recognition that women do not command power in the public realm, while her marriage, a rather complete abdication to the private one, suggests that her immense energies find their appropriate role in relation to a powerfully benevolent husband who can nourish and regulate her psychological life.

Caroline Helstone is Brontë's mouthpiece for a critique of domestic ideology that is both radical and trapped in paternalist metaphor. Like Trollope's Martha Dowling, Caroline is the passive partner in a doubling of heroines, an unmarried dependant in a household ruled by an inattentive male. Caroline articulates the underside of domestic ideology—the fate of having no sphere at all. "What was I created for, I wonder? Where is my place in the world?" she asks herself (190), and her strenuously consequential thoughts about these questions confront the problem of enforced female idleness with an analytical fervor that—almost—outbraves social pieties. Caroline penetrates the strategies of power fully enough to see that the conventional answer to her questions—doing good for others— is one invented by the powerful to bend their subordinates into service; and she goes futher, to the recognition that submission only intensifies the hold of power: "Does virtue lie in abegnation of self? I do not believe it. Undue humility makes tyranny; weak concession creates selfishness" (190).

Moreover, Caroline rejects the idea that charity work is a solution in the lives of single women; for her such a life looks like the death of the soul. The superb studies of the "old maids" Miss Mann and Miss Ainsley are portraits of isolation endured. They form stark counterparts to the conventional fictional plotting that celebrates domestic ideology by sketching an inevitable passage from charitable maiden to happy wife.

Caroline's meditation links women with unemployed workers, only to modulate safely back into the key of paternalist appeal. In a chapter describing the different styles in which the two women fill their essentially unproductive days, she muses:

> . . . I observe that to such grievances as society cannot readily cure, it usually forbids utterance, on pain of its scorn: this scorn being only a sort of tinselled cloak to its deformed weakness. People hate to be reminded of ills they are unable or unwilling to remedy. . . . Old maids, like the houseless and unemployed poor, should not ask for a place and an occupation in the world: the demand disturbs the happy and the rich: it disturbs parents. [377]

Although the analysis wavers in its attribution of fault—those in power may be impotent or simply unwilling to remedy—it retains the assumption of dominance and dependence throughout. Perhaps it is therefore inevitable that the passage moves finally to a plea for paternalist attention: "Fathers! cannot you alter these things?" (378) And it promises the fathers that education and activity for women will produce nothing other than the model household angel: "your gayest companions in health; your tenderest nurses in sickness; your most faithful prop in age" (379).

Characteristically, Brontë's analysis of social oppression highlights the muffling of speech: "to such grievances as society cannot readily cure, it usually forbids utterance, on pain of its scorn." For her one of the definitions of freedom is simply the freedom to speak truly. It is a privilege that Caroline, whose theoretical meditations remain unspoken, can take for herself only under the rare conditions provided by domestic trust and affection. Robert Moore in his private aspect can provide such conditions; the dialogues between him and Caroline in the early chapter "Coriolanus" ratify their love affair by showing how playfully and freely they can talk with one another. When

Moore withdraws, Caroline descends into a state of silent self-repression that is broken only by the arrival of Shirley.

Brontë depicts her version of the separate woman's sphere in the friendship of Caroline and Shirley. The friendship is a lifeline for Caroline, releasing her from depression and silence; it is characterized less by shared social knowledge than by an apparently limitless freedom of expression. The conversations between Shirley and Caroline read like love duets or dialogues of self and soul, especially by contrast with the clashes of opinion and character that shape almost all of the other dialogue in the novel. Shirley, the feminist revisionist, indulges in bursts of half-satirical, half-romantic eloquence, asserting a universal female power and mocking male misperceptions of women in myth and literature. Caroline, often skeptical, is nonetheless present in her own force of imagination and intellect. Both women are liberated from the bondage of banal social amenity, free to expand on their reservations about men and marriage and on their private romantic exceptions. The kind of knowledge with which Brontë imbues this female world is not knowledge of the male world; rather it is a zone in which male myths are transformed, fantasies articulated.

But cruelty and tyranny remain even in this paradise of utterance. As though a human relation without those serpents were unimaginable to Brontë, the plot tension on which the developing friendship rides is a purely factitious rivalry over Robert Moore. Shirley knows that Caroline loves Moore, but she torments her friend by bringing him continually into conversation, does nothing to disabuse Caroline of the notion that she is herself accepting Moore's courtship, and then accuses her of allowing a man to make "a perpetually recurring eclipse of our friendship" (264). Caroline's private pain is, of course, amply rehearsed, and edged by the fact that Shirley is her social superior. This apparently gratuitous love triangle is used as a basis for Shirley's indignant refusal of Robert Moore's proposal, in a scene intended as part of his education and reform. Yet the scene itself, highly contrived and anticlimactically placed, does not depend on the creation of pain between women, which deprives the friendship of any privileged status it might seem to have offered. The silence and secrecy enforced by "society" are recreated in the very nature of the women's relation, so that the separate sphere reproduces some of the same tensions generated by the public world.

The fates of both heroines come to rest in comparable fantasies of domestic paternalism. It is worth examining the nature of those marriages beyond the fact of their heroines' submission to them; for in them Brontë creates a psychological dynamic that answers to her initial critique of paternalist inattention. Marriage is imagined as life with a male protector and audience who provides a safe arena for the controlled free play of mind. Shirley's mythic fantasies and Caroline's sensitivity to social oppression, originally expressed in schoolgirl essays or cousinly dialogue with their respective Moores, are granted their best audiences in a promise of perpetual conversation. The psychological paternalism of marriage is rooted in the attention of men who both cherish and limit the rebellious activity of female minds; so domesticated, the violence implicit in paternalism is transformed into a kind of sexual energy which turns the ideal of domesticity into a play of compelling dialogue.

The alternative to domestic paternalism is suggested in the brief portrait of Rose Yorke. With uncompromising integrity Rose attacks the dreariness of domestic confinement, asserts the primacy of her personal talents, and sets a firm limit on her bondage to her mother's rule. The price, as we know from a preview of Rose's future, is lonely emigration: Brontë's fantasy of escape from a world of patriarchal domination is starkly imagined as a severance of all social connection. Trollope's creation of a separate woman's world is one of the fictive solutions that her imagination rejects.

The unrelenting intensity of Brontë's focus on the implications and undersides of social government is dependent on the consistency of her adherence to paternalist models. The strength of *Shirley* lies precisely in that consistency, which could from another point of view be understood as a failure to transcend the limits of paternalist ideology, and the novel's discontinuity of story is part of that strength. *Shirley* breaks open the myth of benevolent social paternalism and reveals its con-

tradictions exactly because it locates no alternative story of social
government. It refuses the power of the middle-class heroine as
a mediator between classes because it insists on the limitations of
her autonomy in the existing social order, denying that women
constitute a "free zone" of moral power and undermining the
story of charitable social rescue. By presenting us with a double
image of workers as deferent individuals and as a powerful
collectivity, the novel also opens the historical gap in the
paternalist model of society. In her refusal to concede the
solution of story line to either side of any issue, Brontë achieves
an anatomy of paternalism more profound and disturbing than
any other in the genre. As *Shirley* demonstrates, the turmoil of
Brontë's social critique emerges from the stability of her social
idea.

Elizabeth Gaskell and the Politics of Negotiation

Read next to the fierce deadlocks of *Shirley*, Elizabeth
Gaskell's *North and South* (1855) can appear a tamer, more
conventional work, one that reaches back to Jane Austen both
for its depiction of strong-minded domestic virtue and for the
social optimism of its *Pride and Prejudice* plot structure.[27] *North
and South* is, however, in serious struggle with *Shirley*: it is more
progressive, more challenging to traditional conceptions of
social order, and more self-conscious about those conceptions. If
Shirley multiplies cases of tyranny and rebellion, *North and South*
offers a comparable range of relations in which we observe the
process of readjustment in patterns of authority and dependence. Where Brontë protests and then subsides in her portraits
of women's lives, Gaskell creates a heroine whose life is respon-

27. Arnold Kettle placed *North and South* in a literary line between Jane
Austen and George Eliot in "Early Victorian Social-Problem Novel," p. 182.
Gaskell's first modern biographer, A. B. Hopkins, calls *North and South* "a
Victorian *Pride and Prejudice*" in *Elizabeth Gaskell: Her Life and Work* (London,
1952), p. 139. W. A. Craik sees the influence of Austen on Gaskell for the first
time in *North and South*, in *Elizabeth Gaskell and the English Provincial Novel*
(London, 1975), p. 94.

sibly and directly entangled with the male world of industrial politics: in fact, Gaskell's climactic scene mixes industrial and sexual politics in a way that speaks directly back to the Luddite attack scene in *Shirley*. If Brontë rests, finally, in the model of paternalism, Gaskell takes the parental metaphor apart to observe its absurdities and insists on the health of ideological change.

The origins of *North and South* lie close to the beginnings of Gaskell's special interest in Charlotte Brontë and may be traced in her correspondence during the summer of 1850—a summer that ended in the first meeting of the two novelists at the home of Lady Kay-Shuttleworth. Writing to this friend in May, Gaskell follows up a previous conversation about *Shirley*; while rejecting the industrial scheme of the novel, she is taken up by its treatment of women's lives. "I think I told you that I disliked a good deal in the plot of Shirley, but the expression of her own thoughts in it is so true and brave, that I greatly admire her."[28] The rest of her long letter is a troubled meditation on the difficulties of life for single women.

Two months later, she responded to Lady Kay-Shuttleworth's suggestion—possibly motivated by their criticisms of *Shirley*—that she write a new novel about manufacturers. Still smarting from the reception of *Mary Barton*, Gaskell wanted someone else to write that book, but her comments set a direction that she was to follow when she took on its authorship herself four years later:

> I can not imagine a nobler scope for a thoughtful energetic man, desirous of doing good to his kind, than that presented to his powers as the master of a factory. But I believe that there is much to be discovered yet as to the right position and mutual duties of employer and employed. . . . I think the best and most benevolent employers would say how difficult they, with all their experience, have found it to unite theory and practice.[29]

The experimental view of social government sketched out here took fictional shape as a challenge to the assumptions of

---

28. *The Letters of Mrs. Gaskell*, ed. J. A. V. Chapple and A. Pollard (Cambridge, Mass., 1967), p. 116.
29. Ibid., pp. 119–120.

both paternalism and laissez-faire: neither the traditional rural paternalism of Margaret Hale nor the market ethos of John Thornton is allowed to stand in its original formulation. Assessed in the context of its predecessors, *North and South* represents a breakthrough in the patterns of conceptualization which dominated the industrial fictions of the 1840s. Revising paternalistic images of government, views of the working class, and the separate woman's sphere, Gaskell's narrative is itself an enactment of the experimental social activity it recommends, for it takes us through a gradual breakdown of traditional ways of thinking about society and into the confusion generated by the process of working toward new ones.

In the opening chapters the myth of old rural paternalist England comes apart, almost literally, before our eyes. Gaskell's heroine Margaret Hale begins as a true believer, imagining her Helstone home as a pastoral condition apparently immune to change, describing it nostalgically as "a village in a poem—in one of Tennyson's poems."[30] She asserts the conventional class prejudices of the landed gentry in a way that highlights their arbitrariness: "I call mine a very comprehensive taste; I like all people whose occupations have to do with land; I like soldiers, and sailors, and the three learned professions, as they call them" (50). And she spends her days in the New Forest of Helstone engaged in a set of traditional charitable and aesthetic activities; the poor are "her people" (48), their broken-down cottages occasions for picturesque sketching.

The novel's first event, Mr. Hale's defection from the Church of England, throws every facet of this pastoral myth into confusion.[31] Hale abandons paternalist roles in several ways at once: he doubts the single authority of the church, withdraws from his

---

30. Elizabeth Gaskell, *North and South* (Harmondsworth, 1970), p. 42. Further references to this edition will appear in the text.

31. This episode has often been criticized as an unmotivated or misleading beginning that sets up implications that Gaskell fails to pursue. Recent examples of that complaint may be found in Margaret Ganz, *Elizabeth Gaskell: The Artist in Conflict* (New York, 1969), pp. 84–85, and in Winifred Gérin's biography *Elizabeth Gaskell* (Oxford, 1980), p. 151. Craik comes closer to a view of its dynamics when she defines doubt itself as the issue raised by Mr. Hale's defection (*Elizabeth Gaskell*, p. 97).

own authority as pastor, and fails entirely to shoulder his proper responsibility as head of his household, forcing his eighteen-year-old daughter to take charge of the emotional and practical difficulties of the family's move to Milton-Northern. In the course of the domestic upheaval, the child quickly grows up and becomes parent to the parent—but for Gaskell this is not the occasion for strong criticism, or even for much satire. The change is painful, but it is a viable readjustment of authority that does not destroy the bonds of trust and affection within the family. What happens in the Hale household is, in fact, a model for Gaskell's vision of larger social change as well.[32]

By the end of the novel the myth of the pastoral world has been radically undermined. When Margaret returns with Mr. Bell to visit Helstone at the end of the novel, change is the major motif of the episode. The schoolchildren have new terms for grammar that Margaret does not know, so that her traditional charitable role is obsolete. The story of the roasted cat speaks for the cruelty and ignorance of peasant life; and when Margaret thinks of the south as a workplace for the unemployed cotton spinner Nicholas Higgins, she recognizes the destitution and solitude of agricultural labor as compared with the comradeship of factory life. Once she has been educated by the forthright class antagonisms of the north, the social realities of the south emerge from behind the picturesque sketches.

When Gaskell comes to the central question of industrial government, she does not, then, offer some version of paternal-ism as an antidote to the laissez-faire despotism of her millowner hero, John Thornton.[33] Thornton's task in the story is not to

---

32. Gallagher's discussion of *North and South* occurs in the context of her argument that Victorians used the ideas of family and society in metaphoric or metonymic relation to each other (*Industrial Reformation*, pp. 166–179). In her view, the relation is metonymic in *North and South,* and the moral influence of women is the force that connects the private and public realms. This reading relies on a use of the influence model more straightforward than Gaskell's. Mediation between public and private realms is not limited to the heroine of this novel; Gaskell also reduplicates metaphorical or analogous situations among the Hale family, the industrial scene, and the shipboard mutiny.

33. John Thornton has all too easily been cast in the fictional mold of those enterprising industrialists who are converted to paternalism or Carlylean captaincy of industry through woman's influence—an influence sometimes

take better care of his worker-children but to bend his attention away from his status as a merchant-prince toward a working attachment to his laborers and a genuine encounter with the differences in their points of view. His initial position mixes paternalist discipline and contempt with laissez-faire abdication of personal responsibility to his workers: he imagines them "in the condition of children" while denying that the masters "have anything to do with making or keeping them so" (167). Insisting on absolute authority during working hours, he follows a policy of noninterference at all other times; his definition of government is to know what is best for the factory as a whole and to carry it out by himself. Margaret articulates the contradictions in his stance, wondering how "to reconcile your admiration of despotism with your respect for other men's independence of character" (171).

The lesson we might anticipate for Thornton in the traditional paternalist mode would be that he treat his workers with kindness, using his power to look after their welfare in return for their obedience. Instead, Gaskell focuses on the problem inherent in the paternalist idea itself. In the important "Masters and Men" dialogue of Margaret, Mr. Hale, and Thornton (165–171), the analogy of masters to parents and workers to children is both the vehicle and the target of a conversation about mutual duty and dependence. Mr. Hale, making a comparison with the raising of children in adolescence, argues that workers should be prepared for social adulthood by being given more independent authority. But by the end of the dialogue, the characters' explorations of the analogy have led to a recognition of its absurdity. Children grow up to become adults; and to imagine the working class as if it enjoyed an endless state of childhood is to perpetrate a monstrosity. Margaret implies as much when she tells a story about a savage overgrown man-child

---

linked specifically with Christian socialism. See especially Cazamian, *Social Novel in England*, p. 228; Roberts, *Paternalism*, p. 91; and Kestner, *Protest and Reform*, p. 170. The novel's rejection of the philanthropic relationship is recognized by Brantlinger (*Spirit of Reform*, pp. 143–144), Melada (*Captain of Industry*, pp. 151–152), and Coral Lansbury in *Elizabeth Gaskell: The Novel of Social Crisis* (New York, 1975). Lansbury mixes it, however, with a simplified characterization of Margaret as "a middle-class Christian Socialist" (pp. 117, 127).

who has been confined and protected from the opportunities to learn civilized adult behavior; the example reveals not only the logical limitations of the paternalist metaphor but also the social dangers of paternalist ideology. As the dialogue develops, the contradictions of Thornton's position also proliferate as it becomes clear that he relies on the child-worker analogy when his employees are in the factory but rejects it as an insult to the independence of their moral lives beyond the factory walls.[34]

In addition to dislocating the paternalist metaphor, Gaskell takes the significant step of overturning the paternalist model from the working-class point of view. When Margaret meets the working-class hero Nicholas Higgins, she automatically assumes that a charitable home visit will be in order, only to find her offer interpreted as an impertinence. Inverting their positions, Higgins invites Maragaret to his house because she looks lonely and kind. In the same way he will insist on a reversal of roles in his relations with his employer. When Thornton offers him a job, and again when the dining-room scheme is developed, Higgins refuses the role of beneficiary, turning potential charities into invitations initiated by himself. His assumption of personal equality simply overrides the structure of hierarchy and deference implicit in paternalism.

The dining-room scheme that Higgins works out together with Thornton at the end of the novel is designed to address the problem of reimagining the master–man relationship in terms that are neither paternalist nor laissez-faire. Understood as a kind of symbol, the plan successfully bridges the gaps the novel has brought into view. Rather than charity, it is a plan for collective buying in bulk, carried out by Thornton according to

---

34. This central dialogue has been extensively explored in two other discussions. Ganz reads the complicated interchange about the merits of paternalism and interdependence as essentially paternalist in its assumptions and as an indication of the uncontrolled contradictions in Gaskell's political philosophy (*Elizabeth Gaskell*, pp. 92–96). Gallagher reads the passage as a rejection of the paternalist metaphor in which the uses and the dangers of the analogy are identified before the metaphor itself is thrown away (*Industrial Reformation*, pp. 166–168). While I concur with Gallagher's sense that Gaskell self-consciously undermines the metaphor, I am not convinced that the dialogue puts the family-society analogy to rest; Gaskell is not so definitive a novelist as that theory implies.

the orders of his workers. It both obliterates Thornton's earlier distinction between his men as workers and as human beings and allows for their independence from his management in the running of the dining room. Thornton eats there by invitation only; the principles of deference and leadership are not acknowledged by either class. Once he is there, the dining room is a place to talk, a tentative forum for discussion and the formation of personal respect between Thornton and his workers. Finally, the eating place run by men takes its place in the novel's consistent and deliberate intermingling of domestic and industrial spheres.

In the process of working out this forum, Thornton releases his firm theoretical views in favor of openness to experience and a spirit of concrete social experiment. Defining the present as a time of "men groping in new circumstances" (414), he switches tutors, abandoning the acquisition of gentility offered by Mr. Hale's classical tradition in favor of the keen social intelligence of Nicholas Higgins. When he tells the story of the dining-room scheme to Mr. Bell, Thornton himself turns the child-worker comparison on its head: he confesses that he had resisted Higgins's assumption of authority until "it seemed childish to relinquish a plan . . . just because I myself did not receive all the honour and consequence" (445). Practicality of invention remains the celebrated keynote of progress in Manchester-Milton, but Gaskell embraces it in the recommendation that it be turned to the equally practical purpose of inventing new models of class relations.

The story of adjustment in Thornton's idea of mastery takes place within a network of related stories, each of which depicts a troubled relation between authority and dependence. Mr. Hale's solitary decision to leave the church creates pain and confusion for his family in the same way that the millowners' refusal to publicize economic information creates misunderstanding between classes. The story of Frederick Hale's shipboard mutiny reflects the dangers of Thornton's authoritarian position as well as the corresponding dangers for his striking workers. Margaret's defense of her brother echoes Higgins's idealistic vision of union activism: "Loyalty and obedience to wisdom and justice are fine, but it is still finer to defy arbitrary power, unjustly and cruelly used—not on behalf of ourselves, but on behalf of others more helpless" (154).

Put into action, however, the sailors' mutiny and the union strike take their toll in the form of suffering for those "others more helpless"; Frederick's mutiny results in the hanging of several sailors, while the strike drives the worker Boucher to starvation and suicide. Both plots portray violent rebellion as dangerous primarily to its participants, in particular to those on whose behalf ideals of rebellion are formulated. Gaskell stresses the contradiction between the theory of leadership and the consequences of practice rather than the violation of social hierarchy or the threat to property. Even her riot scene (chap. 22, "A Blow and Its Consequences"), which, recalling *Shirley,* relies on the familiar melodramatic language of bestiality and the evocation of the threatening sound of an anonymous mob, later works against those conventions by focusing on Margaret's identification of human faces and individual sufferings in the crowd.

While paternalist images of the working class necessarily alternate between the obedient, deferent worker and the violent, rebellious mob, Gaskell turns the working class into an autonomous arena in which issues of authority and dependence must play themselves out. Inverting conventional representations of unions as virtuous but hapless masses manipulated by self-serving leaders, she creates in Nicholas Higgins an intelligent, idealistic, and flexible union leader whose plans for a peaceful strike are undermined by desperate members such as John Boucher. The revision alters the almost universal identification of striking and violence in earlier industrial fictions. In *Mary Barton* Gaskell herself made a more conventional move from a strike action to the melodramatically plotted murder of a millowner's son; in *North and South* the violence born of starvation—a thrown stone—is overt, public, and unpremeditated.

As Higgins conceives it, the union is admirable, intelligently directed, and theoretically justified by the masters' oppressions; but it fails to confront the practical fact that such members as Boucher cannot afford to strike. Thus Gaskell's criticism of the union is based on its tendency to create new class divisions with oppressive results within the labor force itself. Consequentially, the responsibility for readjustment also lies within the working class. When Boucher commits suicide, Higgins takes charge of the orphaned children—an act in which the activity of paternalism is assigned to a worker and redomesticated as a literal assumption of parenthood. Meanwhile, Thornton himself is made to concede that new forms of negotiation between management and labor are part of modern life: "this last strike, under which I have been suffering, has been respectable" (414).

Gaskell's revision of paternalism is a theory of interdependence that cuts across class lines by defining adulthood as an acceptance of responsibility both for dependence and for dependants:

> "God has made us so that we must be mutually dependent. We may ignore our own dependence, or refuse to acknowledge that others depend on us in more respects than the payment of weekly wages; but the thing must be, nevertheless. . . . The most proudly independent man depends on those around him for their insensible influence on his character—his life. And the most isolated of all your Darkshire Egos has dependants clinging to him on all sides. . . . " [169]

The mutual interdependence that Margaret is made to articulate in this speech is very different from Brontë's bound hierarchy; here shifts and modifications of positions are assured through vigorous verbal clashes. "I suppose we all *do* strengthen each other by clashing together, and earnestly talking our thoughts, and ideas. The very disturbance we thus are to each other rouses us up, and makes us more healthy," Gaskell wrote in her 1850 letter about Brontë;[35] and that credo, too, informs the plot of *North and South*. Through the ego battles between John Thornton and Margaret Hale, Thornton and Nicholas Higgins, theoretical prejudices of class are broken down into recognitions of individual character and worth. Self-expression is a necessity for psychological survival in Brontë, but in Gaskell it is a recipe for social change.

35. Gaskell, *Letters*, p. 116.

Gaskell's challenges to social formulations that create and perpetuate the gap between the classes extend to her treatment of the gap between the sexes. In the story of her middle-class heroine she deliberately overruns the separation between men's and women's spheres while at the same time showing how conventional domestic ideology molds her characters' responses. Twice Margaret Hale acts visibly and directly in the male world: when she rushes to defend Thornton from the violence of the rioting strikers and when she lies to the police inspector to save her exiled brother Frederick from the prosecution of English law. Both times she suffers the consequences in the form of doubts cast upon her womanliness. Gaskell refuses to retreat, as Brontë does, from implicating her heroine with the moral ambiguity of action in the public realm, nor does she, like Frances Trollope, create a rescuing heroine romantically free from the reverberations of social pressure.

The structure of Margaret's role as a mediator between classes is consequently quite different from the model that follows from a paternalist idea of social relations. Trollope's heroines perform secret acts of rescue in a region somewhere in between powerful masters and working-class victims; Brontë depicts a largely frustrated attempt to assume authority that is sandwiched between two similarly recalcitrant classes. Margaret, Thornton, and Higgins form a triangle of strong-minded figures whose fates become intertwined because each has the power to act independently as an influence on the other; each "saves" the other in one way or another. All three are linked through a mixture of public and domestic roles: the two men have, for example, forged a respect both in the workplace and through their common concern for Boucher's children. Margaret's linking role in the triangle is evident, but it is constructed in a way that brushes aside the antipatriarchal secret societies of female observation and imagination invented by Gaskell's predecessors.

In fact, the woman's sphere as Gaskell defines it is less a resort than an obstruction to Margaret. In her character, the split between activity and passivity, earlier expressed in the doubling of heroines, is represented as a moral and psychological conflict that receives little support from other women. Rather, Margaret's special quality is created by contrast with other women—against the hedonistic London life of her aunt and cousin and against the querulous domestic refrains of her mother, her aunt, and Thornton's sister Fanny. Matrimonial calculation and fusses about weddings, dress, and status are the staples of the female realm in *North and South;* Margaret is drawn away from them, into dialogues with men and social activity.

Margaret's struggle to define her life is also presented as a battle against forms of idleness that are enforced more directly by women than by men. How she is to spend her days is an explicit issue at the beginning and the end of the novel, while the intense activity at the center of the Milton section offers the possibility of active women's lives in connection with the developing industrial culture. The theme is sounded in the first chapter by Henry Lennox, when he asks how Margaret will fill her time in Helstone; it rings again in a more somber tone when she returns after her parents' deaths to live with her aunt in London, where she is "wearied with the inactivity of the day" (459).

Teaching herself that she must take charge of her life, Margaret resists the idle sociability of the household: "But she had learnt, in those solemn hours of thought, that she herself must one day answer for her own life, and what she had done with it; and she tried to settle that most difficult problem for women, how much was to be utterly merged in obedience to authority, and how much might be set apart for freedom in working" (508). Gaskell's way of phrasing the question high-lights her interest in the process of accommodation and her avoidance of the fervor of revolt. For her there is no fantasy of rebellion, subversion, or a separated woman's world; she imag-ines a negotiated settlement that asserts a power of choice even in the acceptance of dependence. The romantic solution with which Margaret is finally rewarded includes such negotiations: Margaret's marriage to Thornton is carefully defined as an economic and social partnership as well as a domestic settlement.

In the Milton sections, however, the problem of idleness and activity disappears, to be replaced by a portrait of the heroine as a fully responsible human being who is forced continually into making decisions, alone and under pressure. At the center of the novel, the built-up pressures of public and private life accumulate to a pitch of almost unbearable intensity. When Margaret goes to Thornton's to borrow a water bed for her mother and stays to protect him from the rioters, she has spent the night attending her failing mother, she is torn by her feelings about Thornton, involved with the dying of Bessy Higgins, upset by Boucher's suffering, and sympathetic to Higgins's view of the strike. That afternoon she confronts the mob in an action that inextricably mixes public and private motives. The next day, hurt and unrested, she refuses Thornton's proposal in an angry interchange, visits Bessy and hears about the workers' suffering, hears her mother's dying plea for a last glimpse of her son, and writes the letter that she knows will put her brother in mortal danger. The rapidity of events, so different from the sparse actions and spacious reflections of Brontë's heroines, does not allow Margaret the leisure to learn; rather it creates a new—and maternal—image of woman's life as a negotiation of simultaneous crises, and a continual pressure of responsibility for actions that bear heavily on the lives of others.

Gaskell's most interesting and contradictory approach to the formulations of domestic ideology emerges in her account of Margaret as a rescuing heroine. Her two actions in the world of men are acts of rescue, taken when her urgings have put a man of her own class in direct danger of social violence. She has asked Frederick to come out of exile to pay a last visit to his mother; she has sent Thornton into a riotous crowd to confront his workers "man to man" (232). The impulse to rescue comes, then, as an instinctive move to save a man from the consequences of a situation for which she feels responsible; it is not an abstract mediation between classes.

Gaskell's analysis of the rescue impulse as a psychological phenomenon begins early in the narrative, in the account of the dream that follows on Margaret's rejection of Henry Lennox: "He was climbing up some tree of fabulous height to reach the branch whereon was slung her bonnet: he was falling, and she was struggling to save him, but held back by some invisible powerful hand. He was dead" (77).

Her guilt at endangering Lennox's happiness becomes a fierce
maternal instinct when her brother and her lover are threatened.
"I will put my arm in the bolt sooner than he should come to the
slightest harm. . . . I will watch over him like a lioness over her
young," she asserts of Frederick (301). And, to protect Thornton
from the "perilous place" where she has sent him, "she threw her
arms around him; she made her body into a shield from the fierce
people beyond" (234). This imperious maternal instinct, a proof
of Margaret's special courage, demands that we redefine women
as strong protectors whose power of love is equivalent to the
power of action rather than a retreat from it.

Margaret's instinctive actions are quickly riddled with ambiguities of interpretation that leave us with a complicated sense of
the interplay between such actions and conventional standards
of womanly behavior. In both cases the actions are given sexual
interpretations by others: Thornton assumes that her defense of
him means that she loves him, and that her secrecy about
Frederick means that she has a clandestine lover; Mrs. Thornton
assumes that her actions denote an "unmaidenly" character.
Thornton also sees all of Margaret's activities on behalf of the
working class as improper "meddling" in a man's world; during
the riot scene his masculinity is threatened by the accusation that
he has been sheltered behind a girl. But Gaskell does not allow
us to rest comfortably in the assurance that Margaret's gesture is
an act of social idealism that is merely misinterpreted by a
conventionally minded world. While Margaret painfully attempts to separate her personal from her morally disinterested
self, Gaskell insists on the ambiguity of her actions.

Emotionally, Margaret suffers exactly the consequences that
Shirley foresees for Caroline were she to rush to Moore's side
during the attack on Hollows' Mill. Margaret feels like "a
romantic fool" for making a scene, and she is overcome with
shame for disgracing herself in public (247). All night she is
haunted by the image of faces looking at her, "giving her no idea
of fierce vivid anger, or of personal danger, but a deep sense of
shame that she should thus be the object of universal regard—a
sense of shame so acute that it seemed as if she would fain have
burrowed into the earth to hide herself, and yet she could not

escape out of that unwinking glare of many eyes" (248–249). The shame of having left a protected place for one of unwomanly publicity assures Gaskell's reader that Margaret is replete with maidenly modesty; on the other hand, it exacts its price. It suggests that Margaret has been seen by crude eyes in an act that unwittingly reveals her secret passional life—one that we have already begun to read as a firmly repressed sexual interest in Thornton.

In that context, Margaret's appeals to the ideology of rescuing womanhood have to be read as retreats from the violent turbulence of mixed emotions to the haven of idealistic theory. "If I saved one blow, one cruel, angry action that might otherwise have been committed, I did a woman's work," she tells herself after the riot, reasoning that from her special mediating perspective "I could see what fair play was" (247). When Thornton confesses his love, she distances herself even further from the possibility of a personal act, claiming that "any woman, worthy of the name of woman, would come forward to shield, with her reverenced helplessness, a man in danger from the violence of numbers" (253). In her self-justification, the rescuing heroine is defined and legitimized by an appeal to dependence and passivity—"reverenced helplessness"—and by the focus on the prevention of action; the idealistic invocation of a myth of passive virtue covers up the act of impulsive emotion. Gaskell allows the ideal of saving womanhood to stand, but she renders dramatically the action and the passion that it fails to account for.[36]

Gaskell's scrutiny of Margaret's psychological confusions and theoretical defenses should especially be emphasized in the face of the melodramatic language in which the two rescue scenes are cast. Margaret is done up much like a heroine of magazine ro-

36. In Gallagher's reading, Gaskell projects a view of female moral power that is undercut by its reception: by the misreadings of those who misinterpret Margaret and by the fact that Thornton is moved not by Margaret's moral power but by her emotional hold over him (*Industrial Reformation*, pp. 168–179). What Gallagher reads as a contradiction in Gaskell's appeal to domestic ideology I see as another example of Gaskell's distrust of any formulaic ideology: she is as canny about the simplifications of domestic ideology as she is about the paternalist metaphor. Margaret's appeals to ideal womanhood may, under the circumstances, be at least partially felt as deliberate comedy.

mance in the riot scene, with its focus on the sentimental force of her trickling blood; in the lie scene we watch the pale impassive queen through the eyes of the police inspector. There are genuine moral questions about each act, but the writing pushes us toward the image of a noble suffering paragon in both. Those simplifications are quickly recovered in the treatments of the consequences. When time for thought returns, the melodrama of action is quickly recomplicated, and we are left to work out the ambiguities along with the heroine. Why *does* she rush into the riot? Should she have lied to the police? The narrative genuinely pulls us in two ways, between explanations that emphasize Margaret's self-sacrificing heroism and those that suggest other, unconscious drives at work under the pressures of the moment. Because the questions are never resolved, Margaret's most significant experience is to become a human agent in her own right—a process that means living with the doubleness of her actions, like the men who act and decide in the public sphere. Gaskell's revision of the myth of the rescuing heroine lies precisely in that refusal to keep her "pure" and separate from the activities generally associated with the male, the public, and the system.

Throughout *North and South,* Gaskell's case for faith in the process of social change rests on the modifications of social theory or ideology through experimental social practice. Her narrative continually dismantles the hierarchical structure of class that supports the theory of paternalism and the separation of spheres that underlies the story of the woman as social rescuer. While earlier novelists relied on the model of paternalism because the agentless "system" of political economy posed so implacable a prospect, Gaskell finds an enabling structure within the model of capitalist enterprise itself. *North and South* registers a belief, or at least a hope, that capitalist energies of invention might be turned in the direction of social relations, in order to develop arrangements and concepts that might reflect the natures of the new classes that industrialization had brought into being.

The meditations on paternalism and industrial capitalism central to the social novels of Trollope, Brontë, and Gaskell align themselves quite clearly in one kind of historical sequence.

Trollope "solves" the ideological incompatibility by inserting her heroines into the gap between new capitalists and old workers, making them play the paternalist roles their fathers have abandoned. Her fictional repair of the fracture is superseded by Brontë's recognition of the powerful, if obscured, alliance between old and new orders; the notion of a revived and feminized version of paternalist benevolence is consequently portrayed as both romantically attractive and socially impotent. Gaskell's narrative moves in an opposing direction: rather than conflating paternalism and capitalism, she wishes rather to dismantle the dichotomy in developmental terms, attempting to work free of the theoretical limitations in models of social order and gender even as she acknowledges their shaping force.

The three stages may easily illustrate the absorption of social change as the 1840s became the 1850s; perhaps more intricately, the stories demonstrate the inextricability of paternalist ideas and conceptions of gender. The rebellious or reformist motion of women is contained and separated to the extent that paternalist models are active; the overtly rebellious heroines are products of the more politically conservative imaginations. Only after the brash and melodramatic career of Mary Brotherton is transformed by the domestic realism of Elizabeth Gaskell does the female paternalist become an independent force in the social order, and she does so by transforming the idea of paternalism itself.

Yet the social oxymoron expressed in the figure of the female paternalist remains an important concept in the imaginative struggle with industrial capitalism. In varying guises the figure shows up frequently in Victorian fiction, not only in such industrial novels as *Alton Locke* and *Hard Times* but also in other portraits of active rescuing heroines whose careers are less charged by specific political content. Always an indicator of the need to split moral from social power, the female paternalist derives her fictional force from the multiplication of ideological pressures bearing on her character and on her story. And, as these novels suggest, she is a formal indicator of the new status of paternalism in the industrial world, a locus for the activity of mediation in a divided class society.

2 Gentility and the Dangers of Aspiration

Frances Trollope filled some of the early pages of *Michael Armstrong* with satirical descriptions of crude and ostentatious display at the dinner parties of nouveau riche Manchester manufacturers. Elizabeth Gaskell's contrasted interiors set the massive and unused weight of Mrs. Thornton's furnishings against the modest domestic charm of the Hale family sitting room. In her own way, each writer was contributing to the debate about gentility and vulgarity which was one mark of the political tension between the landed gentry and their challengers, the entrepreneurial northern middle classes. The constancy of concern for the gentrification of Manchester was only one reflection of a century devoted—as Martin Wiener has recently argued—to the successful enterprise of taming raw ambitious business drive to the standards of traditional genteel conduct.[1]

That enterprise is a central concern of the novels grouped in this chapter: Elizabeth Stone's *William Langshawe, the Cotton Lord* (1842), Geraldine Jewsbury's *Marian Withers* (1851), and George Eliot's *Felix Holt the Radical* (1866). Built on a dichotomy between the amenities of genteel life and the integrity of work, these novels all attempt to define the true nature of gentility and

1. Martin J. Wiener, *English Culture and the Decline of the Industrial Spirit, 1850–1980* (Cambridge, Eng., 1981).

69

vulgarity through the stories of passive middle-class heroines
with aspirations to rise.

As in the female paternalist pattern, the stories of middle-class
heroines are structured so that they combine and appear to
reconcile incompatible social inclinations. Through the educated and refined sensibilities of second-generation factory
daughters, genteel culture is imported into factory life. But the
impulse to approve of the gentrification of Manchester is
checked by the wish to celebrate the industry and invention of
northern industrial life and to contrast it with the luxurious
idleness practiced by the inheriting gentle world. These stories
therefore struggle to imagine what gentility means and what its
social function may be when it is recognized as a quality
separated from its social base in the landed power of the gentry.

In its double representation of gentility as both desirable and
dangerous, the story pattern also exhibits a more general
anxiety about social aspiration and mobility. The moral education of the heroine reconciles her to her class of origin even as it
awakens her to a world beyond its limits, and her moral progress
stands in for a similar development in the working class. Thus,
while the industrial world may be seen as ascendant, the story
works against individual ambitions to rise in class status or social
power. Damping the lust for social mobility, it substitutes a hope
for a gradual evolutionary development of each class within
itself which leaves the hierarchical order of society intact.

The novels collected here elaborate variations of these para-
doxical positions. *William Langshawe* and *Marian Withers* form a
pair of Manchester novels written by proud Mancunians who set
out to combat southern stereotypes of the brash uncultivated
cotton lord. Elizabeth Stone's novel is a conglomeration of
literary formulas interesting exactly because it demonstrates the
compelling hold that the southern ideal of gentility makes on an
unoriginal mind. Geraldine Jewsbury succeeds far better at
animating and sympathizing with the early factory society that
Stone purports to describe; her novel makes a coherent, if
romantic, case for an ideal partnership between industrial
technology and a newly visionary type of the gentleman. *Felix
Holt* is continuous with the earlier works in its single success

story, Esther Lyon's reformed choice against her aspiration to the life of luxury and ease (I discuss *Felix Holt* as a whole in chapter 4). To read this novel in the light of its Manchester predecessors is to see its radicalism newly, as a rejection of the alliances between business and gentility which shape and trouble the fantasies of Stone and Jewsbury.

Elizabeth Stone and the Gentrification of Manchester

William Langshawe, the Cotton Lord appeared in 1842, under the name of "Mrs. Stone, authoress of 'The Art of Needlework.'"[2] Dedicated to Elizabeth Stone's father, John Wheeler, "late proprietor of 'The Manchester Chronicle,'" the novel sets out to examine the image of Manchester that had been popularized by the horrorists of the Industrial Revolution:

> Cotton bags, cotton mills, spinning-jennies, power-looms and steam-engines; smoking chimneys, odious factories, vulgar proprietors, and their still more vulgar wives, and their superlatively-vulgar pretensions; dense population, filthy streets, drunken men, reckless women, immoral girls, and squalid children; dirt, filth, misery, and crime;—such are the interesting images which rise, "a busy throng to crowd the brain," at the bare mention of the "manufacturing districts:" vulgarity and vice walking side by side; ostentatious extravagance on the one hand, battening on the miseries of degraded and suffering humanity on the other; and this almost without redeeming circumstances—we are told. Is it so?—[I, 1–2]

The revisionist argument that Stone sets up for herself here is one that was quite successfully argued in a book of the same year, William Cooke-Taylor's *Notes of a Tour in the Manufacturing Districts of Lancashire* (1842).[3] Stone makes an occasional dutiful bow in the direction of the virtues that Cooke-Taylor revealed to his public, emphasizing the generous hospitality, the musicality, the independently upright character that mark northern indus-

2. Elizabeth Stone, *William Langshawe, the Cotton Lord*, 2 vols. (London, 1842). Further references to this edition will appear in the text.
3. William Cooke-Taylor, *Notes of a Tour in the Manufacturing Districts of Lancashire: In a Series of Letters to His Grace the Archbishop of Dublin*, 2d ed. (London, 1842).

trial society. But *William Langshawe* fails entirely to meet its own challenge.[4] For much of the novel those "interesting images" are either simply denied or, in the case of the working class, implicitly corroborated and extended. Stone's narrative must be read as a symptom rather than as a treatment of the social self-consciousness generated by the critique of industrialism—a self-consciousness concerned especially with the difference between vulgarity and gentility of manner. Alternating between defensive social satire and highly conventional imitations of the sentimental novel, she offers us a glimpse of a mind trapped in literary and social stereotype, struggling to integrate a personal view of Manchester life with the structures of sentimental fiction. In the end, the book looks like nothing so much as an attempt to displace the embarrassingly crass display of wealth in the Manchester middle class with a more elegant display of literary sensibility.

Stone imagines her reader as a genteel southern lady, and she is uneasily defensive about her own standing in the eyes of her audience. The first sentence of her story breaks off to imagine "some *parvenue*" picking up the book and disdaining to read anything that begins "Mr. and Mrs. Langshawe lived in the manufacturing districts. He was a cotton-man, and—" (I, 12). Then the narrator invents a dialogue between a lord and a marchioness, in which he encourages her to read the book: " . . . there'll be some fun in that;—the Cotton-bags enacting the sentimental!" (I, 13–14). Entreating her "courteous reader" to "follow the example thus *nobly* set you and to patronize the plebeian publication" (I, 14), Stone proceeds with her story. The narrative by-play is intended as a satire of the idle rich, but the lines of class consciousness are clearly set in the contrast between parvenu and marchioness; in the midst of her facetious irony, Stone bows to the superiority of the aristocracy.

4. For a dissenting appraisal, see Kestner, *Protest and Reform*, pp. 69–81. Kestner praises Stone for the precision with which she depicts industrialists during a period of "assimilation" and for her treatment of middle-class women's lives in the new industrial order. It is not clear how Kestner defines the concept of assimilation as it occurs in his discussions of Stone and Geraldine Jewsbury (pp. 150–158).

Moreover, she is going to give it just what she thinks it wants; *William Langshawe* could hardly be more accurately described than in her own phrase, "the Cotton-bags enacting the sentimental." In her anxiety to provide something delectable from Manchester, Stone simply transforms the social stereotypes she lists in her introduction into genteel literary stereotypes. Volume I is a series of local portraits that defend or explain the variations of manner among the Manchester nouveau riche. In the second volume the tone changes radically, dialects and crudities disappear, and each chapter offers a new episode of sentimental melodrama: new revelations about old loves, changes of heart in worldly fathers, deathbed scenes, and exotic Italian scenery. The large-scale departure from her social topic is reproduced in every smaller narrative gesture as well. Each of the social issues that Stone takes up—the physical aspect of the town, the character and taste of the manufacturing class, and the state of working-class life—is introduced only to be draped in the rhetoric and shaped to the conventions of "literature" and served up liberally sprinkled with quotations from the masters.

"Setting" is one of Stone's specialties. Moving quickly over the disfigurement of the landscape caused by factories and railroads, she represents herself as a guide to the overlooked picturesque delights of Lancashire (I, 2–9). A sentence may suggest the quality of her eighteenth-century topographical diction: "Lancashire's sparkling rivers flow with life and spirit through jutting banks and lofty crags, which, without having much of magnificence, are yet, with the branching trees which now tower aloft and anon sweep over the water, and the clustering foliage which covers the banks, save where some jutting crag obtrudes its rugged front, sufficiently varied to present a succession of rich and beautiful landscapes."

Although such beauties are said to be threatened by industrialization, the settings she describes are unrelentingly pastoral. Her working-class lovers court along a country lane; the heroine visits two elaborately described rural cottages, one complete with a quite sociable hermit dressed picturesquely in Spanish garb. For a bit of sublime scenery to match her picturesque pastorals, the narrator takes us for a chapter to visit a caller of spirits in the "wildest part of Lancashire, amid those desolate moors and heaths" (I, 276), and constructs endless syntactical chains of post-Wordsworthian cliché. Near the end of the first volume, the hero leaves for Genoa, affording many pages of Italian travel sketch; and volume II is filled with pastoral deathbed scenes. Stone's argument seems to be that natural beauty, mystical traditions, and appreciators of the picturesque are yet to be found in Lancashire. As an attempt to complicate the public image of Manchester, such an effort may be effective: depicting the intimate interchange between the new town and the old rural ways is one of Elizabeth Gaskell's achievements in *Mary Barton*. That kind of integration is beyond the powers of Elizabeth Stone.[5] Her romantic conventionalities simply wipe out the offending factories and railways, smothering the land-scape in swatches of literary flowers.

Stone's concern about the taste and manners of Manchester society is more central to her, however, and elicits a more complicated set of tones. Her intent is to find a balanced view, from which the habits of cotton families are both criticized from a genteel standard and defended on the basis of "an open-hearted hospitality, and . . . a widely-extended and unvarying benevolence which redeems the character of Lancashire 'cotton-folks' generally from much that might otherwise degrade it" (I, 53–54). In fact, however, the attempt at balance veers sharply between one point of view and the other: specific jibes at instances of bad taste are made up for by more piously general statements.[6] After gossiping about the "ignorance" of certain

5. In a letter written shortly after the anonymous publication of *Mary Barton*, Gaskell reports with amusement the Manchester gossip that attributed author-ship to "a Mrs. Wheeler . . . who once upon a time was a Miss Stone" (*Letters*, p. 62). While *Mary Barton* does breathe life into some of the same story patterns that Stone employs, it is difficult to understand how either contemporary or modern readers could imagine an identity of two such different sensibilities. For a modern reader who does, see Monica Correa Frykstedt, "The Early Industrial Novel: *Mary Barton* and Its Predecessors," *Bulletin of the John Rylands University Library at Manchester* 63 (1980), 11–30.

6. My sense of Stone's failure to balance her tones is shared by Angus Easson, who notes that the novel "veers erratically between the satirical and the laudatory in its dealings with the masters and between farcical and scornful with the men" (*Elizabeth Gaskell*, p. 69).

characters and making fun of a person who has not heard of *The Vicar of Wakefield*, Stone goes on to protest that such peculiarities "are but spots on the face of the sun compared with the integrity and radiating benevolence of Manchester character generally" (I, 181). She throws up her hands at the way dinners are given and food discussed, and then defends the objects of her satire by granting them genuine enjoyment (I, 39–41)—and so on through the novel. As she defensively looks at her society through the eyes of the audience she imagines and fears, Stone's praises ring rather hollow; she is far too cowed by the standards of "good society" to convince her readers of the homely benevolence she names. This social discomfort sometimes takes form in little journalistic sketches ("The rise of the Cottonocracy"; "Manchester in the Race Week") written in a mock-heroic style implying that Manchester is a social anomaly fit only for literary parody.[7]

The standards of traditional landed society also inform Stone's attitudes toward the work of business and the accumulation of wealth. In one particularly odd passage two older businessmen are seen planning to expand, going on with the calculations that characterize their lives. According to the narrative, they are doing needless work. They have "more wealth than they were able to spend with any propriety or consistency in the station to which they had been brought up," yet they "did still toil day after day as regularly, as elaborately, as if they really had to earn their daily food" (I, 127–128). The assumptions here are instructive: work is defined as a way to wealth, but it is appropriate only to those who need labor in order to live; accumulated wealth is merely extra, as it is unsuitable to the social rank allowed by trade. The lines betray a social contradiction that often shows up in the novel: in the act of assimilating her businessmen to middle-class standards, Stone reveals that labor and gentility are incompatible concepts.

Similar assumptions shape Stone's attempt to defend and

7. Kestner notes that Stone's sketches of Manchester adopt the tone of her brother James's introductory essay in *Manchester Poetry*, a volume he edited and published in 1838 (Kestner, *Protest and Reform*, p. 70).

domesticate the society of first-generation cotton lords, for she accomplishes that end by transforming Manchester society into a generator of genteel emotion and sentimental melodrama. The appropriate cast of characters is supplied through the creation of a hierarchy of gentility within the "cottonocracy"; Stone postulates three "distinct and separate classes" ranging from "the low-lived and ignorant, though shrewd, millowner of some out-lying district" to "the cultivated denizen of the town," with a middle class, "a connecting medium, partaking in some degree both of the vices of the one and the refinements of the other" (I, 82–83). The three "classes" are distinguished in terms that reproduce the structure of a traditional social hierarchy; and the plot has to do with marriages and business alliances among them.[8]

William Langshawe, the title character, is of the middle type, and practices the rather confused creed we might expect from such an indefinite mixture. Although he educates his daughter Edith in the manners and occupations of a lady, Langshawe is proud of his "sweat-of-my-brow" rise and contemptuous of "any idle gentleman or fashionable spendthrift" (I, 18); he refuses to allow Edith to marry a man who does not work. Predictably Edith is in love with one: Frank Walmsley, a nephew of Mr. Ainsley, who represents the highest class of cultivation in Manchester business. Ainsley's credo is that of Stone herself, complete with the defensive bravado: "Sir, it made my blood boil to hear the sneers and the ridicule cast on the 'cotton-lords.' I did not see why trade was inconsistent with gentlemanly manners and refined habits, and I was determined to prove in my own person that it was not" (I, 66–67). Ainsley, like his creator, sees no contradiction in practicing the arts of snobbery upon his peers: believing Langshawe to be vulgar, he also opposes the marriage of Frank and Edith. At the bottom of Stone's social

---

8. Stone's attempt to make distinctions among different kinds of manufacturers is usually seen as one of her main contributions; see Melada, *Captain of Industry*, pp. 115–117; Easson, *Elizabeth Gaskell*, pp. 69–71; and Kestner, *Protest and Reform*, pp. 75–77. But it is important to notice that Stone makes her three-part hierarchy in terms conventionally associated with the aristocracy, the middle class, and the working class.

scale is Mr. Balshawe, who specializes in all-night drinking orgies, has his wife serve him in the kitchen, and, unrestrained by the civilizing influence of the town, has become a despot in his region (I, 122–123). Balshawe's son John, a seducer of factory girls, plays the role of villain: he and his father plot a marriage with Edith as a business venture, a plan in which the well-meaning and innocent Langshawe concurs.

When Langshawe suffers business losses from speculation, Balshawe puts him in a vise: he will loan money (at a profitable rate of interest) only if the unwilling Edith marries John. And so the issue is posed: will Langshawe sell his daughter in order to maintain his standing on the 'Change? He will, and he does; Edith succumbs to his pressure in a spirit of womanly sacrifice. Only a last-minute altar-side revelation that John has seduced and abandoned Edith's working-class cousin prevents the marriage. Then Langshawe embraces his beloved daughter, the family leaves off vulgar ostentation to economize in a smaller house, and love triumphs over business.

As the plot rolls along, Ainsley has a corresponding change of heart after hearing a touching deathbed story from the man who loved and lost Frank's mother as a result of Ainsley's insistence that she make a better match. Realizing that feeling might take precedence over social status, Ainsley expresses his reform by giving Langshawe a loan in the spirit of fellowship. Thus Langshawe's alliance with the vulgar Balshawe is replaced by a new partnership that raises him, setting up the course of gentrification that Stone seems to endorse, and undercutting the vulgar scorn for gentility that Langshawe initially professes.

The novel's melodramas of matrimony and partnership rely on a familiar literary formula—wrong marriages enforced by misguided fathers—in order to dramatize the conflict between sentiment and shrewd, heartless calculation. Feeling and gentility are equated, the process helped along by the abandonment of social satire and dialect writing in the second volume, where upper-class diction becomes the rule for all characters. In Stone's moral scheme good manners and goodness go hand in hand, while evil breeds naturally in the uncultivated. But the novel has a subtext as well: bad manners and badness are powerful, active, and energetic, while gentility becomes increasingly defined as a state of graceful sufferance. This pattern, set by the passivity of the heroine, also emerges as a strain of rather effete neurosis in the genteel plot, and escalates in the melodramas of volume II, which test the good characters' patience and fortitude in the face of violence and insult.

Despite her invention of a business aristocrat, Stone fails to prove that trade is compatible with gentility; she separates worldly activity from refinement in terms and tones that betray a tremendous ambivalence about whether to accept or to satirize stereotypes of the crude businessman. She wonders

> if, indeed, gentlemanly habits, delicate feelings, and cultivated minds, are not inconsistent with success in Manchester trade . . . on 'Change a man of education and refined manners is looked on as an animal to be stared at and pitied. And so long as the cotton trade exists, it is very possible that the gentleman will be surpassed in the race by the low-born mechanic, whose powers of calculation are not checked, and whose shrewdness in worldly things is not clogged, nor his "push on, keep-moving" course not impeded, by any of those delicate embarrassments which might arise in a refined and cultivated mind.   [I, 138]

Checking, clogging, and impeding, gentility is cast as an enemy of action; whether its "delicate embarrassments" are those of moral compunction or of idle decadence it is hard to discern. Stone cannot sort out the deadlock between business and cultivation: because one seems to exclude the other, her plot simply turns away from one to the other. In her portrait of Edith Langshawe, the potential integrator of business and gentility, refined suffering rules the day.

Edith begins by representing the possibility of social development in "the rising generation [who] enjoy advantages to which their parents had no access" (I, 23). She has been ideally educated by a clergyman's wife who has taught her skills appropriate to her station: household work, "a judicious and discriminating charity," and just the right number of accomplishments to make her ornamental as well as useful (I, 25). When Edith practices charity, Manchester turns into a rural village where choice bits of meat or sets of baby clothes are distributed by a young lady on cottage visits; Stone imagines the rituals of gentility only in the paternalist village modes of the past (I, 76–81). Those pretty habits are the only actions through which our heroine's virtues are ensured. "Woman's lot is on her, and she will yet be proved by suffering" (I, 21), the narrator declares; and for the rest of the novel Edith is an image of helpless but brave endurance. She loses her lover, bows to her father's pressure to marry a man she despises, accommodates herself cheerfully to reduced circumstances, and watches tactfully as her lover returns married to someone else. Even when that wife dies at the end of the story, no reunion is made explicit; Edith is left to represent noble self-suppression. She is allowed only one choice, to sacrifice herself at the altar. When that choice is annulled, she has really nothing to do in the novel except to learn of human woe.

Meanwhile her lover Frank becomes the center of a luxury-line Italian plot that seems designed both to elevate the tone of the novel and to depict the dangers of overrefinement. Sent off by his uncle on a "business" trip, Frank joins the household of a wealthy merchant with a voluptuous lute-playing sixteen-year-old granddaughter. On a trip up Mount Vesuvius, Mr. Luttrell is murdered by an Italian guide. As he dies, the girl, Bianca, attempts suicide in an attempt to blackmail Frank into marriage. Believing Edith to be married, Frank succumbs to the marriage in a kind of passive resignation; his gentility also means that he must sacrifice himself in sensitivity to others' feelings. The melancholy mode in which all this is set is the keynote of the second volume, which is full of sad events befalling innocent victims, and ends with Bianca's death—of exposure to Manchester?—heavily bedecked with flowers. The story of the civilized and hapless Frank begs the question originally raised by Langshawe's rejection of an idle gentleman as a son-in-law.

As the genteel plot proceeds into the sentimental effete, the locus of villainy also makes a significant shift from the wicked Balshawes to a nameless, faceless working class. The elder Balshawe is disposed of with a fit of apoplexy—no doubt a suitably crass punishment for his vulgar excesses—and John simply disappears from the novel after he is unmasked at the altar. He has been guilty of brutalizing the working class: after seducing the working-class heroine Nancy Halliwell, he tries to pay off her lover, Jem Forshawe, so that he will marry her. When Jem finds out the truth and flings back the bribe, he is out of a job as well as a wife. John is also responsible for the despair and decline of the Halliwell family occasioned by Nancy's fall, but that matter proves an occasion for his regeneration. When the Halliwells leave Manchester in disgrace, John uses his business connections to arrange work for Halliwell in a new town. Throughout it all, he is praised for the energy and success with which he takes over his father's business, and no further retribution occurs. Instead, Stone turns her attention to denouncing trade unions, and her scorn for the working class supersedes the melodrama of villainy in the cotton men.

Like the rest of her narrative, Stone's treatment of the working class is confined to the imitation of literary models; three distinct and morally incompatible modes of writing come into play when she approaches "the lower orders." The first, and the most benign, renders the working-class lovers as the clowns and clods of Shakespearian subplot: when Nancy Halliwell speaks to Jem Forshaw in a country lane, the scene sounds like an imitation of something out of *As You Like It* (I, 109–112). The second mode is borrowed from contemporary "condition of the working classes" journalism. In this vein she investigates the domestic economy of the Halliwell family. Taking the reader into the unpaved street of operatives' housing, Stone concentrates on the differences among the conditions of front gardens, "from the state of which might easily be guessed the character of the occupant of the cottage"; they reveal that for the cotton operatives, "as in Milton's Pandemonium, 'the mind is its own place'" (I, 157–158). For the Halliwells the mind seems to be its own time as well; they are depicted as a loving, thriving family of handloom weavers set in the midst of Manchester. When the family moves out of Manchester—demoralized not by unemployment but by shame at Nancy's fall—it would seem that the industrial revolution had just arrived: the family moves from its traditional cottage to "a large manufacturing town about forty miles off" (II, 133). In the end the family is rescued from the evils of factory work and prostitution through Langshawe's charity: he sets them up a social notch in a small shop, neatly disposing of the problems of domestic life and factory labor.

These pious fictions of preindustrial family virtue are the exceptions that prove the rule—the rule being the tone of contemptuous satire in which Stone discusses the working class as a mass. The subject comes up in two quite different ways: in the first volume she spends two chapters sketching the Race Week, and in the second she "explains" the actions of unions and strikes to her audience. The sections are unified, however, by Stone's refusal to take the working class seriously. At the Manchester Races "The GREAT UNWASHED are lords paramount of the time, and for three days they 'fool it to the top of their bent'" (I, 235). At Kersal Moor "the gentility is but a drop in the ocean of plebeianism" (I, 236); as the diction suggests, Stone is relying on concepts of the working class that predate the Victorian anxiety about the social threat of the masses, and she goes on only to parody their entertainments. The section ends with a dialogue between two female operatives enjoying themselves at the races while a husband and child die at home (I, 243–244). To underline the shock, the narrator refrains from comment: the utter insensibility of the working-class mind has been established.

When she arrives at a description of unionization, Stone's most telling gestures again suggest that the phenomenon is not to be taken seriously. Such words as "union," "strike," "secretaries," and "leaders of the people" are placed in quotes, as if to say that they are children's make-believe. The strike she describes is got up by "political demagogues" although there is no present cause for distress (II, 281). At the end of the chapter the union's frustration leads to a fatal resolution that results, some chapters later, in the murder of a popular young cotton lord. Neither agency nor motivation is granted to the workers: the strike is trumped up, and the murder victim is said to be beloved by his workers. Union melodrama is also called in to dispose of Jem Forshaw, the ill-fortuned working-class clown who is Nancy Halliwell's lover: he joins the union only to be rendered permanently insane by a skull-and-crossbones union initiation rite.

Introduced late in the text, the union material serves conveniently to obscure and cancel the question of working-class oppression raised by John Balshawe's treatment of Nancy and Jem. The source of personal violence is relocated in union action, and the understandable violence of retribution that might have been leveled at Balshawe is displaced into a motiveless impersonal attack on another character.[9] These machinations are not simply about Stone's hatred of unions; they represent the moral impasse in her imagination of middle-class culpability. Purged of indigenous villainy, the business world becomes an innocent victim of working-class crime perpetrated by Italian guides as well as by English operatives. The shift of revulsion from the Balshawes to the workers completes the stalemate in Stone's initial attempt to discriminate among the manners and morals of the manufacturing class itself. By the end of *William Langshawe*, genteel sentiment has won the day, at the cost of a complete separation from both the energy and the evil that emanate from the world of calculation.

Stone's inability to shape her story with any consequentiality makes for a very bad novel, yet it is one that helps to define some patterns of social tension that were to be more seriously developed in later fictions. The narrative itself is a drama of conflict between the writer's attempt to value and evaluate the manufacturers and her assertion of the superiority of a feeling, literary sensibility. Although *William Langshawe* gentrifies the industrialists, it can do so only by abandoning their working power. The one-dimensional contrast between genteel feeling and shrewd calculation gives Stone no room to negotiate; her three-level hierarchy of sensibility necessarily fails before that more essential dichotomy. The inadequacy of her definitions does, however, raise the question of how gentility is to be defined, criticized, and fruitfully set in relation to the activities of industrialization.

The plot structure of *William Langshawe* is also of interest

---

9. Easson contrasts Stone's use of an actual incident, the murder of Thomas Ashton of Hyde, with Gaskell's in *Mary Barton*. Stone separates the masters' immorality from the union violence, making the manufacturer's son an innocent victim, while Gaskell makes the arrogant son's behavior the final motive for the murder plot (*Elizabeth Gaskell*, p. 72).

because of the ways it reasserts traditional class hierarchies and social stasis in the face of its ostensible subject: the dramatic social rise of the cotton lords. Although the three "classes" of manufacturers are said to have risen together from the working class, the differences among them are as immutable as those in the traditional class structure they imitate. And the romance plots centering on the heroines serve to solidify that hierarchy. Edith is a heroine of "inner" gentility, for whom the idea of union with Balshawe is repugnant; she is clearly not meant to civilize the savage Balshawes by womanly acts of culture. The Langshawes' swing from the low Balshawes to the genteel Ainsley is accompanied by a compensatory dependence on Ainsley's financial generosity; in the very act of looking upward they are kept in their places.

The working-class love plot is more overtly tied to the question of social mobility. Nancy Halliwell is Edith's cousin, and has seen her aunt rise to middle-class opulence through marriage to a cotton lord. Nancy's story is, in outline, the one Elizabeth Gaskell was to develop carefully in *Mary Barton*: the working-class girl, aspiring to ladyhood herself, is caught between the seductive rhetoric of a factory owner's son who means to trifle with her and the genuine affection of a working-class lover. In both novels the pattern warns against the dangers of social aspiration even as it records the reality of class rise. But in Stone's version, the working-class choice has no worth in itself: Jem Forshaw is a figure of pathos. Nancy, like her cousin, is not given the stuff of moral agency that would make her actions into genuine social choices. She simply falls into disgrace, disappears, returns for a moment to save her cousin from marriage, and is finally set up again with her family, through her uncle's charity. On both levels of plot, the urge to look upward leads to a fall and is ultimately replaced by the receipt of charitable help from above. Social movement is downward and then upward; social dependence is the price of restored repectability; in these ways the hierarchy is reaffirmed.

William Langshawe ends in stasis. The pastoral deathbed scene on its final pages is an inadvertently appropriate conclusion to a work in which the wish to raise Manchester into literary gentility erases the social energy and mobility that brought it into being. But the impulse to separate real social mobility and power from a rise in standards of interior cultivation is not special to Elizabeth Stone. A similar tension prevails in later and better novels that set themselves firmly against just those standards of self-conscious gentility that hold Mrs. Stone in thrall.

Geraldine Jewsbury's Romance of Work

Marian Withers, like *William Langshawe*, is a novel written by a Mancunian about first-generation factory owners in the 1820s; Jewsbury, too, wants to create a revised image of that society and to chart the course of its future in plots of marriage and business partnership. But Jewsbury's novel, though it has appeared fragmentary to its critics,[10] is a work of far greater seriousness and integrity. *Marian Withers* does tell several different stories in a short space, in a style of rather fast-moving summary that does not specialize in the patient development of character. Nevertheless, the narrative is original, attractive, and psychologically acute, and the various stories are closely connected by analogy or contrast in order to work out several aspects of a single cluster of ideas. Its frame is clear: Jewsbury contrasts the passion of work in productive manufacturers' lives with the waste of passion in the lives of the idle rich. Each of her little life histories gives us a character who, with the help of an older guide, moves toward selfless productivity or toward the waste of rich inner endowments. This moral scheme, Carlylean in its worship of work and its hope that the industrious classes may come to rejuvenate society, is complicated and enriched by Jewsbury's fresh pictures of the manufacturing class, by her quite modern sense of adolescent psychology, and, more problematically, by her struggles to balance passion, work, and status

10. Jewsbury's biographer Susanne Howe records critical reactions to *Marian Withers*, among them her own: "the material was there, but the book is fragmentary and unsatisfactory." See *Geraldine Jewsbury: Her Life and Errors* (London, 1935), pp. 111, 114–115.

in the lives of both male and female characters. Finally, the novel is a clear instance of a structure in which the abstract hope for the education and development of the working class is embodied in the story of a middle-class heroine.

Jewsbury dismantles the stereotypical portrait of the Manchester businessman with very little noise. Where Stone obfuscates her historical perspective, Jewsbury uses it clearly, inviting the reader into the world of 1825, and into the wild hilly country north of Manchester, where small industrial communities cluster at the bottom of valleys, as yet unconnected by rail with the greater world.[11] Here she finds plain gray stone houses and factories mixed with domestic agriculture and a group of simple, well-meaning factory owners who have risen through the ranks of cotton spinners. In place of the conventional dinner-party scene designed to satirize the nouveau riche, she gives us a sympathetic account of a homely dinner put on in the kitchen by a nervous and disorganized owner's wife, much in need of the neighborly help she gets from the heroine and her aunt (II, chap. 1). In place of the factory tour that reveals the agonies of working children, she takes us on a tour in which each stage of the mechanized spinning process is explained to the visitor; as the machines get more complex, the workers are said to look healthier and more advanced (II, chap. 2). The ideology of technological progress is absolute; it hardly seems accidental that *Marian Withers* was commissioned for publication in the *Manchester Examiner and Times* during the year of the Great Exhibition. Yet there is none of the rhetorical fanfare about magical transformation that characterizes the industrial fantasies written by visiting observers of the Manchester scene. Jewsbury was the granddaughter, daughter, and sister of successful and flexibly entrepreneurial businessmen; practical knowledge and inventiveness were in the family blood.[12] Her refreshingly concrete descriptions of machines capture the

11. Geraldine Jewsbury, *Marian Withers*, 3 vols. (London, 1851), I, 68.
12. Biographical information comes from Howe, *Geraldine Jewsbury*, pp. 4–6, 28–38.

accessible mechanical contrivances and the practical tinkering that characterize the history of early textile machinery.

This perspective allows Jewsbury to separate two responses that coalesce in more conventional myths of Manchester, such as Stone's: the worship of technology and the worship of wealth. Her manufacturers, proud of their stubbornly independent rises, scorn joint stock companies because they make money without work and worry little about wealth itself except when a short supply threatens the ongoing work of the factory.[13] Among themselves they discuss improvements in machinery or accommodations for workers, and argue about the proper treatment of the working class. But such episodes of general discussion are almost pro forma; Jewsbury's real contribution is the tone of affectionate respect in which she presents the unpretentious practicality of her manufacturers. Her argument is perfectly expressed in a short episode during which a minor manufacturing character, Mr. Wilcox, comes to pick up the heroine, Marian Withers, from a wealthy manor where she has been visiting. Marian's hostess, a social-climbing snob, is horrified by Wilcox's "vulgarity," but Wilcox is unembarrassed. He is delighted by the new idea the visit has inspired: an ornamental fountain has given him the idea of setting up public washhouses for his workers, and he has inquired about the mechanics of the piping. Innocently oblivious of the social messages expressed in the spectacle of beautifully wasted water, Wilcox leaves only his hostess convicted of vulgarity.

These portraits of socially innocent first-generation millowners represent an inversion of Elizabeth Stone's view of gentrification. Stone's backwoods Balshawe is a savage; Jewsbury's rural industrialists have not yet been corrupted by the urban rage for wealth. Nevertheless, they have risen—a not entirely innocent venture. In the portrait of her manufacturer-hero, John Withers, Jewsbury creates a model of exemplary aspiration that makes a moral counterpoint to the merely social ambitions

---

13. Melada's summary of *Marian Withers* includes a useful review of the fictional treatment of financial speculation throughout the century (*Captain of Industry*, pp. 43–46).

she describes in the "genteel" part of her novel. It is a model that centers on the passion for creative work.

John Withers' rise from beggar-child to millowner is told in a fairy-tale-like "prologue to the play" (I, 67) separated from the main plot, which centers on his daughter Marian. The fairy godmother, the first of many guides who appear just in time for a charitable intervention, is herself an exemplar of female paternalism in the novel: she moves from "solacing herself with a novel" (I, 6) to rescuing "two of the outcast children of vice" (I, 18) from the den of thievery in which they are beaten and exploited by adults. The two children are named John and Alice Withers, although they are not siblings. Their educations are supported by the workhouse and, for John, by apprenticeship in the cotton mills; Jewsbury offers a meliatory glance at these targets of radical protest, after the stormy decade of the 1840s has come to its end. John burns with the desire to rise to fame and fortune, and contrives to be taught to read. The critical moment of his life occurs when he has become a cotton spinner, and "the visions of making his fortune had long since been blotted out by the monotonous taskwork" (I, 26). His spinning mule breaks, and he discovers by himself how to improvise a repair. It is a moment of essentially religious revelation: "Henceforth all his labour was in a new spirit. The machine had become to him a living creature; he had obtained an insight into the power which moved it" (I, 27). Now Withers' conventional desire to make his fortune is subsumed in a passion for science, described in near-religious terms. He becomes obsessed with an idea for a simpler spinning mule, sacrifices his job, and spends years in a freezing garret on the verge of madness; "his IDEA possessed him like a demon, and haunted him night and day" (I, 29). On the verge of collapse, this Manchester Frankenstein finally makes a successful model. Jewsbury describes the feat in terms of incarnation that reveal *her* model of work as spiritual exercise:

> He had compelled his idea to assume an adequate shape, to interpenetrate the wood and iron, and to work them flexibly, as the body is wrought by the soul.
>
> The demon which had possessed him, which had fed upon his

life and upon his reason, was now exorcised: it had entered into
his work, and he beheld it peacefully and orderly performing that
which he had given it to do.   [I, 36–37]

Work allows interior passion to find external form and
psychic rest. That highly romantic fusion of interior genius with
practical invention is an ideal of power beside which the exterior
changes in Withers' life looks pale.

The story of the rise itself keeps Withers innocent of concerns
with class or status. Deferentially he sells his invaluable invention
to a "gentleman" for a thousand pounds; the gentleman makes
a fortune and takes the credit.[14] When Withers uses his money
to buy a factory, he prospers less than he might have done
because he is more interested in making machines than in
making money. Later in the novel his business is threatened by
failure, and he transcends his sorrows in a communion with his
arrested machines, feeling as a father does among sick children;
this Frankenstein, at least, is full of concern for his creation.
When he finds a spindle in need of repair, his mind turns again
to mechanical invention: "As his thoughts rose to the region of
science, his mind grew calm" (II, 107). John Withers' most
important "rise" is the ascent to that romantic region which soars
gloriously above such petty concerns as class and status.

The historical prologue substitutes the romance of science for
the romance of rise, creating a standard of inattentiveness to
wealth and power.[15] The main plot is, however, about the next
stage of industrial development: how are these provincial industrialists to be brought into relation with gentility? What is true
gentility? And how is social rise to be positively imagined? These
questions are put into action through Marian Withers' second-
generation struggle between her loyalty to the provincial virtues

14. Jewsbury may have found precedent for this story in John Aiken's *A
Description of the Country from thirty to forty Miles round Manchester* (1795). Aiken
describes the inventor of the spinning mule, who did not seek a patent, but sold
his invention to a Manchester gentleman for 100 pounds. The account is quoted
in J. T. Ward, *The Factory System*, 2 vols. (New York, 1970), I, 146.
15. Melada asks a pertinent question: Why is John Withers the only self-made
man whose early career is told in fiction? He speculates that the favorable
reception of the Withers story had to do with its celebration of creative genius
and dedication, rather than the accumulation of capital (*Captain of Industry*, pp.
47–48).

of her father and aunt and her ambivalent attraction to "good society."

Like Elizabeth Stone's heroine, Marian is her father's pride, "a high-water mark which showed how much he had risen'" (I, 81). She too returns home from a good education meant to ensure her social superiority—and here the resemblance ends. Stone invents the melodrama of Langshawe's misguided marriage choices for his daughter; Jewsbury puts the conflict in the adolescent confusion of a young girl who does not know which society she should grow up onto: "it was doubtful whether the education bestowed upon Marian might not tend to make her dissatisfied with the society she was likely to be thrown amongst" (I, 82). On her extended visits to the social-climbing world of her schoolmate Hilda at Carrisford Manor, Marian is both enthralled by beauty and flirtation and horrified by the heartless materialism of the marriage market. When she returns to her father's house, she sulks, wastes time, feels ashamed of her neighbors, and yearns for the romantic stimulus of the Manor. Benevolent but puzzled, her father and aunt encourage her in their ways and their work, but they can give her little social guidance. Marian brooding, withdrawing, and resenting makes for one of the more convincingly impossible adolescents in Victorian fiction. For much of the novel, however, her search for a coherent self takes the form of watching other women who surround her and reflect her possibilities.

In the portraits of those women Jewsbury conducts her most fervent and troubled attack on the tragic waste of women's lives in marriages made for social status. The synthesis of passion, work, and idea that fulfills John Withers is precisely what is absent in women's lives. Led by false guides to believe in the necessity of "a good establishment," these childless women drug themselves with social climbing and escapist romance. Jewsbury's stories reflect her own trouble in imagining solutions for women's lives; she condemns society for teaching women to want the wrong things and sympathizes with the waste of life that ensues, yet places the responsibility on women for failing to consecrate their misguided choices with dutiful good works. Perhaps because of that very doubleness, the novel is marked by an unusual evocation of women's sexual and creative energies fighting hopelessly for unified forms of expression.

The portrait of Mrs. Thomas Arl articulates the shape of a career devoted to social rise. Nancy Arl, the older sister of Marian's friend Hilda, exemplifies repressed natural feeling and energy channeled into ruthless social climbing. Brought up by strictly repressive Calvinist parents, Nancy finds a mentor in a worldly aunt who introduces her to the joys of luxury and good society. She wastes no time in snagging a successful merchant for the sake of the establishment he can afford her. Fueled by her intense wish to be accepted into landed society, her energies are absorbed in an almost frantic obsession with dress, furnishing, and entertainment. In the service of that same doctrine she forces her younger sister, Hilda, into a marriage with a wealthy but aging roué who has wasted his life and strength in dissipation.

This liaison is a grotesque parody of the pattern in which experience guides innocence. In a hypocritical flight from the sins of his youth, Glynton sees indiscretion everywhere he turns; to satisfy and buy him, Hilda dresses as an innocent maiden in white muslin with a single rosebud. Her revulsion from his touch is quite real, however; and Marian watches her force herself to the altar, unable to see an alternative to her sister's mania for social status. Once she has committed this sin against natural feeling, however, the narrative pressure leans on her to make her marriage into a field of good work, an errand of mercy to the wretched. Like her sister, Hilda has been pressured to waste her natural resources, yet both women are subtly criticized when they fail to make their husbands happy. A similar circularity shapes the more fully developed story of Lady Wollaston, the secondary heroine whose career holds the most portent for Marian.

Lady Wollaston is a figure of romantic melodrama whose story outlines a "high society" version of what might happen to a lady of true gentility in a perfunctory marriage. She functions as a warning figure for Marian: both women have "real" taste, expressed in the arrangements of their private rooms; both have highly romantic natures; both have erotic capacities suggested through responses to music; and both fall in love with the same irresponsibly flirtatious young man, Mrs. Arl's cousin Albert. In Marian's story Albert is an adolescent crush, but in Lady Wollaston's he creates a serious romance that teeters crazily on the verge of adultery. Lady Wollaston's starved feeling erupts in a yearning for passionately courtly love games that eventually overwhelm her; when she throws herself upon him, Albert reveals the flimsiness of his nature, flees from her demands, and sends her into despair. Shortly afterward her husband is shot in the course of military duty in Ireland; he reveals to her on his deathbed that he has been followed by a young woman who is in love with him. Lady Wollaston takes charge of the mistress without reproach, seeing in the girl's vulgarity a humiliating mirror of her own behavior. The heroine's repentance has begun.

Repentance is simultaneously a commitment to work. Horrified by the waste of her life, she decides to devote herself to charitable work among the wretchedest of the wretched—the Irish poor. "Now I dread to die before I have expiated my life of self-indulgent indolence," she exclaims (III, 226); the melodramatic self-condemnation is also a conversion to the novel's ideal, labor in a new spirit. The conflation of purposes highlights the discontinuity in Jewsbury's imagination of women's stories. Idle romantic fantasy must be replaced by social service; the moral is clear enough. Yet while male passions are embodied in work, female passions are suppressed, forgotten, or expiated in work. There is no solution to the waste of women's lives, except in the futuristic fantasy allotted to Marian herself.

Marian's solution arrives in the form of an ideal guide who reconciles all the contradictory pulls of the novel, both in the public industrial sphere and in the private romantic one. The genteel and wealthy Mr. Cunningham finds his life's work when he decides to devote his intellect and his wealth to the future of the industrial society. He goes into partnership with John Withers in order to study the relations between capital and labor, and to prepare both of the industrious classes for their futures. It is a marriage of practical industry with visionary intellect; unlike his social equals who live in scorn of trade,

Cunningham sees that the real life and energy of England have passed from the decadent gentry to the industrialists, and he proposes to place the greater intellectual and moral capabilities of the genteel tradition in their service. This, Jewsbury suggests, is the proper relationship between the antagonistic classes: that the gentry should recognize its spiritual obsolescence and serve the new world in the roles of guide and educator.[16]

From the vantage point of 1851, Jewsbury endows her '20s hero with historical prescience. Cunningham foresees the necessary years of antagonism between labor and capital: "*antagonism* is the only process by which a fresh growth is possible in this world" (III, 110). With Jewsbury, he locates the source of value in work, defining "property" as the recompense of labor and "the rights of labour" as the right to the dignity of work (III, 112–113). This apparent amalgamation of the propertied and the working classes under the umbrella of labor presumably underlies Cunningham's idealistic hope that association will replace antagonism as the spirit of commerce in the future (II, 25). He also hopes to guide the manufacturing class away from the principle of self-interest, toward the principle of cooperation: "These men have the old barbaric force of undisciplined life; they need educating; they need civilising; but they will change the face of the world" (II, 29). But "they must be purified from the cupidity of blindly and greedily following their individual interest" (II, 28). The revelation of labor that transforms John Withers' life must be effected in the mass by guidance from above.

Through Cunningham's millennial perspective Jewsbury pays lip service to the convention of the barbaric millowner in need of culture, though the most her hero will do in that line will be to marry the industrialist's daughter, bringing his personal refine-

16. Cunningham's stress on labor as an end in itself is a vague version of Thomas Carlyle's doctrine of work in *Past and Present* (1843); rpt. London, 1912). In particular Jewsbury follows Carlyle's chap. 12 ("Reward"), in which he attacks the concept of money wages as reward for labor. Cunningham's ideas about education are ones that Jewsbury had been writing up with similar idealism in essays titled "The Lower Orders" and "The Civilization of the Lower Orders," published in *Jerrold's Shilling Magazine* in 1847. See Howe, *Geraldine Jewsbury*, pp. 90-94.

ment into her world. Meanwhile, the great task of civilizing and educating is to take place in a more immediate way, through the disciplining of the new industrial work force. At this juncture the implicit analogy between middle-class women and the factory population begins to emerge.

Jewsbury does not even pretend to offer an independently drawn account of the industrial working class. In a single sentence, she notes that exclusion as a form of respect for the differences in class experience and imagination: "The condition of the working-classes was of course very distressed, as the weight of suffering pressed into their daily lives with a minuteness and heaviness of which those above them cannot form an idea" (III, 99–100). The sentence betrays a belief in the immensity of the gap between classes that more abstract wishes in her text deny—yet it may also be a measure of Jewsbury's tact that she did not attempt a working-class subplot in a novel devoted to the glory of technology.[17]

Throughout *Marian Withers* the working class exists only as an occasional topic of discussion for the millowners. Withers and his colleagues are given a passage of "discussion" which raises the conventional questions: Should workers be encouraged to think well of themselves by being given public laundry and bathing facilities? Should children be given time to play during breaks in the working day? Should factory wives stay at home and learn domestic skills? Should the working class learn to save money against lean times? Should they be educated? The good characters answer yes to all these questions, while the harsh treatment meted out by the one recalcitrant master is said to provoke hatred, unionization, strikes, and personal violence. Jewsbury records her attitudes efficiently: organized working-class action is a natural response to oppression, but it only increases the suffering for both masters and men (II, 37 and III, 100). Sympathetic to social traps, she is unsympathetic to anti-

17. Howe defends Jewsbury's actual aquaintance with workers against the emphases in her writing, describing jaunts with Jane Carlyle which included friendly visits with cotton spinners (*Geraldine Jewsbury*, p. 134).

social actions: the response echoes the structure of her women's lives.

Through Cunningham's ambitions, Jewsbury records historical differences in ways of talking about the working classes. Her first-generation millowners worry about physical conditions of labor and domestic life; Cunningham speaks for the 1850s and the decades to follow, stressing the need for education. Representing guidance rather than paternalism, Cunningham aims not to restore feudal relationships between the classes but to raise the level of civilization within the working class itself. In his policy, the ubiquitous paternalist metaphor appears and then disappears: "I should wish our workmen . . . to be educated on the same principles as those on which we would wish our children instructed. Until the state provides against the starvation of the mind as it does against that of the body, it is our duty, as masters, to see that those who work under us shall have that instruction to which they are entitled as rational and accountable beings" (III, 107–108).

Cunningham practices his educational ideals more concretely on another troubled, rebellious, confused, and envious subject: Marian Withers. Predictably, he is the solution to her social dilemma. In marrying him she painlessly aquires a perfect blend of the irreconcilable: genteel social status and respect for the world of her father. But before she is allowed to recognize her love for him, Cunningham becomes the guide and mentor who teaches her Jewsbury's morals. He brings her books, listens to her woes, and warns her against the deceptive lure of romantic fantasy, exhorting her to self-discipline and self-control, "the first law for both man and woman" (III, 130). Dropped at a propitious moment, a word to the wise is sufficient: Marian finds the advice revelatory. She rouses herself from her adolescent slumber, disciplines her dreaminess, and makes a useful woman of herself. With equal alacrity, the manufacturing population begins to thrive during the two-year period following Cunningham's move into the valley:

> With education came also enlightened ideas of self-control and self-government; they no longer spent their wages in sensual dissipation; their notions of enjoyment ceased to be idleness and

drunkenness; ideas of thrift and foresight kept pace with an improving trade and increased wages; unions and benefits-clubs they had as before, but the improvement in education and intelligence enabled them to make a wiser administration of the funds. . . . [III, 242]

The sentence is a particularly comical instance of Jewsbury's impatience as an artist, but it also reveals an essential despair that connects her view of class conflict with her view of women's lives. Cunningham is in the novel as the embodiment of a wish for a personal savior, a Carlylean hero who will add the raising of women to his goal of raising the dignity of labor. His job is to discipline both the idle and dangerous romantic fantasies of women and the thriftless dissipation of the working class. Although he is made to assert the equality of men and women, he is given a status that implicitly exalts the upper-class male: he is the creature whose impassioned guidance may raise the unruly to order, forestalling the threat of rebellious actions such as strikes and adulterous affairs.

Jewsbury's ideals may be distantly egalitarian, but her practice is not. Marian's marriage matches an older, wiser man with the girl he has brought up to be his companion; the working class must also be educated to an appreciation of its place. At the same time the novel yearns in its self-division for a hero who will reconcile its contradictions in his very being: Cunningham asserts the identity of love and status marriage, industry and gentility. With those identities in place, Jewsbury's hero can accomplish the novel's most interesting social task: to activate a fantasy in which "being raised" means a moral and social elevation that keeps its subjects right in place.

Despite their ideological differences, *William Langshawe* and *Marian Withers* exhibit common responses to the initial premise of rapid social rise. Both novels block or displace the fantasy of simple social ascent through plot structures that reassert traditional class hierarchies in which wealth and value flow downward, to raise subordinate characters. And—with rather different degrees of moral control—both Stone and Jewsbury imagine true gentility as a quality of feeling or being that is necessarily in conflict with the energies of upward social aspiration. Stone attacks the image of crude Manchester power with the most simple form of resistance: denial. Her work covers over industrial disturbances in a sentimental literary language that represents Stone's idea of gentility; nevertheless she cannot conceal the radical gap between that fantastic world of sentiment and the effective world of business. Jewsbury carefully separates the will to social power from the passion for scientific power that she idealizes in John Withers. When she reintroduces social leadership to her valley of manufacturers, it comes in the form of an ideal gentleman with a new idea of dedication to the historical battle against the principle of self-interest. The fantasy of union is perfectly designed to combat the fear that technological power and social responsibility are necessarily antithetical. Taken together, both narratives express an intense resistance to social mobility concealed by a romantic, sentimental, or moral ideal that fuses business and feeling.

George Eliot and the Choice against Gentility

The context provided by these earlier novels helps to make some new sense of George Eliot's concerns in *Felix Holt the Radical* (1866). *Felix Holt* is not about the early and highly visible clash of cultures that accompanied the dramatic rises of northern manufacturers, but it does take up issues continuous with those of its predecessors: the morality of business calculation in aspiring men, the status of the landed gentry, and the reeducation of a heroine who yearns for a genteel life. In her Midlands setting, where mining, business, and agriculture gradually impinge upon one another, George Eliot investigates the phenomenon of social ascent from the perspective of the mid-1860s, as a later phase of class realignment moved into view. From that perspective, Eliot's story of middle-class power is a devastating critique of the fantasy of accommodation between old gentility and new business.

Like Jewsbury, George Eliot scorns Stone's conventional distinction between bad business and good manners—but she does so in order to assert the obverse: that the principle of self-interest runs both genteel and business power. *Felix Holt*, an experiment in showing what a genuine battle against self-interest might look like, is a rebuke to any idealizing concept of gentility as the moral salvation of business: for all his own idealism, Felix Holt stands clearly for the necessary incompatibility of social status and moral power.

Felix Holt's political beliefs have always presented a frustrating vagueness to readers who expect working-class radicalism to stand for a shift of power to the disenfranchised; the novel has been described as antipolitical and socially conservative.[18] Eliot's fears about political change and working-class suffrage are only part of her portrait, however. Felix's story, together with Esther Lyon's, can also be usefully understood as Eliot's most direct and theoretical attempt to look at the issues of social rise, gentility, and aspiration. What Felix's life expresses most clearly, and what Esther learns from him, is that true elevation resides in the choice not to rise. Eliot works out that definition of radicalism by juxtaposing the careers of Felix Holt, Harold Transome, and Matthew Jermyn.

The novel opens on two returns: both Felix and Harold come home to lonely mothers, confronting them with unexpected and unwelcome opinions. Harold labels himself a Radical, takes to himself the powers and luxuries of his position as landowner, and goes on to run an utterly conventional electoral campaign in the first post–Reform Bill election. Felix has given up his medical training to remain a member of the working class; he now supports his mother by repairing watches and teaching children. His political goal is to educate some miners in the ways of saving their money and educating their children, but he does

18. For such discussions of Eliot's politics in *Felix Holt*, see Arnold Kettle, "*Felix Holt the Radical*," in *Critical Essays on George Eliot*, ed. Barbara Hardy (London, 1970), pp. 99–115; Graham Martin, "*Daniel Deronda*: George Eliot and Political Change," in the same volume, pp. 133–150; William Myers, "George Eliot: Politics and Personality," in *Literature and Politics in the Nineteenth Century*, ed. John Lucas (London, 1971), pp. 105–129; Fred C. Thompson, "Politics and Society in *Felix Holt*," in *The Classic British Novel*, ed. Howard M. Harper, Jr., and Charles Edge (Athens, Ga., 1972), pp. 103–120; and Linda Bamber, "Self-Defeating Politics in George Eliot's *Felix Holt*," *Victorian Studies* 18 (1975), 419–435.

not label his stance; we are left to discern the intent expressed by
the novel's title. And what seems most "radical" about Felix is his
wish to divert the flow of upward social aspiration. "If there's
anything our people want convincing of, it is, that there's some
dignity and happiness for a man other than changing his
station," he says in a late summing-up speech.[19] That belief rests
on a personal mistrust of the consequences of gentility, which he
describes in terms of bondage:

> "Let a man once throttle himself with a satin stock, and he'll get
> new wants and new motives. Metamorphosis will have begun at
> the neck-joint, and it will go on till it has changed his likings first
> and then his reasoning, which will follow his likings as the feet of
> a hungry dog follow his nose. I'll have none of your clerkly
> gentility. I might end by collecting greasy pence from poor men
> to buy myself a fine coat and a glutton's dinner, on pretence of
> serving the poor men." [58]

Since gentility itself generates wants and desires, its "wearers"
are no longer free: first their own minds, then other people
become victims of its demands. Felix himself has been saved
from the genteel bondage by a prevision of his own course,
which he decribes to Mr. Lyon as a "conversion." In that vision
he has seen the absurdity of "wanting to turn my life into easy
pleasure. Then I began to see what else it could be turned into"
(56). As he understands it, his freedom rests on that moment of
consequential vision: he will determine his life by choosing the
right, rather than having it determined for him by the strangu-
lating demands of class.

Like Jewsbury's heroes, Felix stands for the dignity of labor
against the scramble for status and ease. His doctrine of choice
has more particular resonance, however, in the context of
electoral politics. All of his political activity has to do with his
sense of the working class as a group who do not yet know
enough to choose. Even the newly enfranchised electors of 1833
have no idea how to use their power of choice, as Eliot suggests
in her portrait of Mr. Rose at the polls, canceling out his votes by
trying to please everyone (255–256). The working class, repre-

19. George Eliot, *Felix Holt the Radical*, ed. Fred C. Thompson (Oxford, 1980),
p. 364. Further references to this edition will appear in the text.

sented as ignorant even of what the Reform Bill enacts, is subject
to even greater mass manipulation: the election agent Johnson,
who treats the miners whom Felix wants to teach, sets up the
electoral riot that Felix will later attempt to control and waylay.
Because they do not have a real power of choice that would allow
them to exercise the true power of public opinion, "the ruling
belief in society about what is right and what is wrong, what is
honourable and what is shameful," Felix tells a workers' crowd
that they cannot yet use the lesser power of the vote (249–251).
In his and Eliot's view, the conditions for choice lie in a
disinterested moral region somewhere above and beyond the
pulls of need or class.[20]

Felix's radicalism represents a wish to go to the roots of social
injustice by conflating self-interested gentility with self-interested politics and replacing them with disinterested morality.
Harold Transome's radicalism is its antithesis: an unreflecting
condition in which self-interested politics is a conventional move
in a genteel career. For Harold the luxuries of gentility are
simply assumptions of life, like the air he breathes. As to his
opinions, George Eliot is at pains to suggest that they result from
no choice and that they represent only an instinct for adaptation
and survival. "How Harold Transome came to be a Liberal in
opposition to all the traditions of his family, was a more subtle
inquiry than he had ever cared to follow out," the narrator
declares, and since Harold—unlike Felix—cannot account for
himself, she goes on to explain him (96–98). His "change" is
merely a continuum: "the man was no more than the boy writ
large, with an extensive commentary." He had always been
inclined to opposition that will assert independence and power
"without throwing himself into that tabooed condition which
robs power of its triumph." He "meant to stand up for every
change that the economical condition of the country required,"
but as the narrative implies, this is no more than an opportu-

20. Gallagher discusses Eliot's depiction of Felix as an Arnoldian "best self"
distinguished both from religious transcendence and from conventional social
culture. Concluding that "Felix's politics consist solely of the recommendation of
culture," she shows how, according to Felix, the uneducated worker has no
politics to be represented (*Industrial Reformation*, pp. 243-252).

nistic instinct to go along with what "the increasing self-assertion of the majority, peremptorily demanded" (98). In short, Harold plans to ride to power on the energies and policies of the newly empowered middle classes. The whole matter is told in a way that slyly erases Harold's political opinions by reducing them to his earliest formed tendencies of character.

Harold's failure to comprehend Felix's doctrine of choice is directly reiterated late in the story, in an interchange between Harold and Esther: "'Felix has chosen his lot. He means always to be a poor man.' 'Means? Yes,' said Harold, slightly piqued. 'but what a man means usually depends on what happens. I mean to be a commoner; but a peerage might present itself under acceptable circumstances'" (352). Harold's conflation of personal intention with what is already socially determined may be the most pungent formulation of what is wrong with his politics. It is doubly ironic because he is at that moment acting out his dependence on "what happens" in his "intent" to marry Esther simply because her claim to his estate threatens him with a social fall.

The contrast between Harold and Felix defines social heroism as active personal resistance to conventional models of social aspiration and power. The career of Harold's father, Matthew Jermyn, is there to prove Felix's theory that the rise to respectability necessarily corrupts. Mrs. Transome's sufferings at his hands exemplify the "bondage" to appearances that Felix anatomizes, and Jermyn's precisely delineated career exemplifies the dangers of social aspiration that Felix eschews.

In this portrait George Eliot attacks the entrepreneurial ideal with a vehemence equal to that of any earlier and cruder vilification of the businessman. Jermyn is set in the fictional tradition that links business malpractice with sexual violation: with infinitely more subtlety Jermyn and Mrs. Transome are drawn in the line of melodramas that include such calculating seducers as the Balshawes. Because their sexual relationship lies in the past, smothered by their need for genteel respectability, the plot can center on the psychological drama of concealment rather than on direct sexual manipulation. It is no less melodramatic for that: Eliot loads her narrative from the first moment of

Mrs. Transom's appearance, to suggest and withhold the guilty secret of Harold's paternity. The often-admired scene that closes chapter 8 is, for example, redolent of the staginess characteristic of Eliot's presentation of the guilty pair. The narrator gives us a family scene that "would have made a charming picture of English domestic life" except that the handsome woman's face is turned the wrong way, away from her family. She is therefore startled at the sound of an approaching footstep. It is not her son's; nevertheless she can identify it. And the chapter ends on an unmistakeable note of foreboding: "It was Mr. Jermyn's" (100).

Jermyn's appearances as a villain of business are less titillating but equally damning. He appears in Treby Magna as a new man: "a young lawyer who came from a distance, knew the dictionary by heart, and was probably an illegitimate son of somebody or other" (41). His first move is a failed attempt to turn the old-fashioned town into a fashionable watering place. The advertising is good but the enterprise fails: a preview of Jermyn's career. With his Latin tags and ponderous diction, Jermyn is the image of the parvenu, despised by the gentry as "one of your middle-class upstarts" (30) and by his son as a businessman to be used and then thrown away. Harold's scorn only demonstrates that he has inherited his father's instrumental way of seeing other people along with his physical attributes; here Eliot's irony points to the amoral coalition of entrepreneurial calculation with the power and traditions of the landed gentry. At the same time she shares and endorses the scorn poured upon Jermyn by "gentlemen," shoving him out of the novel in the end with the words of the local baronet: "Leave the room, sir! This is a meeting of gentlemen" (383). The narrator's are, if anything, more damning: "Moral vulgarity clung to him like an hereditary odour" (101). As always Eliot wishes to replace social terms with moral ones, but in this case the tone of social disgust rings clearly through her phrase.

Jermyn's "moral vulgarity" lies in his personal insensitivity to Mrs. Transome's feelings. Dominating her through fear, he is "beneath her in feeling" (102); that is, his moral class belies the social pretension and the slavish devotion to repectability that is the only ground of his morality: "with no glimpse of an endurable standing-ground except where he could domineer and be prosperous according to the ambitions of pushing middle-class gentility, such a man is likely to find the prospect of worldly ruin ghastly enough to drive him to the most uninviting means of escape" (332).

That ground proves shaky when Jermyn relies on it for the fealty of his underling Johnson: "Being a man who aimed at respectability, a family man, who had a good church-pew, subscribed for engravings of banquet pictures where there were portraits of political celebrities, and wished his children to be more unquestionably genteel than their father, he presented all the more numerous handles of worldly motive by which a judicious superior might keep a hold on him" (238). It is clear enough that for Eliot, "gentility" is a bankrupt concept; it is also an invidious one. Johnson learns not only to be respectable but to "act with doubleness towards a man whose own conduct was double" (239); through him the narrative arranges for the world of calculation to perpetrate and then to lash back at itself. Jermyn's long rise ends in a ruined reputation and expulsion from the community.

Taken together with the novel's representation of the stifled life at Transome Court, Jermyn's career is a crucial piece in Eliot's portrait of the new middle class. The plot so intertwines the parvenu and the landed class that an attack on one is equivalent to an attack on the other. Business and gentility are implicated with one another not only in the sexual link between Jermyn and Mrs. Transome but also in the inheritance plot, which legally invalidates the Transomes' "hereditary" claim on their estate, rendering their status doubly questionable—a matter to be sustained only through the manipulations of business. The conflation of these normally opposing social categories obviates the need for a choice or a balance between them; rather the middle class is rejected as a body with neither legal nor moral claim to its power. This plot structure suggests that Eliot criticizes the Reform Bill not only as a failed attempt to impose change through politics but also because she retrospectively rejects the alliance of classes that the bill brought into power.

Two arenas remain for the breeding of virtue: Felix's classless ideal and the rank that cannot corrupt itself with aspiration: the aristocracy. Sir Maximus Debarry's "antediluvian" idea of life is cause for narrative irony (87), but it is the Debarry family that produces the novel's only shadow of a hope for leaders who combine power with disinterested sensibility. "One of the new Conservatives" (39), Philip Debarry is praised by the narrative at each of his appearances. He is a moral aristocrat who represents the possibility of rising standards made possible by a stable class hierarchy.

In the story of Esther Lyon the narrative drive to substitute moral elevation for social aspiration receives its most fairy-tale-like expression. In a novel full of thwarted plans and suppressed actions, Esther is the single medium for change: within six months the heroine undergoes "something little short of an inward revolution" (389). Through this highly tractable character, Eliot offers a version of "revolutionary struggle" (389) that amounts to the emergence of the best womanly self from an adolescent overlay of self-conscious social aspiration. Just as Jewsbury's Mr. Cunningham effects in *Marian Withers* what he wishes for the working class, Felix Holt teaches Esther the essence of his politics: to choose correctly between Harold Transome's luxurious ease and his own strenuous resistance to the bondage of gentility.

The story of Esther and Felix is heavily charted through Esther's changing uses of metaphors of superiority and inferiority. Like those of her fictional predecessors, Esther's story begins when she returns from a fashionable education and "situations where she had contracted notions . . . above her own rank" (67) to a humble home that grates on her fastidious sensibilities. She is full of superiorities, "never doubting that hers was the highest standard" (68). The moment Felix appears, flaunting his sense of moral superiority, Esther's certainty begins to falter: their early dialogues are battles about what is "higher," "lower," or "the best" which quickly chasten Esther's sense of herself. By the time she goes to visit Felix at his house, "it seemed to her as if her inferiority to Felix made a great gulf between them" (193); when he is imprisoned she thinks of him as "an influence above her life, rather than a part of it" (302).

Esther's hero worship is presented as an appropriate womanly feeling, the obverse of Mrs. Transome's yen to rule. She is also given her chance at equality with Felix when she reenacts his rejection of gentility by coming to understand her "sudden elevation in rank and fortune" (304) as a fall. As the process unfolds, the word "vulgar" is attached to Harold (340), and Transome Court looks like "moral mediocrity" and "middling delights" against the "high mountain air" of Felix's sensibility (341, 357). Finally Esther arrives at Felix's own terms for gentility: she "saw herself in a silken bondage that arrested all motive, and was nothing better than a well-cushioned despair" (390). Esther is clearly an exemplary student—but George Eliot is particularly didactic in her application of this scheme. The terms Esther learns may be moral ones, but they attest to an impulse that Eliot shares with her more class-bound predecessors: to reassert revised hierarchies in the face of social mobility.

The didactic form of the educative romance is intersected by the inheritance plot, which gives Esther the luxury and the burden of choice between one kind of romance and another. She is indeed "a remarkable Cinderella" (106)—one who is allowed to go and live in the castle for a while to see what it's like before having to make up her mind about what constitutes a prince and a kingdom. In so outplotting the fairy tale, Eliot creates the opportunity for Esther to redeem herself through that centerpiece of Felix's radicalism, the doctrine of choice. During the walk by the river when Felix expounds the doctrine, Esther demurs: "A woman can hardly ever choose in that way; she is dependent on what happens to her. She must take meaner things, because meaner things are within her reach" (225). But the inheritance plot gives her the opportunity to sacrifice the elegant circumstance within her reach for something she thinks to be beyond it: Felix's love. And the choice, of course, brings Felix within her reach.

The compelling outline of that fantasy conceals the truth of Esther's claim that "a woman can hardly ever choose in that way." When Eliot imagines Felix's liberation from social constraint she portrays him choosing against gentility because he sees it consequentially, as an inevitable process of corruption.

When Esther chooses, she chooses between two men who represent love and status. Felix's scolding has the effect not of changing her thinking but of changing her feeling so that womanly affection triumphs over her social ambition: the first effect of his medicinal talks is that Esther begins to pay tender attentions to her father. Because she loves Felix, she sees Transome Court through his eyes. If that were not enough, the figure of Mrs. Transome looms as a warning that female ambition ends in loveless bondage to more powerful men, while Harold underlines the lesson by revealing that his first wife was a bought slave. Transome Court is a nightmare parody of what Esther imagined; how could she choose it? She flees from it at the moment when it definitively reveals the failure of domestic affection.

Esther's "womanly" version of the doctrine of choice asserts a traditional hierarchy of gender: she chooses her dependence on a moral superior.[21] Her only alternative, represented in Mrs. Transome, suggests that ambition in woman is illusory, ending only in a worse dependence. For Esther, and for the working class that is Felix's other, remoter audience, to acquire the power of choice is to abandon the quest for direct social power. Freedom lies in the choice to submit to a higher "good" rather than to a lower, more manipulative power. The rigidly limited choice asserts a familiar paradox: to rise correctly is to stay in place.

Unlike earlier fantasies, however, Eliot's maintains the separation between virtue and power. The kind of "good" that Esther learns can be socially channeled only in unconventional,

21. For a discussion of Esther's story which emphasizes Eliot's antifeminist reliance on the doctrine of influence through submission, see Bonnie Zimmerman, "*Felix Holt* and the True Power of Womanhood," *ELH* 46 (1979), 432–451. Zimmerman links Eliot's sexual politics with her conservative electoral politics, also making the connection between Eliot's hopes for the working class and Esther's education. In her view, the metaphors that permeate the courtship of Felix and Esther evoke relations of mastery, conquest, revolt, and submission. A similar argument is made by Sally Shuttleworth in *George Eliot and Nineteenth-Century Science: The Make-Believe of a Beginning* (Cambridge, Eng., 1984), pp. 128-141. Shuttleworth draws attention to the parallel between Eliot's Comtean organicism and the ideology of woman's sphere, and links *Felix Holt* with *Shirley* in its treatment of female rebellion and submission.

unpredictable ways. When, for example, Esther exerts her womanly influence to speak for Felix's character during his trial, she also exemplifies that power of public opinion on the side of right which Felix claims as the greatest potential power of the working class (250–251). But the force of feeling with which Esther prepares the way for the town fathers' pardon of Felix is not challenged by any interested opposition. No one has a motive for keeping Felix in jail; he is not one of those guilty secrets that are in this novel practically synonymous with genteel life; and Esther's power is hardly put to the test. More to the point, Felix and Esther are simply rewarded for their visions of middle-class bondage by a providential release from its conditions, just as George Eliot releases other characters—such as Dorothea Brooke—who have learned her lessons. In this novel, however, the relief of Felix's and Esther's magical escapes attests above all to the severity with which the moral conditions of middle-class life are imagined.

In the light of earlier fictional accounts of emerging and conflicting kinds of middle-class power, the radicalism of *Felix Holt* comes to look a little sharper. Carefully set at just the historical moment when it was to become clear that middle-class radicalism had relied on working-class issues for the ends of its own power, the novel virtually ignores indigenous working-class politics (giving it only a brief appearance in the pre-Chartist speech that Felix rebuts [246-248]) but it focuses the matter of middle-class manipulation through the electoral riot plot. Thus, while it is true that *Felix Holt* rejects politics altogether, it is also important to notice that it is aimed at something more particular: the politics of class rise, the shifts and realignments of power that were expressed in the passage of the Reform Bill.

The radicalism of that more particular attack lies in the way Eliot makes combinations of social categories and ideas that were conventionally imagined as dichotomies. Politics, business, and gentility are given the same moral shape, not opposing ones. Like *William Langshawe* and *Marian Withers*, *Felix Holt* examines the tensions between old gentility and new business; but where the Manchester novels imagine business recast in a mold shaped by the virtues of true gentility, *Felix Holt* looks in horror at the coalition, seeing business as the concealed serpent at work behind the scenes, repairing the fading tapestry of genteel life. Where earlier visions of the middle classes set working energy against idle luxuriance, calculation against sentiment, Eliot displaces the virtues of honest work and feeling onto the unworldly region inhabited by Mr. Lyon, Felix, and Esther. Meanwhile, in the middle-class story, an effete gentry imaged in the mental weakness of the Transome-Durfey line does receive a shot of energy from the entrepreneurial character that flows from Jermyn through Harold into the revitalized Transome estate. But that flow is quite literally defined as illegitimate: shady business practice shores up the ruins of a decadent claim to landed power. In *Felix Holt* the calculating and the genteel dissemble and fall together. Looking back thirty-odd years, Eliot sees no thread of historical virtue in the coalition of old and new middle-class attributes.

Eliot's social skepticism is similarly expressed in the way she treats the idea of hierarchy and social ascent. In the earlier stories, Stone and Jewsbury oppose the threats of calculation or sexual aggression posed by middle-class social climbers with imagined versions of social hierarchies that are intrinsically virtuous. Stone ends with a business aristocracy supporting a newly sentimental middle class, which in turn supports a decent preindustrial working class. Jewsbury imagines a genteel hero descending to the support of a working manufacturing population. In both fantasies, wealth, power, and gentility are ultimately merged; their favors flow downward in the social scale in order to raise each class within its station; and an idealized traditional model of social rank is reestablished. For all her conservatism, Eliot's imagination is not stuck in social hierarchy in the same way. Her story insists on a radical separation between social statuses and moral ones; the Felix-Esther romance opposes those ideas, teaching us to see social elevation as moral vulgarity. With the exception of Philip Debarry, a last hope for the aristocratic ideal, Eliot portrays the social hierarchy as a labyrinth of traps and dead ends which necessitates the invention of a moral hierarchy that opposes it from no clearly defined social place.

Felix Holt is radical, then, both in resisting the way power flows within the middle class and in refusing to fantasize about virtuous arrangements of power within conventional structures of social order. Esther, the legitimate heir to Transome Court, does not go there to effect a moral transformation, to infuse a "real" gentility of feeling. True, her romance with Felix offers us a fantasy equivalent in its sentimental idealism about womanly submission to the one imagined by Geraldine Jewsbury. But Eliot's is a fantasy of virtue severed from social power. If Felix and Esther represent the hope for historical renewal, it is not because they have refilled genteel status with gentle power but because they will survive in a kind of moral guerrilla warfare with gentility, choosing to live in some unplaced territory of resistance.

Just as the social philosophy and practice of "systemic" political economy generated a need to refurbish and redefine images of paternalism, unprecedented rises to power and wealth precipitated reevaluations of the meaning of gentility. In fiction the topic was an old one, of course: making moral distinctions between true and false gentlemen and ladies had long been an important theme in novels of middle-class life. But the novels I have treated here address something more threatening than questions of individual moral discrimination within a variegated middle class. The problem they recognize is new in scale: the release of a strong source of wealth and authority which had nothing to do with the order of inherited rank or station, which posed the possibility that real social power might be separated from the codes of upper-class behavior. What was more, the industrialist's display of wealth and respectability threatened to undermine the symbolic power of the traditional gentry by revealing that its signs of entitlement—its luxuries, estates, entertainments—did not necessarily signify the levels of breeding they were meant to express.

Getting the "upstart phenomenon" into a fictional frame of judgment therefore required more than assessing, controlling, or denying the self-interested power of business morality. It also meant that an opposing ideal of gentility could not be simply seen to reside in a certain social class. In order to go into battle with the powers of calculation, gentility itself had to be purged of calculation. And so the idea of gentility has a fate rather similar to that of paternalism: its "real" intrinsic virtue is disentangled from the status-conscious society that claims it, and it is idealized at the cost of separation from a basis in social power. In the very act of reasserting the moral force of gentility, the novels betray a sense of its irrevocable dependence on other sources of social energy and power.

PART TWO

Narrative History and the Social Record

In Part One I have been interested in the ways in which romantic story lines centering on middle-class heroines create fictional zones for fantasies about social order. Because they can be seen as undetermined by the laws of the marketplace and even as marginal to legal process, the rules that govern the progresses of these heroines form alternatives to those that shape stories about the role of paternalism or the rise of business in a political economy. But, as I have suggested, the fantasies are in themselves symptomatic of contradictions between middle-class wishes and fears about the reorganization of social power. Female questers turn out to embody ideals of paternalism purged of power, of gentility purged of social aspiration. The story lines they sketch out tell us both about the special perspectives of the middle-class and female imaginations that created them and about their ideological entrapments.

The focus on womanhood is a powerful way to locate a space for alternative activity and social criticism in the midst of the social order itself. Other social-problem novels create comparable alternative or dissenting spaces by sketching out histories of value beyond the boundaries and outside the terms that define life in society. Such realms of discourse are rhetorically shaped in two major ways: through appeals to nature and through invocations of a "true" history. The chapters in Part Two are concerned with texts in which the pastoral or the retold past is an essential technique of narrative argument against the assumptions that shape Victorian social discourse. Both nature and history work in these novels as forms of romantic resistance to the idea that character is either defined or determined by its social circumstances and constraints. Despite the differences in their overt topics—which range from Chartism to the plight of the fallen woman—all of these fictions participate in a discussion that has its roots in the conflict between romantic ideas of human freedom and the philosophy of social determinism.

The novels grouped in Chapter 3 rely on post-Romantic pastoral writing to free their characters from the social circumstances that create their shame and their imprisonment. Consistently, the appeal to nature is linked to the creation of tainted heroes and heroines who raise the essential problem of social determinism: are they helpless victims or responsible agents? I will not try to answer that question: the narratives reveal exactly how unanswerable it was for the Victorians, and how deeply they were divided between their simultaneous beliefs in the power of character and the power of circumstance. Rather this chapter explores the ways in which pastoral works within the narratives to deflect the question itself, so as to free its readers from the conventional social responses generated by the problem, and thus to make a place for a genuinely radical critique. Each of the novels I discuss makes this effort with a different kind of effect. As a whole my discussion aims to take pastoral writing seriously, to see how it may successfully penetrate conventional social ideas, and how it can be used to perpetuate reigning ideas of social place and order.

Like the appeal to nature, the invocation of "true history" calls upon the authority of temporal courses that make sequence and meaning of human experience in larger-than-social perspectives. Chapter 4 is devoted to novels in which the moral life of character—and by extension of society—is intertwined with the capacity for connection with the past. In all of them contemporary politics is associated with a present that is discontinuous with a value-laden past, while history and personal story are endowed with a separate temporality extending before and after the course of political life. As in the pastoral chapter, my intent is to explore just those fantasies of continuity and value that are often rejected as deflections from social realism, in order to identify what they are made of, what they betray, and their structural relationships with those parts of the novel that directly evoke social life. What then emerges from the grain and texture of the narratives is something quite different from nostalgia or a flight to the past. Rather the stories trace out an intense conflict about the nature and the possibility of social change, expressed as a deadlock between histories of continuity and the temporal fragmentations of political life.

3 The Pastoral Argument

Descriptions of nature in fiction cease to be simply atmospheric, ornamental, or even symbolic once they are read in relation to the social terms for which they provide ideological alternatives. Charles Dickens's *Oliver Twist* (1837), Charles Kingsley's *Alton Locke* (1849), and Elizabeth Gaskell's *Ruth* (1853) are all social-problem novels in which Romantic ideas of nature play major structural roles. Each of these writers develops a kind of pastoral that sets nature in antithetical or dialectical relation to social constructions of characters or events, though each calls on somewhat different meanings of nature. My initial definition of pastoral will therefore be a broad one: by post-Romantic or post-Wordsworthian pastoral I mean a kind of writing that asserts or implies a continuity between the human spirit and the natural universe that is distinct from social definitions or placements of character.[1]

---

1. The emphasis should fall on "writing"; for I am interested here in narrative developments of the "green language" that Raymond Williams named and identified as Wordsworth's contribution, "in which the affirmation of Nature is intended as the essential affirmation of Man" (*The Country and the City* [New York, 1973], p. 132). J. Hillis Miller has differently stressed the need to examine Victorian nature writing not as it indicates concern for nature but as a metaphor for subjectivity; see "Nature and the Linguistic Moment," in *Nature and the Victorian Imagination*, ed. U. C. Knoeflmacher and G. B. Tennyson (Berkeley, 1977), pp. 440–451.

In the context of a novel otherwise committed to social analysis, post-Wordsworthian pastoral can be a great cleansing agent. It is a commonplace in Victorian fiction that sensitivity to nature is a sign of interior virtue; pastoral writing can also erase the social stains of working-class origin, illegitimacy, or sexual fall by relocating those experiences in a classless, lawless, natural realm. In the novels discussed here, fallen women, illegitimate children, and class-tainted men are rendered pure and placed beyond the scope of social condemnation through pastoral affiliation. Creating a history of character that is separate from its social surroundings and actions, the pastoral makes a serious argument against conceptions of socially determined development. The argument depends, however, on a conflation of opposing constructions of nature: it evokes the idea of nature as an analogue for the uncontrollable forces in human character, and then muffles that meaning in a Wordsworthian idea of nature as the emblem and guarantor of the highest motions of the human spirit. In the conflicts between the social and the pastoral parts of their novels, Dickens, Kingsley, and Gaskell carry on Romantic critiques of social determinism, with varying degrees of control over the tensions held within the idea of nature itself.

William Empson's work on the social implications of pastoral offers a rich collection of formulations that still prove suggestive in new contexts. Three of his points in particular are exemplified in these fictions, though in ways he does not specify or develop. Empson's notion of "the child as swain" touches on the antideterminist argument I have outlined, for it "depends on a feeling . . . that no way of building up character, no intellectual system, can bring out all that is inherent in the human spirit."[2] Oliver Twist, an exemplary child-as-swain, marks out a territory bounded not only by nature but by childhood. Pursuing the descriptive writing itself, we can further see that Dickens works Oliver's story as well as his character, creating an alternative history for the spirit Oliver enshrines, while Kingsley and Gaskell play out the complications of a similar argument in

2. William Empson, *Some Versions of Pastoral* (New York, 1974), p. 260.

characters who grow out of childhood into the world of social consequentiality.[3]

Empson also defines the "proletarian pastoral" as a process "based on a double attitude of the artist to the worker, or the complex man to the simple one," and shows how it works to "imply a beautiful relation between rich and poor" by combining simple, feeling characters with educated language, and so merging the best parts of worker and aristocrat.[4] Something like this appears in Victorian narratives as an almost automatic connection between a character's experience in nature and reading. At the same time that pastoral sections provide a character with a best self that is not socially conditioned, being in nature leads without pause to education through books; the love of nature, the desire to read, and the cultural improvement achieved through reading are rendered as though they were virtually equivalent. It is precisely through these applications of "literary pastoral" that Victorian characters are transformed and given histories that reject the consequentiality of their social records.

Such arguments have obvious political implications. Any claim that a concept or way of life is "natural" defends some social structure by defining it as inevitable and right. As Jerome McGann argues, the Romantic notion that the soul contains the elements of its own transcendance in communion with a natural world conceals its own base in social conservatism.[5] The pastoral writing in these novels displays its unquestioned social assumptions with great clarity: Dickens's pastoral is an individualistic middle-class retreat; Kingsley's nature is inseparable from aristocratic ownership and cultivation; Gaskell's is melded with the ideology of motherhood. All of the writers imagine a split between the socially determined body and the naturally asocial soul which seems to constitute an argument for

3. Barbara Hardy calls upon Empson's formula in a discussion of Dickens's early pastoral; she limits its role to the "reinforcement of character" in support of the claim of unconditioned goodness through "a stereotyping of sweetness, simplicity and rural innocence" ("The Complexity of Dickens," in *Dickens 1970*, ed. Michael Slater [London, 1970], p. 44).

4. Empson, *Some Versions of Pastoral*, pp. 14, 11–12.

5. Jerome McGann, *The Romantic Ideology* (Chicago, 1983), pp. 67–70.

Romantic transcendance even as it works to empower a conservative social contruct.

Yet it is important to see the difference between a Romantic poem that celebrates the dialogue of mind and nature and a pastoral argument that works in a dialectical relationship with an account of conflicts in the social realm. Pastorals are withdrawals from social consequentiality cloaked in green; at the same time the withdrawal may establish a separate ground for social judgment. Another of Empson's points is relevant here: the idea that realistic pastoral expresses social injustice by identifying a poor person outside society's benefits with the independent critical stance of the artist, and by making the poor character forced into crime "the judge of the society that judges him."[6] I would extend that notion from character to the workings of nature writing itself. Within the whole fantasy of the fiction, it creates another way of talking, enabling social attitudes and assumptions to be made visible and declared arbitrary. While the final effect may be to combat one ideology by substituting another, the pastoral strategy has a special power to isolate determinist social rhetoric and lay it bare.

Paradoxically, the most uncritical reliance on the myth of a separate realm can go hand in hand with the most radical social perception. Dickens's nearly absolute division between a pastoral haven and a criminal society allows him to make a clear case against the flaws in the idea of social determinism. Kingsley, on the other hand, is so self-conscious about the social constructions of nature that he cannot separate it from social bearings; his text manages to reveal the contradictions in his ideas of nature at the cost of a consistent social vision. Gaskell, somewhere between the two, argues her defense of Ruth twice, first in pastoral, then in social terms. All of these texts finally submit an absolute dichotomy between social rhetoric and an alternative one; yet each has a characteristic way of positioning and maintaining the border between these two linguistic realms.

6. Empson, *Some Versions of Pastoral*, p. 16.

The Natural History of Character in
Oliver Twist

Halfway through *Oliver Twist* its young hero is absorbed
into a pastoral world evoked in fragments of Wordsworthian
language and echoes of an idealized eighteenth-century village
order. From that point on Oliver, cleansed of his tainted past, is
permanently ensconced at the heart of a domestic pastoral
warmed by generosity on one side and gratitude on the other.[7]
His own adventures end; the stories center on Rose and Nancy,
Fagin and Sikes; and Oliver remains of interest primarily as he
raises the question of his birth. The moment of idyllic transformation looks like the novel's great evasion, the point at which, as
Arnold Kettle argues, Dickens retreats from his critical investigation of pauperism and crime to create a symbolic battle
between good and evil which ends in a solution redolent of
genteel respectability and virtue.[8]

Yet once Dickens's—certainly derivative—nature rhetoric is
taken seriously, *Oliver Twist* becomes a relatively coherent and a
radically antisocial novel. Through repeated allusions to
Wordsworthian concepts, Dickens posits the idea that nature,
inheritance, and spirit combine in a natural history of character
that is betrayed by social circumstance and that must be read by
means other than those afforded by social evidence.[9] Character
in this sense is under attack from all forms of social interpretation—whether perpetrated by workhouse guardians or by the

7. Charles Dickens, *Oliver Twist* (Harmondsworth, 1966), pp. 290–292. Further references to this edition will appear in the text.

8. Kettle forcefully establishes this central line of criticism in *An Introduction to
the English Novel*, 2 vols. (New York, 1968), II, 115–129. He argues that the
narrative of *Oliver Twist* represents a struggle between the "pattern" of social
protest and the melodramatic plot, which transforms social issues into a facile
battle between good and evil.

9. For a related discussion of nature as a realm of freedom in *Oliver Twist*, see
John Lucas, *The Melancholy Man: A Study of Dickens's Novels* (London, 1970), pp.
32–38. Lucas maintains a continuous sense of Wordsworthian echoes through-
out Dickens's work; other critics who link Wordsworth and Dickens have focused
largely on work written after the publication of *The Prelude* in 1850. U. C.
Knoeflmacher makes such connections in "Mutations of the Wordsworthian
Child of Nature," in *Nature and the Victorian Imagination*, pp. 422–425; Carl
Dawson draws parallels between *The Prelude* and *David Copperfield* in chap. 6 of
Victorian Noon: English Literature in 1850 (Baltimore, 1979).

gang of thieves—which read the evidence of action as a record
of character, and imprison their victims in that record. Pointing
to a pre- or posthistorical mode of being, the pastoral rhetoric is
there to make a place for a nonenvironmentalist interpretation
of character. It is supported by the meaning of the inheritance
plot, which makes the most forthright statement of the assumption on which the novel takes its stand: that social and legal
legitimacy are the channels of injustice and evil, while "illegitimate" nature is the conduit of affection and virtue. Thus
Oliver's status as a "natural child" of love becomes a source of his
goodness; at the same time the pastoral language evokes the
virtue and acts as a cleansing agent, erasing the social stigma of
Oliver's illegitimacy and his mother's sexual fall by referring
them to an asocial realm of judgment.

To pursue such a reading requires not only that we overcome
our resistance to "the sentimental Dickens" but also, more
important, that we readjust the well-known criticism that
Dickens presents a contradiction between freedom and necessity, undermining his investigation of social corruptibility with a
saving vision of unconditioned goodness.[10] What if *Oliver Twist* is
symptomatic not of escapism or inconsistency but of Dickens's
resistance to the environmentalist view of character itself? It
then becomes a more profound and interesting attack, not only
on the local injustices of the workhouses and the courts but on
the determinist ideology that framed the New Poor Law of 1834
in such a way that the indigent would be conditioned out of their
reliance on the parish, or punitively "reformed" by the regulations of the union workhouses. The large structure of the novel
implies, first of all, that to treat poverty as a sign of criminality
makes real crime a preferable choice: who would choose the
workhouse against the activity of Fagin's gang? Within that
structure Dickens combats the assumption that a person's spirit

10. Critics have often argued around the problem of unconditioned goodness by noting how vulnerable Dickens makes it, how threatened by forces of
social corruption. For a direct exploration of the contradiction between freedom
and necessity in *Oliver Twist*, see Brantlinger, *Spirit of Reform*, pp. 49–55. He
suggests that a "double psychology" of free agents and social victims in reform
novels allows the writer both to expose injustice and to undermine the threat of
political action on the part of the victims.

is shaped or controlled through social interventions, by repeatedly inventing scenes in which some visible behavior that comes
from "natural character" is misread as a sign of social depravity
and punished with the intent to reform.[11]

The effort saturates all parts of the narrative: Fagin's social
assumptions parallel and parody those of the utilitarian social
reformers, while the pastoral characters deliberately overlook or
deny social evidence in order to protect natural character from
the misinterpretations built into social law. Nature writing
creates a realm incommensurate with the social, postulating an
absolute gap between social experience and the moral shape of
spirit. Asserting an asocial core of being, the pastoral language
acts itself as a form of narrative resistance to social interpretation. If the result looks like a picture of genteel middle-class
individualism, as indeed it does in *Oliver Twist*, we must nevertheless credit Dickens's attempts to unclass and dehistoricize it;
give credit, that is, to the wish for a utopia cleansed of *all* the
paraphernalia of social control.

The gap between nature and society opens at the moment of
Oliver's birth and is extended throughout his story in terms of a
split between the body and the spirit. Oliver begins his life as he
is to continue it, "rather unequally poised between this world
and the next"; and Dickens facetiously attributes his existence to
the absence of social intervention: no anxious relatives or
doctors get in the way, so "Oliver and Nature fought out the
point between them" (45–46). The moment he is born, he is
"badged and ticketed" (47) as a parish burden and starved
according to the workhouse system, which stunts his body but
not his soul: "nature or inheritance had implanted a good sturdy
spirit in Oliver's breast" (49). As the phrasing hints, the event
will prove that Oliver's inheritance *is* nature; in the mother's case
as well as Oliver's, Dickens separates the socially fallen body
from the naturally loving spirit, which remains safe in a pro-

11. A corroborating view of Dickens's attack on utilitarianism may be found
in George Goodin, *The Poetics of Protest: Literary Form and Political Implication in the
Victim-of-Society Novel* (Carbondale, Ill., 1985), pp. 30–34. Goodin argues that
for Dickens "social problems were caused, not solved, by engineering circumstances and encouraging people to act in accord with them" (p. 33).

tected place, buried in the woman's grave and the child's breast. In the single significant episode where Oliver personally fights back against oppression, Dickens allows that force to show its power. Noah Claypole insults Oliver's mother, and Oliver is transformed: "his whole person changed, as he stood glaring over the cowardly tormentor who now lay crouching at his feet; and defied him with an energy he had never known before" (88). The preservation of the natural inheritance is later transferred to the protectionist activity of the Brownlow-Maylie group, but not before Oliver sets the limits of his toleration at the border between body and spirit.

Dickens focuses often on the disjunction of physical circumstance and mental freedom, as though he is seeking a naturalistic explanation for a phenomenon on which his argument depends. Oliver's face (as distinguished from his body) is the book of nature and inheritance, both because it is a "living copy" of his mother's (132) and because it retains its innocence in despite of his social experience. Haunted by it, Brownlow's mind revives the images of other dead faces: "There were [faces] that the grave had changed to ghastly trophies of death, but which the mind, superior to its power, still dressed in their old freshness and beauty, calling back the lustre of the eyes, the brightness of the smile, the beaming of the soul through its mask of clay. . . ." (119).

What the "superior" imagination does to mortal and changeable physical reality is like what it evokes: "the beaming of the soul through its mask of clay" is a spiritual penetration of physical circumstance. The doctrine of the unchangeable natural face is reiterated when Dickens meditates on death, asserting that "the troubled clouds" of earthly experience pass off the faces of the dead and "leave Heaven's surface clear" (223). The metaphor extends the pattern in which social experience is subject to erasure in the light of a larger experience generated by memory, imagination, or the idea of Heaven. It is that perspective which can properly be called the pastoral of *Oliver Twist*, representing not a retreat to the suburbs but a reach for some rhetorical tradition that might act as a counterweight to social explanations of character and personal history.

Despite the vaguely religious overtones in the separations of body and spirit, the appeal of the pastoral is not to a Providential deity that uses social life as a test or that sets right what social life sets wrong. Dickens reaches not for God but for something akin to the myth of origin that Wordsworth elaborates in "Intimations of Immortality"; he wants to imagine a prehistory of natural innocence that is slowly worn down and covered over by social experience. Thus, when the Maylies first look at Oliver's sleeping face, their sympathy gives him unconscious access to some prehistorical place of origin:

> Thus, a strain of gentle music, or the rippling of water in a silent place, or the odour of a flower, or the mention of a familiar word, will sometimes call up sudden dim remembrances of scenes that never were, in this life; which vanish like a breath; which some brief memory of a happier existence, long gone by, would seem to have awakened; which no voluntary exertion of the mind can ever recall. [268]

The presence of this passage gives a frame of irony to the discussion that follows over the sleeping boy; Rose makes an "environmentalist" plea for saving Oliver and the Maylies begin the plot to rescue him from the machinations of the law. Oliver has always existed in the special temporality of pastoral, impervious to all forms of social discipline and indoctrination, presumably because his head is full of prehistory. He needs no saving, only a place that will welcome and extend his natural disposition. When the Maylies provide it for him, Dickens awkwardly echoes language that in "Tintern Abbey" celebrates a return: "Who can describe the pleasure and delight, the peace of mind and soft tranquillity, the sickly boy felt in the balmy air and among the green hills and rich woods, of an inland village! Who can tell how scenes of peace and quietude sink into the minds of pain-worn dwellers in close and noisy places, and carry their own freshness, deep into their jaded hearts!" (290).

As the passage proceeds, it turns, as if by an automatic association of Wordsworthian ideas, into a vague and generalized reiteration of the myth of primal memory: "there lingers, in the least reflective mind, a vague and half-formed consciousness of having held such feelings long before, in some remote and distant time, which calls up solemn thoughts of distant times to come, and bends down pride and worldliness beneath it" (290).

Dickens's persistent connection between pastoral and death is often noted; it pervades the pastoral section of Oliver Twist, particularly in the story of Rose's brush with death.[12] The association of ideas that controls the direction of this particular paragraph does, however, introduce the pastoral as a kind of rhetoric rather than as a place. At the same time as it withdraws from the social conflict by evoking a classless sense of common mortality, this writing suggests that all human beings are linked in a temporality that extends before and after the conditions of social life.

While it is easy to dismiss the pastoral pastiche as the least believable style and the most evasive social strategy in the novel,[13] Oliver Twist is full of evidence that Dickens was genuinely interested in plotting the clash of histories represented by the ideas in his nature language. Each time that Oliver is nearly apprehended as an accomplice in a criminal act, he falls into a faint followed by an illness that erases his immediate past like a little death. After a rebirth, he wakes up among the social remnants of his natural history—Brownlow and the Maylies. While he convalesces at Brownlow's, he "recognizes" the portrait of his mother (128–129); when he awakens in the ditch and sees the Maylie house, "a feeling came over him that he had seen it before" (258); he has temporarily forgotten the robbery, and the sentence hovers upon the suggestion that the house exists in a deeper kind of memory. There is a curious moment when Oliver's London past seems to have been literally wiped away: when he takes Dr. Losberne to find Brownlow, he seems to have misremembered the house where the thieves took him, and Brownlow himself has disappeared (286–288). Dickens contrives

12. The connection between the idyll, the death wish, and sentimental writing is pursued by Steven Marcus in Dickens from Pickwick to Dombey (New York, 1965), pp. 129–151. For James Kincaid, Oliver Twist "comes about as close as is possible to building its final society literally in heaven . . . the morally approved people . . . exist on the edge of the grave" (Dickens and the Rhetoric of Laughter [Oxford, 1971], p. 51).

13. I have done so myself, in "Dickens and the Art of Pastoral," Centennial Review 23 (1979), 452–467.

to "explain" such occasions in realistic terms, but not before he plays on the mysterious incompatibility between Oliver's social and "real" pasts.

This dance of memory and erasure culminates in the scene where Fagin and Monks peer at Oliver through the window of his pastoral haven (308–311). Carefully ensconced in a natural setting, Oliver falls asleep over his books. Attempting again to ground his mind–body split in naturalistic terms, Dickens prepares the scene "scientifically," describing the kind of hypnotic state that always fascinated him; the visions that occur in it, he asserts, may be influenced by external objects that we cannot hear or see. In such a condition Oliver has a vision of Fagin and Monks discussing him in London, and wakes to find it truth—at least to find the figures staring malevolently in at him. Yet they leave no external evidence; not even a bent blade of grass testifies to their intrusion. The internal impression is another matter: "But they had recognized him, and he them: and their look was as firmly impressed upon his memory, as if it had been deeply carved in stone and set before him from his birth" (311).

Dickens is tuning up the melodrama here, but the fatal recognition is not without a context. Monks is there because he is part of Oliver's true history, the sinister part of the story that Oliver must sleep and awake to discover as his natural heritage. The syntax conflates the "new" experience with memory and recognition, making it, like so many other moments, a return to the conditions of Oliver's birth. The incident is another "scene that never was," a step in Oliver's recovery of an original past. And, in a way that also resonates with other scenes in the novel, the absence of "evidence" is a sign of its deeper truth.[14]

The active part of Oliver's story is a series of incidents in which he is misread according to circumstantial evidence. He asks for more gruel in the workhouse, he attacks Noah Claypole, he runs

14. John Lucas reads this as a central scene because it attests to Dickens's sense that withdrawal into a state of nature is impossible. See *Melancholy Man*, pp. 30–38. For psychoanalytic readings of it, see Marcus, *Dickens from Pickwick to Dombey*, pp. 358–378; and John Bayley, "*Oliver Twist:* Things As They Really Are," in *Dickens: A Collection of Critical Essays*, ed. Martin Price (Englewood Cliffs, N.J., 1967), pp. 83–96.

from the scene of the bookstall theft, and he appears at the Maylie house after the burgalary attempt; each time he is taken into custody and treated as a criminal by those who represent the social order, but each time his apparently antisocial behavior represents a courageous effort to protect what is naturally good. Dickens's broad satire obviously attacks those who equate poverty and criminality, and uncovers the materialism of interventionist social theory: Bumble's interpretation of Oliver's defense of his mother is that he has been fed on meat, which has "raised a artificial soul and spirit in him" (93). It is very important, then, that those who read Oliver correctly believe his face and his story despite incriminating circumstances, and that they go out of their ways to defy evidence and the law. Brownlow fights with the magistrate Fang and strives to believe in Oliver's innocence against the justified suspicions of Grimwig. Dr. Losberne schemes to baffle the investigation of Blathers and Duff, who will comprehend Oliver's story only according to what can be proven; he pays off Giles to muddle the evidence. When Oliver points out the house in London that fails to corroborate his story, Losberne decides to believe him anyway. And when Brownlow goes about the business of restoring Oliver to his inheritance, he avoids entanglement with the authorities; the "truth" is established in the private ritual of questioning Monks, after the "evidence" of the mother's wedding ring and the father's will have been destroyed. In action, then, the pastoral characters do not provide an easy view of benevolent middle-class individualism;[15] they are depicted in a defensive posture, carrying on a kind of guerrilla warfare with the assumptions and the institutions of the state.

Fagin's gang, on the other hand, is Dickens's most brilliant "representation" of the utilitarian state: they act the roles of the so-called legitimate world better than its own equally hypocritical actors do.[16] When Nancy plays the role of Oliver's older sister

15. Brantlinger calls benevolent middle-class individualism the only solution that Dickens can see for the social problems he raises (*Spirit of Reform*, p. 49).

16. Because the struggle for Oliver pits Fagin's gang against the pastoral characters, these worlds are generally discussed as paired opposites. The bureaucracy is usually related to the thieves through social continuum or

rescuing him from thieves, she is more convincing than Mrs. Mann is when she pretends to mourn Oliver's departure from the orphanage. The Artful Dodger on the stand can manipulate legal jargon better than the court officials can. When Oliver is returned to Fagin after the Brownlow interlude, Fagin lectures him on "the crying sin of ingratitude" and the threat of the gallows in terms that perfectly parody the attitudes of the Poor Law officials (177–178). And when Fagin instructs Noah Claypole about the principles of society, he gives an impeccable rendition of the contradiction at the heart of utilitarianism, developing a theory in which looking out for number one is identical with the mutual interests of the "little community" (387–389). By implication, what is literally the case in the self-protective loyalty of the community of thieves is also true of society at large.

Fagin's design on Oliver is a reduplication and a literalization of the design on which the workhouse system is conceived. Like the parish officials, he is a behaviorist: he wants to give Oliver a "record," to create circumstances that will alter his character and enforce his loyalty to the little society. He puts Oliver in solitary confinement to create a yearning for *any* society; he sets up Oliver's role in the burglary to make him socially irredeemable. His tactics are smarter than those of the parish bumblers, but they rely on a similar assumption that circumstance creates character. If the workhouse turns people into protocriminals, Fagin turns them into real ones; his superiority lies in his penetration and use of the social principles on which he preys. Yet his vulnerability stems from those same assumptions: he is finally betrayed by his model student, Noah Claypole, rather than by his incorruptible failure, Oliver.

The state and the gang form a social continuum, creating and replicating each other. Both attempt to erase natural character by grafting social records upon their victims. Thus the struggle over Oliver which occupies the second half of the plot is really a

---

causation; Brantlinger, for example, says that "workhouse and prison help to cause the conditions they are meant to correct" (ibid., p. 48). The worlds are linked in a more symbolic and sinister way through utilitarian practice.

battle between a history of social circumstance and a socially unreadable heritage. Although the plot turns into a simplified tug of war between good and evil, Dickens does not abandon his interest in the potential complexities of the dichotomy between nature and society. He writes them into the stories of the two young women who function as Oliver's extensions and doubles, Nancy and Rose. Nancy plays out the drama of social corruptibility while Rose, embodying a domestic pastoral that is also out of world and time (264), pulls steadily toward nature. Like the young child, the two women are automatically endowed with original innocence; each of them represents a possible direction for the life of natural being.

Nancy is an Oliver who has become irrevocably implicated in the social record, yet retains "something of the original woman's nature," of which "her wasting life had obliterated so many, many traces when a very child" (361). Fagin—the novel's most self-conscious social conditioner—recognizes that Nancy can still be moved by "some long-forgotten feeling" (194), although Nancy's acting convinces him that it is a feeling soon dispelled. In challenging Fagin's view of Nancy, Dickens also challenges the respectable middle-class code of condemnation for the fallen woman. Nancy's nature is essentially incorruptible; she is naturalized through her maternal protection of the child and her womanly care for Sikes, while her degradation is attributed to Fagin's design. Her story charts the fate of natural virtue captured by a social system: undercover goodness makes heavy demands on her acting abilities, and her reward is to be murdered by the man to whom she has been loyal at the price of imprisonment in the gang. Her true attachment to Sikes is punished as a betrayal of the gang so that her fate becomes an enlarged and horrific version of Oliver's social dilemmas: a necessary collision between interior virtue and the social code through which it is interpreted.

The murder of Nancy marks the extremity of the pattern in which social orders extinguish the natural being they fail to alter. Rose's encounter with death sketches an antithetical extreme: to embody the pastoral is to hover on the margin between life and death, reminding people of a "brighter world than this"

(295). Her nearly fatal illness opens a theoretical gap between human mortality and obliviously beautiful nature, yet its effect is to bring the idea of pastoral closer to human life: Rose has been almost to that brighter world and returned, all the more like a newborn child trailing clouds of glory.[17] Replicating the states of unconsciousness and illness that mark Oliver's transitions between the social and the pastoral, the sudden inexplicable illness is nature at work, creating the fertile melancholy of human sorrow. It forms the "plot" of pastoral, shaping a sentimental action that draws members of the community together in common sympathy and memory; this is the tie that must substitute for self-interest, or Fagin's little community of number ones.[18]

Rose's illness also links her to Oliver and to his mother—her sister—in a different way: in all three characters a sexual stigma is overridden and cleansed by an immersion in the stream of that remembered presocial life. From it the younger sister returns to complete the interrupted movement of the elder's life: because she refuses to mix marriage with her (falsely perpetrated) history of doubtful birth, she draws her lover out of the social and into the pastoral realm, where they are immune to the destructive power of social interpretations. Absurdly as it reads, this little plot deepens yet again the absolute gap between nature and even that "best" society in which Harry Maylie moves.

The world to which the good characters retreat at the close of *Oliver Twist* is therefore characterized most fully by the fantasy that there is a place outside of organized society in which people may protect and nourish their natural inheritances. Dickens attempts to make his paradise classless by filling it with the universal threat of mortality; timeless, by setting it in the past, in

17. In "'The Parish Boy's Progress': The Evolving Form of *Oliver Twist*," *PMLA* 93 (1978), 20–32, William T. Lankford argues that Rose's illness alters the course of the novel by challenging the paradigm of providential protection which has functioned up to that point in the narrative.

18. John Kucich makes a helpful point about sentimentality in Dickens, suggesting that the threat of death or loss secures the sense of community even as it seems to enjoy the emotions of grief. See *Excess and Restraint in the Novels of Charles Dickens* (Athens, Ga., 1981), pp. 52–57.

an eighteenth-century educational and recreational community where the pious middle class and clean laborers exist in harmony with nature and the church. He does this badly; his pastoral rhetoric, pasted together from preromantic and Romantic sources, betrays a lack of imaginative resonance in Dickens himself.

Yet if the Brownlow-Maylie world is a dreamworld, it is not "merely the romantic escape-world" that Kettle rejects.[19] It wishes to escape not only from brutal social interplays but from the powerful idea of social circumstance as it is used by controllers upon the controlled. Precisely as fantasy it has its importance, making an imaginary place from which the social doctrine of necessity may appear unnatural and therefore arbitrary; and in which characters may be imagined as offering it some resistance. As a sentimental predecessor to more originally conceived separate worlds that perform comparable functions in Dickens's later narratives (the circus in *Hard Times* is discussed in chapter 4), this pastoral marks an early stage in Dickens's development of fictional structures that allow him to penetrate and denaturalize middle-class ideologies by looking at them from a place outside.

The seriousness of Dickens's pastoral design may be measured against other pastoral writing that makes cruder attempts at social erasure or transformation. In *Michael Armstrong, the Factory Boy*, Frances Trollope attempts to imitate *Oliver Twist* in some aspects of her story about a child abused by the factory system.[20] The imitation comes off as parody because Trollope exaggerates Dickens's rhetorical gestures without controlling the social, or asocial, attitudes they imply. Her pastoral rhetoric wipes the mud off working-class oppression only in order to provide her hero with a ticket of admission to gentility; her explanations of his special nature are opportunistic applications of pastoral rhetoric without the resonance of a contextual frame.

19. Kettle, *"Oliver Twist,"* p. 123.
20. Cazamian speculates that Mrs. Trollope's decision to write *Michael Armstrong* was influenced by the current popularity of *Oliver Twist* (*Social Novel in England*, p. 236).

Like Oliver Twist, Michael Armstrong is depicted as a naturally incorruptible child who is continually placed in situations that misrepresent his nature and his origin. He is "adopted"—that is, torn away from a loving mother and brother—by his sadistic employer, Sir Matthew Dowling, who wishes to advertise his benevolence by pretending compassion for the boy. Reviling him all the while, Dowling forces Michael to dress like a genteel child and to act the part of a rescued and grateful factory child in a home theatrical. When his presence becomes an embarrassment, his mother is blackmailed for the signature that will allow Michael to be sent away as a pauper apprentice to an inaccessible fortress of a mill in Deep Valley. Even so cursory a summary of the events in volume I reveals the extent to which Trollope is incapable of systemic analysis: every one of these incidents is atypical, a special form of personal evil rather than an effect of social condition or philosophy.

After Michael is incarcerated in the Deep Valley mill, he is absent from the narrative that bears his name for many chapters while Trollope pursues the adventures of her middle-class heroine, Mary Brotherton (see chapter 1). After she has rescued Michael's friend Fanny from the mill, Michael comes in for some third-volume dramas: an independent escape scene and a liberation from the factory world. The tale begins as he is almost literally raised from the dead, a single live body among rows of children extinguished by a fever epidemic in the mill, looking "for all the world as if he had been buried and dug up again" (III, 64). With this rather gruesomely literal rebirth upon him, Michael manages to spend a number of years working in the mill without incurring the physical damage that cripples and deforms the other children. Trollope accounts for this immunity through a parodic version of Dickens's mind–body distinction: after arranging for Michael to get extra food from a kindly source, she moves into an explanation of how his strong spirit prevents his limbs from bending so that, at fourteen, he is "both tall and straight": "Nature and accident together had been stronger than the tendency of his employment to cripple his limbs . . ." (III, 78–79). The argument recalls Dickens's coupling of "nature and inheritance"; but the new combination betrays

Trollope's ever-materialist mind. Michael's survival is "just a piece of good luck, really"; an accident, much like the misfortune of falling in with Sir Matthew in the first place. And Michael's clever escape from his factory-prison follows in a similar mode: he does the impossible, and is turned into a glamorous hero who outwits the evil world. Shedding his childish passivity, Michael becomes, in fact, a counterpart to his adventurous middle-class patroness, Mary Brotherton.

Once out in the world, he is due for another rebirth that will purge him of the interior as well as the bodily signs of his class and history. For this rebirth only pastoral will do, and the appropriate rhetoric is applied in liberal doses. Returning home to find that his mother has died and that his brother is presumed dead, Michael attempts suicide by throwing himself into a river, from which he is rescued by a group of shepherds led by an "old Westmoreland statesman" (III, 120). Although this scene takes place only a mile from the factory world, his life instantly turns into a pastoral one. Trollope sprinkles her pages with quotations from Wordsworth's poems, and we next see Michael "sitting upon the hill-side in one of the most romantic spots in Westmoreland, a shepherd's maud wrapped round his person, a sheep-dog at his feet, and his master's flocks nibbling the short grass around him on all sides" (III, 126).

This "mountain occupation" with its neighborhood of "mountain torrents, glassy lakes, stupendous crags, and sylvan solitudes" is Michael's timely salvation: it recalls him to his early religious training and inspires many "improving processes" (III, 127–128). He educates himself by reading among his flocks, taking holidays only to climb some notable Wordsworthian hills. Four years later, when he sets forth on the journey that will ultimately reunite him with his brother and friends, he seems to have turned into the great poet himself; Trollope endows him with a version of the feelings Wordsworth records in the opening of "Intimations of Immortality" (III, 130). Thus, in five short pages, Michael's mind is gentrified and made ready for inclusion in the educated, cultured milieu that Mary Brotherton has established in her German retreat.

While Dickens's Wordsworthian meditations point us to a

mythical state of preexistence, Trollope's obtrude as an inadvertently comic interlude in which a screen of literary pastoral is lowered in front of the industrial world, blotting it out as a serious threat for the rest of the novel. Where Dickens adds a genteel village culture as a social context for Oliver's attachment to feeling and learning, Trollope would have us imagine a self-made man performing an educational odyssey in the guise of a pastoral life. For her, putting on the pastoral means throwing a shepherd's cloak over her actual belief in the ethic of social aspiration—the kind of aspiration that in its middle-class versions forms the target of her earlier satire.

In both Dickens and Trollope, the invocation of post-Wordsworthian pastoral places the single human and the natural world on one side, society on the other. A significant contrast is provided by the distinctly eighteenth-century pastoral in Charlotte Elizabeth Tonna's *Helen Fleetwood*, published at the same time as *Michael Armstrong* and often paired with it for discussion.[21] Tonna's novel is really a religious tract: the factory system appears as the work of the devil, and its most dangerous aspect is the cynical and immoral environment that turns children away from religious faith. The plot events are for the most part organized around successes or failures of religious conversion effected by members of the pious, country-bred Green family during their devastating encounter with Manchester life. Tonna is good at exposing specific failures in the administration of the 1833 Factory Act, but the frame of her novel exhibits a wish to annihilate the factory system entirely: the story begins in a struggling rural world threatened by the New Poor Law bureaucracy, moves to the factory town, and returns to the country, now transformed into a successfully harmonious paternalist community.

---

21. Charlotte Elizabeth Tonna, *Helen Fleetwood* (1840), 4th American ed. (New York, 1848). For introductions to the novel which include comparisons with *Michael Armstrong,* see Cazamian, *Social Novel in England,* pp. 237–240, and Ivanka Kovačević and S. Barbara Kanner, "Blue Book into Novel: The Forgotten Industrial Fiction of Charlotte Elizabeth Tonna," *Nineteenth-Century Fiction* 25 (1970), 152–173.

Like the pastoral sections in Dickens and Trollope, Tonna's occurs more than halfway through her novel, after the general evils of the factory system have been exposed. Her transforming diction creates neither an otherworldly paradise nor a coat of literary gentility; she paints an "old English hedge-row" firmly rooted in the language of the eighteenth-century landscape poets, with ancient generations of "patriarchal trees" giving way to equally grand young successors, under which vines, berries, and streams offer their bounties to children. One side of this bounded protectionist field opens upon "the mighty main" whose "magnificent distance" connects the ordered landscape with heaven. In this place the village squire is holding the festival of harvest home for parishioners enumerated in neoclassical categories: here are "the sun-burnt peasant," "the sober matron," "the stout boy," and "the sprightly girl." Meanwhile the daughters of the squire assemble village urchins of the infant school in orderly procession. This, the narrator asserts, is the order that God intended (177–180). From it she summons up her young hero Richard Green and sends him on a mission of rescue to the city, to return with all the members of the family who have not already gone directly to God. The novel does not end in the social paradise sketched here; too many losses have been incurred, the family is broken up, and the evils of the factory have permanently scarred the minds of the survivors. But even so attenuated a rescue is equivalent to being snatched from the jaws of hell.

Tonna's pastoral signifies a refusal of history far more profound than the asocial otherworld of Dickens or Trollope's fantasy of upward mobility.[22] Her book says stubbornly that the whole course of industrialization has been a mistake; that preindustrial patriarchal society is equivalent to the timeless and always reproducible course of nature. The effect of her rural scenes is to renaturalize an old vision of a social order rather than to provide an interior pastoral from which the workings of the social order may be observed; believing that all human nature is fallen, Tonna cannot place any faith in individual or asocial

22. This assessment is shared by Angus Easson in his brief account of the novel (*Elizabeth Gaskell*, pp. 66–68).

virtue. Her work offers a good example of something that is not common in Victorian industrial fiction: a direct yearning for a golden age imagined as a social and historical reality and summoned up in the language of preromantic poetry.

The Aristocratic Pastoral of *Alton Locke*

Charles Kingsley linked his novel *Alton Locke: Tailor and Poet* (1850) with *Oliver Twist* when, in imitation of Dickens, he inserted a scene exposing the unsanitary conditions on Jacob's Island, dramatizing there the death of his derelict tailor, Jemmy Downes.[23] The two narratives are also more deeply and problematically related. Each makes a structural opposition between a free pastoral world and an imprisoning urban one; each struggles explicitly with and against the doctrine of environmental determinism. Dickens, as we have seen, constructs the opposition in two clearly demarcated zones. Kingsley does not; *Alton Locke* oscillates wildly between its commitment to the circumstances of working-class life and its yearning for a pastoral world, until it finally collapses into a dream vision that resolves the conflict by changing the meanings of its original terms. In the process Kingsley inadvertently deconstructs the ideological opposition between social conflict and pastoral harmony, producing versions of pastoral that reveal on the one hand its reliance on aristocratic society and on the other its evolutionary connection with human drives to lust and power.

Alton Locke was composed in unchronological fragments during 1849 and 1850,[24] and its chapters alternate between scenes

23. Charles Kingsley, *Alton Locke: Tailor and Poet* (Oxford, 1983), pp. 325–334. Further references to this edition will appear in the text. Dickens's "Preface to the First Cheap Edition" of *Oliver Twist*, also published in 1850, was, like Kingsley's episode, a response to the cholera epidemic of 1849. In it Dickens mocks government officials for thinking that Jacob's Island existed only in his fiction. The Preface is reprinted in the Signet Classic Edition of *Oliver Twist* (New York, 1961), pp. xi–xiv.
24. Susan Chitty, *The Beast and the Monk: A Life of Charles Kingsley* (London, 1974), pp. 133–134.

of working-class life, scenes of upper-class life, and social or
philosophical dialogues. It is therefore almost always praised—
when it is praised—in pieces. Carlyle called the whole "a fervid
creation still left half chaotic" but praised the Sandy Mackaye
character who represents him;[25] later critics single out the set
pieces of social exposure—the tailor's attic, the sweater's den, the
Bermondsey scene—or Kingsley's descriptions of nature.[26] Yet
Kingsley insisted formally on the psychological and chronolog-
ical significance of his narrative by choosing to write it in the first
person, as the fictional autobiography of a working-class tailor
and poet. The result is indeed chaotic: Kingsley does not know
what he thinks, and Alton is created in his image. Critics who
wish to talk about the guiding ideas in the novel can do so only
by ignoring the flow of Alton's story; indeed, Louis Cazamian,
Kingsley's most enthusiastic defender, explicitly disregards the
chronology in order to analyze events "all together in the light of
intentions which reflect equally upon them all."[27]

Cazamian supplies a causality far firmer than Kingsley's to
explain how Alton becomes a Chartist in response to specific
social and religious restrictions in working-class culture.[28] The
conclusions that emerge from such readings outline the ideas
loosely associated with the beliefs and activities of Kingsley's
Christian Socialism: his wish for an equal distribution of education and access to aesthetic beauty; his critiques of rigid non-
conformity, the commercial and industrial bourgeousie, and
physical-force Chartism; his exposure of working conditions in
the tailor's trade and unsanitary conditions in working-class

25. Carlyle's letter is quoted in *Charles Kingsley: His Letters and Memories of His
Life*, ed. Fanny Kingsley (1876; rpt. and abr. New York, 1877), p. 133.
26. For an amusing Victorian response, see Peter Bayne, "Charles Kingsley,"
in *Essays in Biography and Criticism*, 2d ser. (Boston, 1860), pp. 9–51. For
discussions of Kingsley's overt social targets, see Cazamian, *Social Novel in
England*, pp. 268–288; Larry K. Uffelman, *Charles Kingsley* (Boston, 1979), pp.
54–55; and Sheila M. Smith, *Other Nation*, pp. 52–69 and 110–115.
27. Cazamian, *Social Novel in England*, pp. 268–269. Uffelman also finds it
necessary to separate his plot summary from his summary of Kingsley's social
recommendations (*Charles Kingsley*, pp. 48–56).
28. Cazamian, *Social Novel in England*, pp. 268–276.

districts; and, finally, his vision of an egalitarian Christian state based on aristocratic paternalism.[29]

Once Alton's story is read as a story, Kingsley's mind begins to emerge as a field of intense conflict. Alton's confusions, supposedly the misguided conflicts of a talented worker drawn at the last to a Christian Socialist conversion, are in fact mirrors of Kingsley's own very middle-class Victorian conflict between social duty and Romantic poetry. Rather than offering an account of experience and error told by an enlightened and understanding retrospective voice, the first-person narrative works as a conduit for Kingsley's acute ambivalence, allowing him to move rapidly from one side of an issue to another. Not only is he unable to separate himself from Alton enough to create a believable working-class character and voice, but he uses Alton, ostensibly his greatest gesture of sympathy with the working class, as a stick with which to beat workers and exalt his own idea of a "democratic" aristocracy. In the flow of the narrative—a process characterized by Alton's swings between guilty loyalty to one class and guilty betrayal of the other— Kingsley reveals a middle-class sensibility in which the tensions created by class sympathy have deepened into something like pathology.

The failures in Kingsley's creation of Alton have been well described in recent discussions of *Alton Locke*. Patrick Brantlinger shows how Alton, torn between his own class and his desire to rise, is a character "who is caught up in a perpetual social identity crisis" expressing the oxymoronic doubleness of Kingsley's vision.[30] Catherine Gallagher clearly delineates the terms of Kingsley's split between Romantic antideterminism and scientific determinism, showing how that contradiction makes it impossible for Kingsley to create Alton as a fictional character.[31] Yet for all its incoherence, the narrative reveals patterns that articulate Kingsley's imagination of social conflict and his fantasies of resolution. The most dominant of these imaginative

29. Ibid., pp. 268–286; Uffelman, *Charles Kingsley*, pp. 53–56.
30. Brantlinger, *Spirit of Reform*, pp. 137–141.
31. Gallagher, *Industrial Reformation*, pp. 88–110.

structures is the recurrent image of psychic imprisonment: urban entrapment in class-bound circumstance vibrates against the wish for pastoral escape to an aristocratic world of aesthetic appreciation.[32] Alton's story is also set alongside the calculated rise of his tradesman cousin, George Locke, in such a way that the two stories become insidious counterparts. Finally, in a gesture that undermines all the novel's earlier patterns, the dream vision redefines both nature and social collectivity, providing Alton with a new history shaped in a way that supersedes yet oddly recapitulates the old.

The essentially Romantic structure of Kingsley's imagination pervades the early chapters, in which Alton Locke records his childhood. Repeatedly Alton represents himself as a great yearning bounded by the prison of working-class circumstance; the terms of his opening paragraph stand for almost everything that is to follow:

> I am a Cockney among Cockneys. Italy and the Tropics, the Highlands and Devonshire, I know only in dreams. Even the Surrey Hills, of whose loveliness I have heard so much, are to me a distant fairy-land, whose gleaming ridges I am worthy only to behold afar. With the exception of two journeys never to be forgotten, my knowledge of England is bounded by the horizon which encircles Richmond Hill. [5]

Alton's initial claim of identity with his class and place of origin is immediately contradicted by his counteridentification with distant beauty and romantic sensibility. He goes on to describe London not as a Cockney but as a prisoner, attributing to himself a Keatsian longing to escape into a pastoral of death (6) and a Ruskinian power of concentration on minute details of the natural world as though they were symbols of spirit and romance: stray wild flowers, beetles, and butterflies "were to me God's angels shining in coats of mail and fairy masquerading dresses" (9). When, overtaken by a sense of horror at the ugliness of his urban surroundings, Alton yearns for the Pacific

---

32. In *Victorian Noon*, Carl Dawson describes Alton's "psychic battle between social activism and pastoral escape" (p. 201). Dawson does not elaborate, although he implicitly connects the battle with an interesting account of Kingsley's character (pp. 182–186).

islands and the "free, open sea" he reads about in missionary tracts, he is rebuked by the coarse sensuality of actual missionaries (13–17); when he tries to imagine himself as a young David, he breaks neighbors' windows with his slingshot (17). Nature and books are not only parallel but essentially equivalent terms, both invested with the power of forbidden fruit: pastoral scenes are "a forbidden El Dorado" (9), and reading is forbidden by the strict terms of his mother's Calvinism. Nevertheless, his "soul escaped on every side from my civilized dungeon of brick and mortar, into the great free world from which my body was debarred" (80).

This structure exhibits some familiar characteristics: the intertwining of literature, pastoral, and transcendance; the distinction between the physical bondage of circumstance and the free mind. Presumably they are meant to "naturalize" Alton for middle-class sensibilities, to suggest a source of character beyond circumstance, and, as the story progresses, to demonstrate the injustices in the educational system which keep talented Alton out of Cambridge. But Kingsley is so ambivalent about all of these matters that he turns the configuration in contradictory ways. Alton is less an unconditioned spirit trapped in a social body than a being intensely conscious of his own imprisonment, whose yearning increases with his distance from the objects of his desire. His intellectual ambition is saturated with social guilt, first because it is a betrayal of his mother and then because it is a wish to escape his class. His story demands that he subdue ambition by harnessing his genius to working-class subjects (to which he has to be introduced as though he were a middle-class observer), while at the same time it chastises him for seeing his life as socially conditioned and identifying himself with Chartist politics. Alton is wrong when he acts like a part of the working class and wrong when he aspires beyond it. Associated from the beginning with the world of nature and books, his dilemma—like Kingsley's—is that he has a gift without a conviction about how it should be used.[33]

33. Yet Kingsley's account of Alton's conflict does in some measure correspond with the choices faced by Chartist and working-class writers and poets.

The imagery of freedom and imprisonment that pervades *Alton Locke* can be traced elsewhere in Kingsley's writings during the year of European revolution and British hysteria over Chartism. On April 12, 1848, two days after the final presentation and failure of the Chartist petition, Kingsley posted a placard in London addressed to the workmen of England, in which he advocated moral rather than political reform and challenged the Chartist view of political freedom. It includes this sentence: "That, I guess, is real slavery; to be a slave to one's own stomach, one's own pocket, one's own temper. Can the Charter cure *that* ?"[34] Kingsley's freedom seems to mean a freedom from economic and personal circumstances achieved through sheer personal force; elsewhere he represents freedom and a consequent class brotherhood as attainable in the transcendance represented by aesthetic appreciation.

In the essay "British Museum," published around the same time, Kingsley advocates free museums of science and industry for the people. An illustrative anecdote tells a story of Kingsley admiring a display of hummingbird specimens in an Oxford Street shop window, and finding himself standing next to a coalheaver who is doing the same thing. Full of his best naturalist's rhetoric, Kingsley extends his own elation to his neighbor; above all he feels in that shared moment the meaning of fraternity: "that the party-walls of rank and fashion and money were but a paper prison of our own making."[35] Aesthetic transcendance (as Kingsley experiences it) makes him feel that the economics of class is not only slavery but imaginary slavery; his idealism does not mean, as it does in Dickens, that the party walls are unnatural and evil, but that they are unreal—mental barriers that imagination and kind feeling can overcome. When

---

Martha Vicinus points to the contrary pulls of aesthetic pleasure in traditional "high" forms and political commitment, to conflicting desires to radicalize or to elevate working-class readers, and to the difficulty of finding patrons and publishers without seeming to abandon working-class associations. See *The Industrial Music: A Study of Nineteenth-Century British Working-Class Literature* (New York, 1974), pp. 94–184.

34. Quoted in Kingsley, *Letters and Memories*, pp. 95–96.
35. Quoted in ibid., p. 104.

the imagery of freedom and imprisonment is worked out in the plot of *Alton Locke,* it turns out to mean something similar: that freedom is the aristocratic privilege of appreciation, prison the consciousness of working-class life and politics. In all of these texts Kingsley's conflict between the politics of circumstance and imaginative freedom lands him finally in the most conservative of social positions.

The aristocratic pastoral shapes the "two journeys" that are announced as key episodes in the novel's first paragraph. In the first journey, Alton's innate craving for pastoral beauty is rewarded, while it turns before our eyes into a justification for the institutions of upper-class life. Alton walks from London to Cambridge in order to get support for the publication of his poem from his rising cousin George. The journey occurs at a moment when Alton has recognized his economic kinship with his fellow tailors and has refused to do piecework; he has begun "to look on man . . . as the creature and puppet of circumstances" (110) and (a corollary for Kingsley) to describe himself as a Chartist. Although the narrative immediately dis-avows the doctrine of circumstances (only to espouse it a few pages later in a less politically charged context), the journey episode develops the argument against Alton's Chartism by wrapping him in blankets of pastoral and sending him into the upper-class world.

Alton's walk restores his body (he instantly loses a lifelong cough) and liberates his spirit: he describes nature with a rhetorical exuberance that suggests Kingsley had been reading the early numbers of *David Copperfield,* and himself "in the temper of a boy broke loose from school" (116)—no matter that he has never been to school. Yet it is not long before nature becomes property, out of bounds again: Alton can indulge his literary ecstasy in his first wood only after asking permission to enter from its gentleman owner (117). Like a free museum of natural history, the wood, he thinks, should be open to all his fellow Londoners; he does not imagine that nature belongs to them (118). As he approaches Cambridge, the objects of his admiration and envy grow increasingly social and institutional: a fisherman father joins a loving upper-class family; a new village school releases happy children and a kindly parson whose wife is seen "popping in and out of the cottages" (121); and the Cambridge boat races inspire Alton to produce some muscular Christian rhetoric. He is finally taken under the wing of Lord Lyndale, a paragon of "innate nobleness and grace" (146), and comes to pay a long visit to the elaborate household of Dean Winnstay of D——, who becomes his patron. It is embarrassing to read these pages, in which Kingsley (the fisherman, the parson, the athlete, the Cambridge man) fantasizes about how his own life should look in working-class eyes and indulges his penchant for upper-class idolatry. Sensitivity to class difference is placed almost entirely in Alton's mind; Kingsley suggests that his social defensiveness is a paper prison of his own making. The whole episode makes it uncomfortably clear that Kingsley is using the first-person narrative partly in the service of his own need for working-class love and approval.[36]

During this first journey, Alton's craving for natural beauty is implicated with his guilty admiration of class privilege and with his betrayal of the working class. Agreeing to expurgate the political parts of his poem in return for patronage, Alton associates himself with the apparent transcendance of material life which characterizes the aristocracy, and which makes it in Kingsley's view potentially "democratic." Beauty becomes an intrinsic part of upper-class social order, marking out no separate or asocial zone. In one sense, then, Kingsley's shaping of the first journey unmasks the fantasy of the asocial pastoral by insisting on its basis in social privilege and power. Nevertheless, that connection seems an inadvertent by-product of his own guilty participation in the Romantic yearning for a sensuous and aesthetic transcendance rooted in the ease of aristocratic life.

36. On 19 June 1848 Kingsley wrote a letter introducing himself to the Chartist poet Thomas Cooper, who was, according to Robert Bernard Martin, one of the models for Alton Locke. See *The Dust of Combat: A Life of Charles Kingsley* (London, 1959), pp. 112–113. In this letter, quoted on p. 108 of *Letters and Memories*, Kingsley demonstrates the peculiar tone of defensiveness about his class which pervades *Alton Locke*. Assuming that Cooper will reject his advances, Kingsley reveals that he feels misunderstood by working-class radicals who see him as an aristocrat, and appeals to Cooper as a fellow poet for a working-class hearing.

The second journey out of London appears to be a correction and a social inversion of the first. Until this point, Alton has been full of scorn for country laborers, imagining them as "coarse men and sluttish women" (5) who fail to appreciate the beauty of the nature that surrounds them. Now he reenters the country-side of D——not as a poet but as a Chartist organizing agricul-tural workers. This journey, like the first, is a flight from one class identification to another. His working-class fellows, having discovered the disloyal expurgation of his poem, turn on him with accusations and abuse. (Although both classes expurgate Alton's writing—Dean Winnstay of his working-class politics, O'Flyn the radical editor of his upper-class sympathies—it is consistent with Kingsley's vision that the working class be represented as more punitive in its class antagonisms.) After a public recantation, Alton undertakes this mission to prove his solidarity with his own class. The second journey is a penance for the first, but in the end it only deepens Kingsley's original identification of nature and aristocracy.

Alton's first "poetic" vision of the fens landscape of D—— empties it of the rural working class that makes a blot in his pastoral. His language works toward the transcendant:

> The vast height and width of the sky-arch, as seen from those flats as from an ocean—the grey haze shrouding the horizon of our narrow land-view, and closing us in, till we seemed to be floating through infinite space . . . the little island knolls in that vast sea of fen, each with its long village street, and delicately taper spire; all this seemed to me to contain an element of new and peculiar beauty. [156–157]

On the second journey, to the same part of the country, "I arrived in the midst of a dreary, treeless country, whose broad brown and grey fields were only broken by an occasional line of dark doleful firs, at a knot of thatched hovels, all sinking and leaning every way but the right, the windows patched with paper, the doorways stopped with filth, which surrounded a beer-shop" (255). The Malthusian desolation of the winter landscape is described as a hardening of nature: "the earth was iron, and the sky iron above our heads"; deserted plows stand frozen, the fields are "burnt black with frost." Now the absence of people becomes a matter for comment; there are no villages, just an occasional "great dreary lump of farm-buildings"; the only people Alton and his guide encounter on their way to the workers' meeting are two freezing children (256–257). Seen through the eyes of working-class politics, nature becomes associated with an iron law of minimal survival.

In one sense, Alton sees on this journey the social suffering he had failed to see as a poet.[37] Yet as the speeches of the farm laborers spin out, decrying absentee landlords, the New Poor Law, and seasonal wage labor, it becomes apparent that the significant absence in the landscape is that of the aristocratic landlord who orders and cultivates land and people together. When Alton incites a bread riot, its target is a symbol of that absence: the Hall farm is a "huge square corpse of a hall" whose window makes "a black empty eye-socket"; its own park is overgrown, its mistress is "a fat virago" (269). The neglected estate is the key to the look of the countryside: Alton's "re-vision" is merely an inversion, a pure negation of the properly aristocratic pastoral. Rather than broadening Alton's social sympathies, the incident deepens his disgust with the rural laborers, who turn away from his political rhetoric and follow the needs of their stomachs, creating an incendiary riot at the hall. Thus the shape of the second journey finally corroborates that of the first: as a poet Alton walks out of the prison of London into pastoral privilege; as a Chartist he walks into a world shaped by people enslaved to their stomachs—and suffers a literal imprisonment.

Once Alton is in prison, the original contradiction between imaginative freedom and environmental determinism returns with all the ferocity of a literalized metaphor: "I was a brute animal, a puppet, a doll. . . . And yet my whole soul was as wide, fierce, roving, struggling as ever. Horrible contradiction! The dreadful sense of helplessness, the crushing weight of necessity, seemed to choke me" (283). The landscape he sees from his cell

37. Uffelman contrasts the journeys in order to prove that Alton learns to correct his Romantic visionary response and to see the actual human suffering in the countryside (*Charles Kingsley*, pp. 51, 54).

window is not the desolate moorland of necessity but his soul's pastoral, a rich and fertile country enclosing the house of Dean Winnstay and his beautiful daughter. Alton's imprisonment is a sign of his identification with working-class politics; it seems to cut him off forever from the aristocratic pastoral that he watches from afar. The "contradiction" he names here marks the climax of his whole earthly existence, in which a tormented search for escape from the limitations of social conditions only tightens the noose of social guiltiness around his neck.

The frenetic history of Alton's class oscillations and betrayals is partially controlled by another, more rigidly allegorical structure that might be called the novel's family romance. Alton has two fairy godparents who nurture him without constraining him, and who invariably produce rabbits out of hats at just those moments when Alton comes to the end of each of his many ropes of despair. The first is Sandy Mackaye, the Carlyle figure, who recognizes Alton's genius, houses and educates him, and pushes him toward working-class poetry while keeping a skeptical eye on working-class politics. Sandy dies on the eve of the final "physical-force" Chartist demonstration; his era of compassionate rationalism has reached its symbolic limit. After his death Alton's aristocratic mentor, Eleanor Staunton, comes to the fore as the goddess of Christian Socialism, to preside over Alton's dream, guide his conversion, and embody Kingsley's religious and social ideals.

Eleanor replaces Sandy because social reform must come from the upper class and from a redeemed Church of England. The switch of mentors is accompanied by a switch in Alton's object of desire. Eleanor's cousin Lillian has been throughout the novel the lodestar of his poetic and sexual fantasy; now he learns to reject her worldly and carnal lures for a new idolatry of the chaste, motherly, spiritual beauty of Eleanor. The hopeless romantic quest for physical beauty which torments Alton in the prison of working-class life is—so the narrative insists—translated and redeemed in the worship of Eleanor.

The more interesting part in the family romance is played by Alton's cousin George, who combines the roles of villain and double. George's history reveals why it is essential to Kingsley that Alton get nothing that he wants: George gets everything that Alton wants, in a social rise represented as the most despicable form of calculated ambition. The intelligent, athletic George, supported by his father's grocery fortunes, makes himself successful at Cambridge and in the church, wooing and winning Lillian while Alton pines. His life is a series of social strategies that have no end but status: he takes orders because the status of churchman will ensure his treatment as a gentleman, and he shapes his opinions to flatter the vanities of his aristocratic patrons. While Alton's earnest and divided loyalties ruin his relationships with both classes, George's cynicism leads surely to a brilliant career in the church.

In George, Kingsley manages to combine his attacks on competitive middle-class utilitarianism and on the Puseyite wing of the Church of England. He also betrays the depths of his scorn for the risen tradesman and the depths of his fear of rise itself. The apparent contrast between George's cynicism and Alton's confused integrity pretends to honor the artisan at the expense of the parvenu, but George is at the same time a sinister double to Alton's desires. His lascivious pursuit of Lillian is the underside of Alton's "Petrarchan" love; the hypocrisy of his opinions is only a calculated version of Alton's successive sellouts; and he literally shadows Alton, following him into the favors of the Winnstay family and into the Chartist world, where he mysteriously appears to spy on Alton's recantation of his upper-class sympathies. In fact, George is a double agent who tells the aristocracy of Alton's Chartism and the Chartists of Alton's capitulation to upper-class pressure—a figure of paranoia who exposes Alton's own hapless need to please both aristocracy and working class. As an image of Alton's desires empowered, George reveals Kingsley's actual horror at the idea that working-class talent might be translated into legitimate social agency; for him Alton's yearning remains sympathetic only so long as it is hopeless.

Alton's predicament is rhetorically soluble only through the final dream vision, which repeats even as it revises his history of romantic yearning and social imprisonment. In this remarkable piece of writing Kingsley purports both to satisfy the cravings of Alton's imagination and to recast its categories. Its beginning is the culmination of his central conflict: "my fancy, long pent-up and crushed by circumstances, burst out in uncontrollable wildness" (335); at its end "the past seemed swept away and buried, like the wreck of some drowned land after a flood" (353). In the delirious dream Alton sees the beauteous forms he has been longing for all his life; but in them nature is transformed from a romantic image of escape to a predatory world of lust and power in which the past conflicts of Alton's life are obsessively played out in each of the stages of a drama of evolutionary development.

Alton's first nightmares find him in exotic landscapes—a teeming volcano, a Himalayan ridge inhabited by Hindu gods—in which he is tormented and threatened; they are emotionally turbulent, flowing naturally out of the chaos of his history. Choked, blinded, and burned, he is saved by Eleanor, who drops his soul into the sea. As he falls "for ages," her voice explains that he must climb the "golden ladder" of the species in order to make himself a whole man. The fantasies that follow fall into two groups. In the first Alton is a defenseless creature—a crab, a remora, an ostrich—crushed and hunted down by the forces of lust and ambition, represented by Lillian and George in various guises. Then Alton himself becomes implicated with desire. As a South American mylodon, he tastes the delight of sheer animal strength, getting pleasure from destruction. A special, distant tree marks itself out as a target; he finds it surrounded by treasure and full of erotic flowers: "from among the branches hung great sea-green lilies, and, nestled in the heart of each of them, the bust of a beautiful girl. Their white bosoms and shoulders gleamed rosy-white against the emerald petals, like conch-shells half-hidden among sea-weeds, while their delicate waists melted mysteriously into the central sanctuary of the flower" (340). Attempting to get at this beauty, he destroys the tree and himself while George pockets the gold and the Lillian-flower. Finally, Alton is an ape, struggling toward intellect but dominated by lust, envy, and rage: Lillian appears as an exotic jungle maiden wreathed provocatively in flowers and suckling George's baby, George as a missionary of civilization who carelessly kills Alton in his tree.

These violent and erotic fantasies recast the story of Alton's social struggle as masochistic sexual fantasy, in which the guilt associated with class affiliation is transposed into the guilt of sexual power and desire. In them Alton dies many times, but the series ends with the "scientific" dissection of his monkey body: Alton's journey to "whole manhood" requires that he leave his lustful, violent, envious body behind. This story recapitulates in sexual terms the earlier struggles for release from circumstance, but now Alton's desires are associated with his imprisoning "natural" body, while his "manhood" is released to take up its role in the collective activity of human social order.

Recast as the nature of the body, nature is the new prison of Alton's dream. As the body is broken up into parts, Eleanor saves Alton's soul for a second time, and a new story, the story of civilization, begins with the dawning of the idea of "the All-Father" (343). In this extended symbolic history, the evolved Alton is the hero of his race: transcending the economic conflicts of rich and poor, rejecting the temptation of Lillian, he adheres to the work of moving toward God. The fantasy imagines social harmony in the form of a community that divides its time between two kinds of work: boring through the mountain that obstructs the human race in its westward spiritual journey toward the place of origin and destiny, and cultivating the land of the valley to ensure its physical survival. Class conflict begins when the work on the mountain is forgotten or abandoned. When the poor finally rise up against the injustices of the rich, Alton—who has remained faithful to work on the mountain—becomes their leader; when they follow him, the original state of equality and harmony is restored. The story recreates the original antinomies of Alton's story by presenting another world divided between the body and the spirit, and a landscape in which the mountain plays the role of the imprisoning wall.

In this fantasy, the imprisonment earlier associated with the idea of mass politics is transformed into an ideal of social collectivity and freedom controlled by the authority of God. The ideal seems to resolve the novel's contradictions by inverting their terms: first nature is an escape from or a transcendence of the circumstances of class; now collectivity is a liberation from the lures of nature. Although Kingsley wishes in theory to reconcile the miraculous God with the concept of an evolutionary ladder (as Eleanor argues in the anti-Straussian dialogue in chapter 38), the narrative postulates an apparent progress from animal to God which conceals the essential disjunction between body and soul.[38] Moreover, Alton's leadership is possible only because he has made the greatest transcendance of them all: beyond both class and sex, he eschews social power even as he embodies the spirit of collectivity.

The dream vision is the most original writing in the novel,[39] perhaps most congenial to Kingsley's sensibility because it allows him simultaneously to release and to chastise his powers of fantasy. As a narrative act, it is Kingsley's grandest gesture of escape from the circumstances of Alton's social dilemmas and from the consequentiality demanded by the novel form itself. But it reproduces both the flight from circumstance and the failure of that flight: Alton's dream invents a new human hero forged outside of human history in evolution and biblical myth; and yet each part of that history repeats the structure of desire and frustration which characterizes Alton's story from the beginning. Even the fantasy of Alton's heroism as a spiritual leader recapitulates the structure of divided loyalty (the mountain and the plain; the high and the low) and frustrated imprisonment (boring through the mountain wall that locks in the journey toward God); it cancels Alton's earlier social oscillations with a transcending stance of disengagement and withdrawal which is only a rewriting of the earlier ideal of aristocratic democracy. Like the two earlier journeys, the dream vision escapes from the prison house only to land in a world elsewhere that is itself built on the pattern of restriction and escape.

38. Cazamian treats the dream vision at some length, taking Kingsley's word that the fantasy exemplifies a reconciliation of evolutionary theory with the story of fall and redemption (*Social Novel in England*, pp. 282–284).

39. For a discussion of *Alton Locke* as a self-conscious array of "writing," see Gallagher, *Industrial Reformation*, pp. 101–109.

Dickens's simple division between the pastoral world and the imprisoned social one is more unbelievable, more fairy-tale-like, than Kingsley's strife-torn depiction of Alton's divided loyalty and hopeless romanticism. Yet the apparent simplicity of Dickens's design makes it possible for him to "see" social institutions: the unchallenged Wordsworthian myth creates a dialectic that lights up the assumptions of social manipulators. Kingsley's work creates and breaks down the idea of pastoral harmony, lighting up its basis in aristocratic hegemony; yet his inability to distinguish or delimit the meanings of nature and society adds up to a rehearsal of the most conventional fears and prejudices about class and, in the end, about sex. *Alton Locke* suggests that a Victorian as permeable to currents of thought and rhetoric as Kingsley was would find it impossible to maintain a conventional literary pastoral in the face of pressures from evolutionary theory on one side and theorized working-class protest on the other. The contrast between it and *Oliver Twist* also makes it possible to see the power of a pastoral mode that functions as a stable antithesis to social interpretation, even if it depends on a claim to a transcendant discourse.

The Maternal Pastoral of *Ruth*

In Elizabeth Gaskell's *Ruth* (1853), pastoral writing functions as in *Oliver Twist* to create an alternative interior realm that protects its subject from the conventional language of social judgment. In Gaskell's work, however, the natural world is not a utopia in which the narrative may find a place of rest but a realm of images for the emotional life which must give way to a confrontation with social life as it stands. In this second of her social-problem novels, Gaskell relies on the asocial pastoral as a way of reformulating the loaded social questions raised by a highly conventional story: the seduction and abandonment of a young seamstress. Gaskell's defense of the natural virtue of a "fallen woman" and her bastard child put her up against one of the most rigid Victorian social codes, and one of the most formulaic story patterns, in which the seduction of an urban working girl is followed by prostitution and/or death.[40] The pattern is one that Gaskell herself had used in *Mary Barton* (1848) to shape the fate of Esther Barton and the threat to her niece Mary; in "Lizzie Leigh" (1850), it lies behind the main story of a young prostitute rescued by her country mother. It is therefore of special interest to see how she set out to question and complicate the story in *Ruth*.

The novel was written as a kind of negotiation between two pressures: the strong sympathy Gaskell had developed for a sixteen-year-old prostitute whom she had helped to emigrate, and the knowledge—based in part on the public reception of *Mary Barton*—that she would be the target of intense social criticism when *Ruth* was published. Gaskell first told the story of her young protégée in a letter to Dickens asking his advice about the arrangement of an emigration plan. The child had lost her father at two; her mother was indifferent to her. Her uncle had placed her in an orphan school and then apprenticed her to a fashionable Manchester dressmaker. The business failing, the girl was placed with another dressmaker, who

> connived at the girl's seduction by a surgeon in the neighborhood who called in when the poor creature was ill. Then she was in despair, and wrote to her mother *(who had never corresponded with her all the time she was at school and an apprentice;)* and while awaiting the answer went into the penitentiary; she wrote three times but no answer came, and in desperation she listened to a woman who had obtained admittance [to the penitentiary] solely as it turned out to decoy girls into her mode of life. . . . [41]

The final twist, as Gaskell told Dickens in a postscript, was the return of the seducing surgeon in the role of physician to the prison where the girl was being held for theft. When she fainted upon being brought before him, the story emerged, and the doctor was dismissed from his position.

As Gaskell unfolds it, this is clearly a "story"—the return of the seducer as physician makes a compelling ironic climax that

40. Coral Lansbury suggests that "prostitution was not merely a social condition but a literary convention with accepted modes of expression to mark the progress from virgin to harlot and eventual suicide" (*Elizabeth Gaskell* [Boston, 1984], p. 25).

41. Gaskell, *Letters*, pp. 98–99.

was turned, in *Ruth*, into the fictional return of Bellingham as a parliamentary candidate. It is, in particular, a story of parental abandonment. Of all the misfortunes in the tale, Gaskell underscored only the parenthetical clause about the mother's failure to correspond. Her horror arose especially from the initial violation of parental responsibility, which was repeated over and over in the failures of the adults who were in charge of the child. With its elements rearranged and romanticized, this story, and this emotional focus, formed the basis for *Ruth*.[42]

Gaskell's personal and maternal commitment to the story took a very different form, then, from the fictional terms in which the "problem" of the fallen woman was usually conceived—as an indication of personal weakness, depravity, or social victimization; as a threat to "pure" women and a shame to the family; as an inexorable path toward hardened or despairing isolation. Her fear of the collision between the two conceptions is strikingly apparent in the letters written just before and after *Ruth* was published. In a letter to her daughter Marianne, Gaskell is evasive and nervous:

> when Ruth will be published whether this year, next, or ten years hence I don't know. It is not *written* yet—although Agnes Sanders was told at a Leamington library that it was coming down next day. I have never asked for any copies for myself. But, as I say again, *when* or *if ever* I shall finish it I don't know. I hate publishing because of the talk people make, which I always felt as a great impertinence, *if they address their remarks to me* in any way.[43]

The gap between her private sense of the book and its public life was very real to her even before publication; she dreaded public discourse as a direct personal "impertinence," a violation of her privacy. Since at this time the first two volumes were already at the publisher's and she was to send off the completed manuscript a month later,[44] her claim that the novel was not yet written is particularly odd, suggesting that she still imagined it as tied to her internal life rather than as an externalized, "written"

42. Winifred Gérin sketches the story in *Elizabeth Gaskell*, pp. 104–105.
43. Gaskell, *Letters*, p. 209.
44. Gérin, *Elizabeth Gaskell*, p. 137.

object. Her fears were to be justified by the actual reception of
Ruth.[45] But the split between Ruth as a private conception and as
a public issue had already been inscribed in the text itself. It
takes form as a division between a pastoral argument about
private feeling, which occupies the first nine chapters, and a
social argument about the treatment of fallen women, which
dominates the rest of the novel.

This division makes a discontinuity in the novel; it also
contains and rebukes the contradictions that have always been
noted in the novel's argument. These contradictions may be
readily summarized in the form of two questions: If Gaskell is
intent on showing Ruth's utter innocence and ignorance by
arguing that she is simply a victim of Bellingham's seduction,
what are we to make of the early passages that suggest her
suppressed sense of guilt and her intuition that what she is doing
is wrong? And if Gaskell presents Ruth as an innocent, how can
the bulk of the book be devoted to the proposition that she is a
sinner who may expiate her sin and be recovered as a valuable
member of society?[46] Precisely such formulations of the case are,
I argue, what Gaskell's pastoral aims to challenge and set aside.
The alternatives they offer are based on socially determined
views of the fallen woman: either Ruth must be a victim of social
forces beyond her control or she must be guilty of sexuality. The
pastoral writing recasts Ruth's fall in a different language, one
that relies on the Wordsworthian conflation of nature and
individual psychology. Her pastoral sensibility is not simply a
guarantee of some innate, asocial innocence[47] but a way of
talking about emotional needs so fundamental that they achieve
the status of "nature" whether they are socially named as

45. See ibid., pp. 137–141, and Gaskell, *Letters*, pp. 220–227.
46. Margaret Ganz develops the most extended argument about Gaskell's
contradictions in *Elizabeth Gaskell*, pp. 105–131. Angus Easson makes a succinct
statement of the problem in *Elizabeth Gaskell*, pp. 117–125. Lansbury gets around
the issue by constructing a Ruth so malleable that she is entirely determined by
the circumstances of her surroundings (*Elizabeth Gaskell*, pp. 25–27).
47. Several critics have taken note of Ruth's pastoral nature. See especially
Craik, *Elizabeth Gaskell*, pp. 55–60; Sally Mitchell, *The Fallen Angel: Chastity, Class,
and Women's Reading*, 1835–1880 (Bowling Green, O., 1981), pp. 32–38; and
Easson, *Elizabeth Gaskell*, pp. 115–117.

innocence or as guilt. Thus the pastoral chapters allow Gaskell to describe Ruth's fall as a natural emotional event that has a life independent of the social constructs that are later brought to bear upon it.

Wordsworth's "Ruth" (published in 1800) seems to have provided both a model and an antagonist for the pastoral part of Gaskell's enterprise.[48] In that poem, Ruth is a little girl of six when her mother dies and her father remarries; left to her own devices, she wanders about in nature and becomes "an infant of the woods."[49] When she is grown, she is courted by a Youth from America, who marries and then abandons her before they set sail for the American wilderness, where he has promised that they will share a life in the forest. After a period of madness, Ruth returns to nature to live out the rest of her days, with no other home than barns or greenwood trees; she is, of course, one of Wordsworth's blessed beggars and solitaries who never enters the social realm, but retains the customs of her childhood in "an innocent life, yet far astray!" But the poem does not simply associate nature with this radical and innocent solitude. In the figure of the Youth, nature shows its sinister aspects: lawless freedom, irregular impulse, voluptuous longing. Although Wordsworth does not admit any sexual irregularities into the plot of his poem, his language about the Youth suggests a more conventional context of seduction than he is willing to describe.

Gaskell follows Wordsworth in making her Ruth identify herself with nature in the absence of parental love, in imagining a courtship that seems to offer a pastoral life shared by two lovers of beauty, and in associating with the seducer a more

48. Gaskell's love and knowledge of Wordsworth's poetry are evident in her letters of 12 May 1836 and 18 August 1838, in which she describes working with her husband on prose imitations of the poets and helping him with lectures on the poetry of humble life (*Letters*, pp. 7, 33). Gérin attests to her love of Wordsworth and her excitement at meeting him in 1849 (*Elizabeth Gaskell*, p. 103). Donald D. Stone argues that Gaskell deliberately allied herself with Wordsworthian ideas in order to justify herself as a writer. His analysis of *Ruth*, attributing the flaws in the novel to Gaskell's need to punish as well as to celebrate Romantic qualities, seems to conflate the willful and the quiescent romanticisms his book intends to distinguish. See *Romantic Impulse*, pp. 144–153.

49. *The Poetical Works of Wordsworth*, ed. Thomas Hutchinson (New York, 1933), pp. 192–195.

rebellious and voluptuous idea of nature. Once Bellingham is disposed of, however, she has very different ideas about the continuation of Ruth's life. Even for Ruth alone, images of nature become morally ambiguous, divided between the innocent and the dangerous. And Gaskell, arranging for her heroine's rescue and socialization, argues not only against the unhappy endings of social seduction-and-abandonment tales but against the Romantic isolationism celebrated in Wordsworth's poem. For her, Ruth must grow up out of the pastoral mode and into the social realm, developing her natural sensibility into domestic virtue.[50] Although Gaskell fails to make a seamless progression from one mode to the other, her pastoral does succeed in making a place from which social responses to sexual falls may be distanced and criticized.

From her first appearance, Ruth is described as a spirit whose home is natural beauty, while the ambiguity of her class status strengthens the sense of an asocial positioning. She is immediately distinguished from her fellow apprentices by the strength of her need to be outside; when a break is allowed, she "sprang to the large old window, and pressed against it as a bird presses against the bars of its cage;"[51] from the window she sees an old larch that is an image of herself, once surrounded by affectionate natural life, now "pent up and girded about with flagstones" (5). Despite bad weather, going outdoors on errands is her only restorative; the place she chooses in the seamstress's attic is the coldest and darkest, but it allows her to look at an old wall panel that depicts a beautiful abundance of flowers (6–7). Unlike the literary flights of the urban Alton Locke, these images connect Ruth in memory to her mother and the country life she has lost with the deaths of her parents; for her the pastoral is literally a lost heritage.

Gaskell understands this heritage not as a symbolic guarantor of virtue and innocence but as an experience that leaves in Ruth

---

50. Sally Mitchell reads *Ruth* as a story about the need to overcome Wordsworthian innocence and to make choices in the knowledge of good and evil (*Fallen Angel*, p. 35).

51. Elizabeth Gaskell, *Ruth* (London, 1967), p. 4. Further references to this edition will appear in the text.

what might be called a pastoral drive. In the life of the seamstresses she is claustrophobic; she needs and chooses to go out whenever she can. Her hunger for beauty is a consciousness that is oblivious of the social: when she goes to the hunt ball she sees the dancing figures as "a joyous and brilliant whole," not caring to separate and name them as her companions do (14); the aristocracy is the stuff of dreams to her because "literally and figuratively their lives seemed to wander through flowery pleasure-paths" (17). In her mind, Mr. Bellingham is quite literally a way to get outside: he takes her for walks in the countryside and nourishes her need for beauty. The kind of innocence that Gaskell creates is not the innocence of utter passivity and helplessness but an obliviousness of social implication. Ruth makes choices according to her very strong need for a natural world associated in her experience with an affectionate and nurturing mother. To call her a Wordsworthian child does not mean that she is innocent the way Oliver Twist is, but that she embodies an actively asocial principle, a singular imagination that works emotionally and aesthetically rather than socially.

Ruth goes with Bellingham not—like her fictional sisters in sin—because she has aspirations to economic status or because she is starving or destitute. Gaskell explains the seduction morally and psychologically, as a result of parental abandonment on a large scale. In passages that most appear to muddle the issue of Ruth's innocence by attributing to her a latent sense of guilt, Gaskell attempts to set the terms in another way: to present Ruth as a presocial being to whom she attributes a "natural" chastity without knowledge of it as a social concept. Gaskell herself naturalizes the concept of chastity, identifying it with a presocial spirit that recalls the legitimizing language of origin in *Oliver Twist*: "a brooding spirit with no definite form or shape that men should know it, but which is there, and present before we have recognized and realized its existence." (43)

This bit of mystification allows her to retain the equation of woman and chastity while separating it from its punitive social consequences. Thus she argues that while Ruth has an intuitive social conscience that leads her to feel some guilt about her outings with Bellingham, she has no concepts to which to attach the feelings, and therefore no reason to value them. Her mother has died when she is at the critical age of twelve, and no other adult in her life will take the responsibility of recognizing that Ruth does not already know what young ladies may and may not do. And, as a presocial creature, Ruth acts according to the nature of a child: her moment of liaison with Bellingham comes after the last in a series of abandonments, when her employer fires her; she gives herself up to him because she feels that no other person will take care of her. The question of sexuality is overridden by Ruth's need for a loving parent; innocence or guilt is subsumed in an argument about psychological need. The seduction episode is correspondingly suffused by Gaskell's emotional appeal to the maternal and protective instincts of her readers.

The integrity of this argument is most brilliantly displayed in Gaskell's treatment of Ruth after she has become Bellingham's mistress. When they appear at the inn in Wales, nothing has changed, no "fall" has occurred; Ruth haunting the Welsh landscapes is, if anything, even more a solitary child of nature than she was before the seduction. Her sexuality is implicitly a part of natural affection, while the real disjunction lies, as before, in the gap between her natural behavior and the social interpretations of it, which begin to trouble her consciousness only now. It is difficult to believe in the extreme innocence that Gaskell portrays here, unless her decision is understood as a narrative move that intends some quietly radical challenges to the doctrine of female chastity. The Wales section implies that a sexual relationship may be a natural fact separate from the social construct of "fall," that social innocence and virginity are not identical. Throughout Gaskell takes care to show that Ruth's primary emotions are the result of her attachment to Bellingham—anxiety, nurture, and the despair of abandonment—rather than the guilt and shame induced by the social code. It is not until Ruth enters society with the Bensons that she begins to feel the socially constructed emotions "appropriate" to her situation.

In the first nine chapters, which tell the story of the seduction and abandonment, Ruth's emotional life is charted almost entirely through her responses to natural scenes, as though her real relationship were not with Bellingham but with nature.[52] The main events in this narrative sequence are descriptive passages that stand in for the development of Ruth's feelings for Bellingham and distinguish her emotional responses from his social ones. When Bellingham takes Ruth to see her old home at Milham Grange (44–50), the house is described as a picturesque overgrown pastoral inhabited only by the Wordsworthian figure of the old deaf laborer Thomas. Bellingham is an intruder in this world; he watches as Ruth is absorbed in a passion of memory and grief, obtruding his alien class sensibility in his repugnance to Ruth's familiarity with Thomas. The old man intuits his threat, but Ruth is oblivious of social distinctions and implications, and cannot translate Thomas's biblical warning into the appropriate social terms.

When the pair leave the cottage, they enter a vast, extended landscape that seems to express a moment of rich, wide possibility and pleasure just before the fatal decision (51–53). Standing on the summit of a hill surrounded by blooming gorse, they see flocks of birds at a pool, the hospitable inn, farm animals, and distant hills and spires; the view perfectly integrates human, animal, and plant life in a kind of open harmony that is shattered by their arrival at the inn and the appearance of social consciousness in the person of Ruth's employer, Mrs. Mason. The wide fullness of this landscape will be replaced by the wide emptiness of the landscapes that will later represent Ruth's loss of place in the ordinary world.

After the lovers appear in Wales, its starker landscapes express the growing gap between Ruth's emotional life and human society. In the "Alpine country" Ruth becomes more of a spiritual Wordsworthian: "vast ideas of beauty and grandeur filled her mind at the sight of the mountains, now first beheld in full majesty . . . the grandeur of this beautiful earth absorbed all idea of separate and individual existence . . ." (64) Now

52. Gaskell's use of "setting" in *Ruth* is discussed in a more symbolic mode in Craik, *Elizabeth Gaskell*, pp. 56–60.

Bellingham is associated with indoor social obligation, sulking and fretting in bad weather, while Ruth goes out and exults in every change of sky and scene. The only recorded change in her consciousness is her intensified wish to fill her being with inhuman images that blot out her own social identity.

The different sensuality of Bellingham is suggested in the "green hollow" where the lovers have their last scene of harmony together (72–74). Only here, in the description of the "green gloom," with its low pond reflecting a tiny fragment of sky, is the lovers' "descent" into sexuality lightly figured. Bellingham, absorbed by the physical beauty that seems meaningless to Ruth, decks her hair with lilies and makes her look at herself in the pool, but she does so only for his pleasure. The underwater quality of this scene—the depth, the enclosure, the secrecy, the narcissistic worship—serves to delineate Bellingham's wanton idea of natural beauty, and to distinguish it from Ruth's.

After Bellingham falls ill and his mother arrives to rescue him, Ruth's relationship with nature begins to admit pain and the possibility of final oblivion. On the night when she crouches beside the door of Bellingham's sickroom, her feelings of woe and loss are caught in the description of the landscape as it darkens, and then as the dawn gradually moves toward a glorious sunrise that prefigures Bellingham's recovery. Finally we see Ruth, Tess-like, on a "bare table of moor" with a white road stretching emptily toward the distance into which Bellingham has disappeared. The desolation and bareness of the scene figures her sense of final abandonment; her consciousness records no feeling except her loss of Bellingham and the movements of insects and birds around her (93). After Thurstan Benson rescues her and takes her in, her suicidal despair takes her again to the windows, where she watches the stormclouds move and wishes to die into "the free, broad world" (99). Her yearning to "get out" reaches its furthest limit here. Yet the suicidal impulse, like all of Ruth's emotions, is not a response to social guilt and shame but an extension of her propensity to respond to pain by merging herself with the inhuman beauty of natural process.

The pastoral writing disappears with Bellingham's disappearance from Ruth's life; the rhetoric that has located her in a realm apart from social interpretation and judgment has served its purpose. It returns only briefly when Bellingham returns, in the scenes on the sands of Abermouth (chap. 23 and 24), where the descriptions mirror the recurrence of painful confusion and conflict in Ruth's feelings. In these scenes the solidity of the humanized, rooted landscape in which Ruth now has her social identity is threatened by the shifting sands of the beach where she confronts Bellingham in his new social identity as Mr. Donne. Once again Ruth is drawn to merge herself in the asocial oblivion of nature; before she confronts Bellingham she tries to walk beyond the human border marked by the black posts of the fishermen, into the ocean (291–293). This time, however, she has an independent sense of morality to defend, and, after the effort of rejecting her former lover, she collapses only after regaining the land, on a rock in which an ash tree is rooted (301). Now nature both images her desolation and comforts her with more clearly religious meanings; her old impulses take only a momentary flight from a steadier social existence.

The crucial elision in the novel occurs at the juncture between Ruth's pastoral existence and her social one—that is, at the moment of her adoption by Thurstan and Faith Benson. During this part of the narrative Gaskell shifts her focus to the consciousnesses of the Bensons, so that Ruth is visible only from their points of view. She is now, for the first time, a "social problem," one that we are asked to consider in the most generous possible way, from the unconventional perspective of Thurstan Benson. When we see her again she is conscious of her "sin" and aware of her social status and that of her child; the baffled perplexity with which she greeted social rebuffs during her liaison with Bellingham is instantly succeeded by an absorbing attitude of humility and repentance. This discontinuity in Ruth's moral life signals the essential contradiction of Gaskell's argument; it is not a matter of guilt and innocence but an unacknowledged shift from the natural to the social definition of what has happened.

Yet Gaskell proffers a bridge over the fissure: Ruth's absorp-

tion in nature is now replaced by her "natural" joy in preg-
nancy—precisely the instinct that is to be the novel's central
argument for her social virtue. Against Faith's conventional
responses to the prospect of a bastard child, Thurstan articulates
Gaskell's creed, calling Ruth's joy a "burst of nature from her
heart," and criticizing "the world's way of treatment" for being
"too apt to harden the mother's natural love into something like
hatred" (118–119). In this way the leap in Ruth's moral life is
buried under Gaskell's strong appeal to the ideology of motherhood and obscured by the leap in her emotional life which
turns her magically from a motherless child of the woods to a
natural mother fiercely devoted to protecting her child from
social castigation and harm.

Once having negotiated these chasms, Gaskell reasserts Ruth's
continuity with an earlier past. In the Benson household Ruth—
still only sixteen years old—completes the growing up that was
interrupted by her mother's death. The narrative reminds us of
Ruth's own protected childhood, and suggests an ascent from
the natural virtue associated with Mrs. Hilton to a higher form
of asocial principle: "it seemed that their lives were pure and
good, not merely from a lovely and beautiful nature, but from
some law, the obedience to which was, of itself, harmonious
peace, and which governed them almost implicitly, and with as
little questioning on their part, as the glorious stars which haste
not, rest not, in their eternal obedience" (141).

Now the world of flowers, too, is contained in a domestic and
social order of household and garden;[53] while Ruth's grief is
chastened and turned to domestic content by the ministrations
of Sally and Faith. Although Ruth's religious education is never
specifically charted, we are meant to understand that Ruth's love
of nature turns into a love of God which, like that of Thurstan,
sustains a higher-than-social morality.

The rest of the novel is about the tension between the natural
virtue protected and nurtured under cover of the Bensons' lie
and conventional social responses to the fallen woman and the

---

53. Craik notes the combination of nature and domesticity at the Bensons'
(ibid., p. 58).

162

NARRATIVE HISTORY AND THE SOCIAL RECORD

bastard child. Unlike Dickens, who creates an absolute split between his pastoral and social worlds, or Wordsworth, who flees the social world, Gaskell develops a genuine strain between the claims of the competing realms, formally containing it in the moral ambiguity of the lie. Like Margaret Hale's lie in *North and South,* the Bensons' representation of Ruth as a young widow is both right and wrong. It protects the naturally virtuous person from the social machinery of interpretation and condemnation which is incapable of reading character, rather like the machinations of Dickens's pastoral characters in *Oliver Twist.* But in Gaskell's work one cannot violate social law or convention without paying for it with social exposure. Ruth's story is designed to make her suffer for her past, yet the act of exposure challenges conventional images of the fallen woman as a separate and tainted being who carries the threat of sin.

In developing Ruth's own character and shaping her end, Gaskell reveals the pressure of her topic. Ruth's meek perfection and selfless motherhood pull heavily at ideological strings, while her death from nursing her former lover falls too easily into the pattern of sacrificial but necessary punishment doled out to fallen women (Dickens's Nancy, Trollope's Jessie Phillips). Through the stories of the Bradshaw children, however, Gaskell makes a more indirect attack on the taboos connected with the fallen woman. In a way that must surely have formed a model for the Gradgrind family in *Hard Times,* Gaskell sets the turbulent careers of the children in a "model" household against the simple domestic generosity of a young woman "tainted" by her earlier experience.[54] Richard Bradshaw's story shows what true social hypocrisy is: Ruth's lie covers an emotional truth, while Richard's apparent dutifulness conceals a life of petty profligacy and business crime. Jemima Bradshaw—one of the novel's most interesting characters—struggles with a conflict between natural love and social expectation which identifies her with Ruth's earlier confusions.

Set tightly within a familial context, Jemima's problem is that

---

54. Numerous critics, including Craik (ibid., p. 72) and Lansbury (*Elizabeth Gaskell,* p. 32), have noticed this connection.

she loves the man she is socially supposed to marry. Her long, moody rebellion is a comic version of Ruth's earlier tragedy: what Ruth does from natural feeling is utterly asocial; for Jemima the social acceptability of a match with Mr. Fahrquar seems to invalidate her feeling for him. Her internal and self-conscious battle with social convention is a limited version of Ruth's unconscious pastoralism, which ends well partly because Jemima learns of Ruth's past, and understands that the apparently perfect Ruth has experienced a more drastic form of her own turbulence. (Like Ruth's, Jemima's older lover partly takes the place of a parent.) Ruth's influence on Jemima therefore inverts the fearful Victorian idea of the tainted woman: only after Jemima learns that Ruth has "fallen" does Ruth's life help her to develop womanly sympathy and successful love: she defends Ruth against her father's righteous condemnation and finds a special connection with her husband in their shared disregard of the public shame heaped on Ruth after her exposure. Gaskell's analogy between the two women's adolescent confusions also brings Ruth's history closer to the normal social sphere, defying the conventional gap that set the terms for so many fictional confrontations between pure and fallen women.

As Ruth progresses from domestic motherhood to her role as private governess and finally to her public social work as a nurse, the pastoral sensibility of her childhood falls almost completely away, raising the question of its final status in Gaskell's work. For her the pastoral is not a place in which a character may abide, nor can it act as a stable alternative realm outside of the social one. In both Dickens and Kingsley, the pastoral blurs into social meanings: Dickens's utopian community, Kingsley's transcendent realm of aristocratic appreciation and his lower world of animal passion. For Gaskell the pastoral is a position of psychological and moral isolation genuinely incommensurate with social life. While sensitivity to nature signals the potential of the spirit, it does not (as in *Oliver Twist*) automatically guarantee ideal character, which can be worked out only within the knowable terms of the domestic and the social spheres. *Ruth*'s pastoral is a screen against which the isolated spirit projects itself when its emotions are uncontained in appropriate social relations. It is superseded by a direct confrontation with social prejudices made visible in a context that is finally committed to the belief that life in the social order is all we have. The difficulty of protecting a generous domestic order from the constructions of social life is delicately rendered in the economic and moral vulnerability of the Benson household; no pastoral havens remain in Gaskell's fictional terrain.

Nevertheless, Gaskell's special reliance on pastoral language in this novel makes an argument like Dickens's, a protest like Kingsley's, against the imprisonment of character in social determinants. She uses it to explain Ruth's fall in a way that pulls clear of the dichotomy between guilt and victimization brought on by economic necessity or social aspiration. Like Oliver Twist, Ruth is given an inner nature made of pastoral language and an emotional heritage of affection that makes her internal history very different from her social record. Her character is firmly set in a wider-than-social world against which conventional social definitions declare their blindnesses. The nine chapters that open *Ruth* render nature as both a consolation and a danger, but they also set up an emotional and moral discontinuity between nature and society which lies at the heart of Gaskell's claims for her heroine.

The pastoral arguments that emerge from *Oliver Twist, Alton Locke,* and *Ruth* all work, in one way or another, to formalize a stance above or beyond an explanatory narrative tied to the consequentiality of social determinism. In the variety of those stances it also becomes possible to see why Wordsworth proved so especially fertile in the imaginations of socially anxious Victorians. Wordsworth offered a "pastoral within," a way of talking that could evoke individual alternatives to social deadlocks without denying that those deadlocks were there, or likely to remain. Furnished in pastoral images, the interiors of characters' minds make separate and finer histories than their social worlds can record. Wordsworthian rhetoric could also sanction the myth of a spiritual inheritance that was not the same as a lost social past and that did not simply yearn for a golden age. So Oliver Twist's prehistory defies social institutions as they develop in history, and Ruth's early childhood sanctifies the socially reprehensible form of her yearning for love and protection. And Wordsworth provided a way to spiritualize wildness, to submerge passional drives of need or sexuality in language that presented the asocial as a transcendence rather than a violation of social codes.

Perhaps most powerfully of all, Wordsworthian language could work as a blurring of class difference: it stood at the same time for literary culture and for the special powers of humble and working-class people. This identification is especially strong in Dickens and Trollope: for Oliver Twist and Michael Armstrong extensive reading is virtually synonymous with life in the country, and their natural affinity for books matches their spiritual affinity with nature. For Alton Locke the worlds of nature and books are always parallel: equally desirable, equally impossible transcendences of social life. Even Ruth, originally formed in the mode of the blessed Wordsworthian vagrant, later manifests—as though inevitably—a special talent for book-learning and a natural gentility of manner. Through the unexamined conflation of nature and culture, all of these characters are rendered socially equal with their appreciative middle-class readers without having followed the same social courses. As Wordsworth sidestepped social guilt by projecting special spiritual and moral powers upon the poor and vagrant figures of his poems, the novelists who followed him entangled nature with education and culture, making fictional pastoral into a rhetorical substitute for social ascent.

4 Politics and the Recovery of Story

The desire to retell and reclaim both personal and cultural pasts may be the most significant mark of Victorian writing. In the novels I have been discussing, pastoral realms perform a double function in relating the past to the present: they account for structures of character that are unreadable from the social perspectives of the present, and they demand recognition as alternative stories, separate from the chains of cause and event that seem to bind contemporary social thought. The doubled stories created in the plotting of *Oliver Twist,* in the dream-vision re-creation of Alton Locke's history, and in the two ways of accounting for Ruth express that stance: the past explains the present while asserting immunity to its ruling explanations.

In Benjamin Disraeli's *Sybil* (1845), Charles Dickens's *Hard Times,* (1854) and George Eliot's *Felix Holt* (1866), the very act of remembering and retelling stories creates alternative narrative zones endowed with value, continuity, and the potential for reform. Perhaps the phenomenon of rapid and visible social change helped to catalyze—and moralize—models of history which stressed its recalcitrances and its continuities; whatever the impetus, these texts, like the pastoral writing, do nothing so simple as to yearn for a preindustrial past. Rather they set political fictions of the present against true stories about the past, in wars of narrative that probe the relationship between the telling of history and the possibility of social change.

The novels are all built on a dichotomy between history and politics. Each of them, in a distinct way, sets an ideal of temporal continuity against political activity or the management of social power. While they take industrialism, class relations, and social government as their material, they are not fundamentally about that material: rather than inquire about how social relations might be readjusted and reformed, they redefine the concept of reform itself. In each novel, the reforming politics of the present functions as a block to the movement of history from the past to the future; it is characterized and condemned by its willful abandonment of the past. In its place the novelists propose a different account of history, one that values temporality, memory, continuity, and loyalty; and they redefine "reform" in terms that embrace those values.

What sounds like simple social conservatism acts more like radical social despair. The novels propose an absolute gap between the value-laden history they espouse and the fraudulent social order they confront. Only in magical terms can they imagine the infusion of history in society, if they can imagine it at all. For the most part, they present us with the proposition that "history" is going on somewhere other than in public formulations or social events, and that the purpose of fictional narrative is to recover, embody, and enshrine that history as a moral and authentically political activity. The direction they gesture is not "back" to a mythically remembered social order but "up" to a realm that can represent history exactly because it is disconnected from the course of social affairs.

The histories that are betrayed or recovered in the stories these novels tell are often personal ones. Disraeli's characters stand for class concepts; in his largely symbolic narrative we are not tempted to make much of a distinction between public and private realms. In *Hard Times* and *Felix Holt*, however, the organizations of the stories seem to separate the private from the public spheres, and discussions of these novels are often divided in one way or another between their political and their personal or familial "halves." Such distinctions miss the connecting narrative structures that test public discourse against private narratives precisely in order to show the fatal discontinuity between them, or that pair individual life histories as examples of true and false relationships with the past. Through such structures—of analogy, metaphor, and narrative commentary—

the novelists consistently establish tensions between practitioners of an "ahistorical" present, who cut off continuity with the past, and those who, confronting and remembering the past, are endowed with the moral power associated with "true history." Their plots (themselves acting as vehicles of history) reward allegiance to the past with the promise of continuity and punish political action with aborted stories.

The dichotomy between politics and history works in many ways like the stories of middle-class heroines I discussed in Part One. Relying on the partial disconnection of women from the industrial sphere, those stories establish an ideal space for action that can embody contradictory social ideas: paternalism purged of power or gentility purged of status. Similarly, Disraeli, Dickens, and Eliot establish spaces for "true histories" that link past and future together; and these ideal spaces are equally caught in contradiction: the only way continuity can be claimed in the face of a contemporaneous politics is through the invention of a realm or a character discontinuous with that society. Moreover, the realms of the ideal—Disraeli's pre-Reformation abbey, Dickens's circus, George Eliot's Felix Holt—are themselves composed of mixed social fantasies comparable to those carried by the female characters. In the contradictions that shape them we may decipher common terms that shape the consciousness of change in these three very dissimilar Victorians.

As commentaries on change itself, the novels define the status of fictional story in ways that have important implications for Victorian narrative theory. In one way or another, all of them identify politics with false fictions and true history with honest storytelling. Implicit in their practice is the assumption that narrative, with its dependence on temporality, continuity, and memory, is an especially privileged moral form that in itself has, or ought to have, reforming power. The dichotomy does not make a simple claim for the novel as an instrument of social reform, although it includes that claim. It points as well to a shared historicist assumption: that history is a narrative that moves to its own ends, and an overriding temporal power within which permanent meaning may be conferred. History in this sense is necessarily beyond the vision of any person located in a particular time and a particular society. But, the novelists suggest, its meanings and its process are discernible and imitable for those who make history not by acting in the realm of politics but by taking the power to face and shape narrative.

Looking Back into the Future: *Sybil*

In *Sybil* (1845), Disraeli's narrator presents himself as a revisionist historian who, by recuperating the suppressed truths of the past, invalidates the politics of the present in the service of an imagined future. His fictional narrative denounces the dominant narrative of English history as "a complete mystification": "Generally speaking, all the great events have been distorted, most of the important causes concealed, some of the principal characters never appear, and all who figure are so misunderstood and misrepresented, that the result is a complete mystification."[1] The successful imposition of such political mystification has, he argues, kept the Whig oligarchy in power

> the last hundred years . . . during which a people without power or education had been induced to believe themselves the freest and most enlightened nation in the world, and had submitted to lavish their blood and treasure, to see their industry crippled and their labour mortgaged, in order to maintain an oligarchy, that had neither ancient memories to soften nor present services to justify their unprecedented usurpation. [12]

Sybil promises a "true history" that will unmask the illegitimate power sustained by historical fictions. Disraeli's version of true history would, however, merely revise the chronology of great men and events by praising suppressed political genius and reinterpreting the significance of major actions; it is part of his program to see no gap between the political narrative of events from above and the experience of a populace. And Disraeli's work is marked by the transparent self-interest of his attempt to impose his own political mystifications in order to legitimize

---

1. Benjamin Disraeli, *Sybil, or The Two Nations* (Oxford, 1981), p. 15. Further references to this edition will appear in the text.

Young England, Tory democracy, and his own Jewish origins. Still, the ingenuity and sophistication of his novel and his ways of using the opportunities of fiction to contain the contradictions of his political position make *Sybil* comparable in energy and interest with *Hard Times* and *Felix Holt*—novels that share its strategy of creating histories that undermine the legitimacy of contemporary politics.[2]

The overt argument of Disraeli's revised English history is impossible to miss. In the name of "civil and religious liberty" the Protestant-Whig line of English politics has contrived to exclude from power two entities linked historically to the church and to each other: the Crown and the People. Two moments in history are the touchstones in this theory of usurpation: King Henry VIII's dissolution of the monasteries and the Glorious Revolution of 1688. The Whig oligarchy that has dominated eighteenth- and nineteenth-century politics is constituted by "the families who in one century plundered the Church to gain the property of the people, and in another century changed the dynasty to gain the power of the Crown" (11–12).

In Disraeli's rhetoric "the subordination of the sovereign and the degradation of the multitude" (38) are concepts mystically and indissolubly paired by the sheer power of syntactical parallel. True aristocracy is by definition a condition that elevates the condition of the people; thus the Whig oligarchy is a fraudulent aristocracy with a claim to power that Disraeli undertakes to discredit by tracing its ancestries. In each case the search for origins discovers ironic elevations of menials through political interest and falsely established claims to title. Such attempts to "dispel the mysteries with which for nearly three centuries it has been the labour of party writers to involve a national history" are

2. Modern critics of Disraeli fall into two camps, one delighting in his self-consciousness and paradox, the other finding in his contradictions mostly muddle. Arnold Kettle expresses the enthusiastic view in "Early Victorian Social-Problem Novel," p. 178; he is followed by Daniel R. Schwarz in *Disraeli's Fiction* (New York, 1979). John Lucas rejects Kettle's valuation of *Sybil* in "Mrs. Gaskell and Brotherhood," pp. 152–161. Brantlinger expands on his argument, articulating the unresolved contradictions in Disraeli's attitude toward hereditary aristocracy, the working class, and the "Two Nations" concept (*Spirit of Reform*, pp. 96–104).

necessary steps, in Disraeli's view, without which "no political
position can be understood and no social evil remedied" (31).
Social reform depends, it would seem, upon arriving at a vision
of the "real" past.

Accordingly the first half of *Sybil* (books I–III) is devoted
largely to setting out a social panorama that elaborates and
animates Disraeli's revisionist view of the Whigs and the people
they fail to rule. *Sybil* aims to retell a contemporary history as
well as to establish and puncture a historical fiction, however.
Beginning with book IV, Disraeli shifts his attention, readjusts
his characters, and centers his novel on a revised history of
Chartism designed to uncover its "true" significance as the
people's quest for a legitimate and noble leader. While the first
three books, set in 1837, criticize the representative aristocrat
Lord Marney along with specific failures of paternalist management—the New Poor Law, factory fines, tommy shops—the
second part follows working-class politics from 1839 to 1842,
tracing its decline into factionalism and violence. In both sections Disraeli sets up a counterpoint between two different kinds
of historical explanation: a satirical account of how things
happen in the illegitimate world of politics and an idealized
vision of a moral succession grounded in "true history." These
separate temporalities are bridged by literary conventions
through which the novelist contrives to symbolize the intersection of his ideal with the present current of events.[3]

Disraeli's task in the first half of *Sybil* was to invent an
authoritative historian's voice that could, through apparently
historical argument, produce a suprahistorical ideal against
which to measure and devalue contemporary politics. His feudal
ideal, represented by the monks of Marney Abbey, is not simply

3. In the most sophisticated account of *Sybil* to date, Catherine Gallagher
accounts for its contradictions in terms of a theory of aristocratic representation
received from Coleridge and Carlyle. In her account Disraeli portrays all
political representation ironically. The autonomous political realm that he needs
in order to assert a vision of true representation threatens his belief in a
historically grounded "territorial constitution," so that he cannot represent it. In
Gallagher's reading even the symbolic ideal expressed through Gerard and Sybil
gives way to an always ironic account of history. See *Industrial Reformation*, pp.
187–218.

a device that permits him to compare the good past with the bad present; rather, he wishes to assert continuity rather than irrecoverable change in the nature of English society. He does so by expanding the historical scale of his narrative in such a way that nineteenth-century industrial and political development looks economically like no change at all, and politically like an unfortunate interruption in a legitimate succession.

The historian-narrator does his best to absorb the social challenges of industrialization into an extended vision of "the preponderance of the landed interest." The Manufacturer is merely one more in a succession of historical characters—the Turkey Merchant, the West India Planter, the Nabob—who have turned commercial fortunes into aristocratic estates, "merged in the land," and, in turn, become extinct (75). Economic tension between land and industry is backdated to the system of Dutch finance imported by William of Orange for his own purposes during "the Dutch invasion of 1688" (19); its roots are not only preindustrial but foreign, not truly English. When Disraeli describes Wodgate, the iron and steel district that serves as his version of an evil empire, he makes it into a region that has "zealously preserved" its original seventeenth-century character: it is a lawless, propertyless agglomeration of squatters who gathered during the Revolutionary War (161–162). Even Mowbray, the new industrial town, is introduced as an expanded village that had "principally belonged" to its aristocratic land-owner, whose rents it has trebled, and whose castle gives its name to the town's main street (79, 85). Industrialization itself is historicized as the narrator takes note of "ancient factories," now eyesores of a flourishing town (85). Once well into the town, the dramatist in Disraeli proceeds to sketch a set of modern, highly urban characters—but not until he has done what he can to pull the town back into a historic association with the land.

The principle of historical continuity would seem, then, to be guaranteed by the flow of new blood and new money into land. But in Disraeli's fictional representation of action there is no way of achieving such continuity correctly in the course of ordinary human history. By tracing the genealogies of his aristocratic characters, he turns them into frauds, servants and sycophants who have played double-edged games of party politics for the sake of title and have bought genealogies that make a perpetual irony of the idea of hereditary dignity. Like Whig historiography, their pretensions are historical fictions that sustain power rather than renewals of the seamless power of the landed interest. And this disjunction between the theory of historical continuity and the drama of usurpation is the central paradox of Disraeli's historical position.[4]

The families of Marney, de Mowbray, and Fitz-Aquitaine are damned for originating as plunderers of monasteries, financial manipulators, and bastard sons of monarchs. They are damned again for having no talent for public affairs; recall that the oligarchy has "neither ancient memories to soften nor present services to justify" its rule. Disraeli has to have it both ways. The genealogical satires assert that the fake aristocrats can be measured against some "real" genealogy that traces an unbroken line back to a legitimate origin.[5] At the same time Disraeli must allow for an aristocracy of talent coming from nowhere, in order to justify his own claim to renew English politics. This talent, exemplified in the stories of suppressed or passed-over geniuses—Bolingbroke, Burke, Shelburne, and, by implication, Disraeli—creates a kind of independent historical succession. Its members are marked by the range of their moral intelligence and rhetorical excellence and by a common fate: their power is usurped by mediocre minds. Real talent and real claims to hereditary dignity are implicitly linked, then, because both are subject to usurpation. Disraeli's political romance works toward a double fantasy of relegitimation, uniting the real talent of Charles Egremont (a younger son of an illegitimately titled family, his talent coming from nowhere) with the real hereditary right of Walter Gerard. It is such a creation of "real aristocracy,"

4. In seeing Disraeli's project in this way I give more weight to his myth of historical continuity than does Gallagher, who describes Disraeli's vision of history as "perpetual displacement," his narrator as "normally neutral about the historical process" (*Industrial Reformation*, p. 207).

5. Gallagher describes Disraeli's Middle Ages as "not so much a historical period as a prehistorical one," stressing its lack of continuity with the present (ibid., p. 213).

rather than a union of classes, that is figured in the marriage of Egremont with Gerard's daughter Sybil.[6]

The "meaning" of this union is compressed in the novel's central symbol, the ruined Marney Abbey, where Gerard and Egremont meet (55–60). The whole description quite brilliantly manages to realize the mythic, ahistorical quality in Disraeli's vision of an ideal society. The abbey buildings both recall and embody the moment before the novel's first great usurpation, the dissolution of the monasteries. The unfinished Gothic spire of the church testifies to the instant of interruption, when Egremont's ancestor Baldwin Greymount arrived in the service of Henry VIII, and when Walter Gerard's abbot forebear, refusing to surrender, faced torture and hanging (82). The encounter of their nineteenth-century descendants is, then, the beginning of a process that leaps over the intervening centuries to the wrongs of that moment, in order to set them right. At the same time the description of arrested motion turns the abbey into a suprahistorical ideal. The church rises "with a strength that had defied time, and with a beauty that had at last turned away the wrath of man"; the tower looks "as if it were hewn but yesterday"; and the whole spot asserts an eternal union of nature, religion, art, and human generosity.

This spot is Egremont's true (and pastoral) parent. "He had almost been born amid the ruins of Marney Abbey"; his imagination is said to have attached itself to its relics in Wordsworthian fashion (57). His indulgent social upbringing has been counteracted by "benignant nature" (28–29); the luxurious idleness of his life is not written in his face (32). So removed from the world of social consequence, Egremont is further cleansed by his position as a younger, disinherited son, his kinship with Marney Abbey strengthened by its historic role as a

6. By identifying Sybil simultaneously with the aristocracy and the working class, Disraeli makes it impossible to read the marriage as a simple symbolic union of the classes. Gallagher, placing Sybil entirely beyond class, reads the marriage as a Coleridgean union of the sacred with its true representative, the state (ibid., p. 215). Brantlinger accuses Disraeli of praising talent at the expense of genealogy and then contradicting himself by raising Sybil to a valued aristocracy; he does not figure Egremont's "non-hereditary" talent into the formula (*Spirit of Reform*, pp. 97–104).

vocation for younger sons of aristocratic families. (Gerard identifies the injustice of primogeniture as a reason that younger sons are "natural friends of the people" [136]). Egremont is thus detached from the false aristocracy and led toward the true—a position in which aristocracy and people are fuzzily indistinguishable. Gerard exemplifies this mystical mixture: his veins hold "the best blood in England" (253), but he argues that most of the abbots were like himself, sons of the people (62). When Egremont pretends to be "Franklin" in order to pursue his friendship with the Gerards, he appropriately and symbolically asserts the same immunity to literal descent, the same magical identity of worker and aristocrat, that the character of Gerard represents.

As a social idea, the abbey stands for a conflation of aristocracy and people in the administration of hospitality to mankind. It succeeds in that task because it also represents landownership without the rights of private property or inheritance. Owned by the church, the land cannot be corrupted by individual greed or by the mixed fortunes of generational change. Gerard's language literalizes the ideal of continuity, turning the abbey into "a deathless landlord" that never dies or wastes; "the abbot was ever the same" (62). Since the monks have no direct descendants, the question of succession is mooted; the people are the direct beneficiaries of the monks' services and buildings, and have "property on their side" (63). The whole description quite ingeniously contrives to defend the inviolable right of property while imagining the poor as its true inheritors.[7]

The monks of Marney Abbey evoke an ideal of landownership purged of its social machinery, possession and primogeniture. As a counterpointed story of spiritual life Disraeli invents an ideal of Christianity floating free of its institutional history. His English Catholic church is neither answerable to Rome nor reformed by Protestantism. Sybil first manifests herself as a voice filling the ruined abbey with religious feeling;[8] throughout

7. In this way the abbey is an attempt to reconcile the contradiction that Gallagher notes between a territorial constitution and an autonomous political realm (*Industrial Reformation*, p. 209).
8. As Ruth Bernard Yeazell points out, Sybil manifests herself "like the

the novel she hovers on the threshold of the convent, as though to emphasize her status as a spirit without institutional embodiment. Aubrey St. Lys, the vicar of Mowbray, is Disraeli's spokesman for an expanded genealogy of Christianity which parallels the novel's political history. Going rather far beyond the influence of the Tractarians,[9] St. Lys argues that the Church of Rome is only a part of an "apostolical succession" that reaches directly back to the Old Testament prophets. The "second Testament is avowedly only a supplement . . . Christianity is completed Judaism, or it is nothing"; the ultimate source is Jehovah, not the authority of Rome (112). Repeating the strategy of writing "true history" by expanding the time scale within which modern events are conventionally judged, Disraeli manages to put himself into the true succession, blurring historical distinctions between Catholicism and Protestantism in his emphasis on the originary importance of Judaism. More centrally, he completes the idealization of Marney Abbey by forging its social and spiritual histories in an original continuum.

In the most apparent plot design, the ancient life of Marney Abbey is set in contrast with the crass political economy of its contemporary inheritor, Egremont's older brother, Lord Marney. The pure social antithesis of Marney Abbey lies, however, in the remarkable sketch of Wodgate. Point for point, the Wodgate chapter inverts the ideal of a unified social order untouched by historical usurpations.[10] The brief fantasy is an attempt to imagine a society developed apart from any traditional human institutions of culture or civil polity, a society in which there is no basis for usurpation. There is no ownership of land, no system of law, education, or religion, no public build-

ancient prophetess whom she resembles in name" ("Why Political Novels Have Heroines," p. 129).

9. St. Lys has been too simply identified with the Oxford Movement, by Cazamian (*Social Novel in England*, pp. 195–196) and by Schwarz (*Disraeli's Fiction*, pp. 112–113).

10. Wodgate is more usually read as a parody of Whig aristocracy: the government of Bishop Hatton exaggerates Whig brutality and misrule, while at the same time Wodgate shows how workers spontaneously create an aristocracy in a vacuum of leadership. See Brantlinger, *Spirit of Reform*, p. 101, and Schwarz, *Disraeli's Fiction*, pp. 115, 117–118.

ing, no municipal service; in short, no public life. No one knows "anything except his business"; work is conducted in the private houses of the master workmen. It is "the ugliest spot in England, to which neither Nature nor Art has contributed a single charm." Its people are animals; violence is its only negotiable social currency (161–165). In Wodgate, then, Disraeli posits an extremity of laissez-faire individualism that must end in dictatorship. Its cheerful inhabitants have no historical, cultural, or moral standard against which they can measure or understand their condition as one of brutal slavery.

In the absence of such standards Disraeli can claim, with an irony so deep it means to sound like truth, that the brutal masters of Wodgate are "a real aristocracy" that "does something for its privileges," possessing "in its way complete knowledge," and imparting it "to those whom it guides" (165). In isolation from society or history, "complete knowledge" of itself and of its craft is indeed possible, for it goes unchallenged by alternative knowledges. And this is the ultimate horror of Wodgate: that the chain of human history might be permanently broken into fragments; that bishops might name themselves and perform marriages that are witches' spells, that Christianity might be the worship of Pontius Pilate—and that it will not matter. Wodgate is the nightmare that pressures Disraeli's plea for the continuity of traditional institutions against what he reads as the usurpations of the historical present.

The juxtaposition of ordinary political temporality and "true history" in the first half of *Sybil* may help to account for the difficulties raised by Disraeli's treatment of his ostensible theme, "the Two Nations." Clearly the narrative does not support the notion enunciated by Stephen Morley that there are two nations, the rich and the poor, separated by an immeasurable gulf (66).[11] Rather it is committed to that mystic duality, "the Crown and the People," which has been excluded from history but which must

11. For Brantlinger, the Two Nations theme is one of Disraeli's unresolved contradictions (*Spirit of Reform*, pp. 102–104). Schwarz argues that the idea is discredited through the character of its spokesman, Stephen Morley (*Disraeli's Fiction*, pp. 120–121). It is certainly undermined through the plot, in the story of Sybil's shift of loyalty from Morley to Egremont.

be made to seem implicit, or latent, in the accounts of contemporary social life. There are no "People" in the novel, nor is there an active "Crown." In the scenes that are intended to compare and contrast the rich and the poor, Disraeli manages to negotiate two quite separate purposes at once. He dramatizes the gap in society by presenting the upper and lower classes in analogical rather than hierarchical relations with one another.[12] And he suggests in the working-class scenes some shadow of the "People" waiting for their true leaders. The incompatible objectives of the satire and the idealization makes it impossible to assign a stable set of meanings to the social contrasts for which *Sybil* has always been famous.

The narrative is put together in such a way that every set of characters inhabits a separate sphere; moving from chapter to chapter is almost invariably a leap from one self-enclosed social world to another. The result is a picture of England chopped up into bits: not two nations but many, each obsessed with the particular politics of its own condition. Yet each of the fragments reproduces a comparable set of social issues and hierarchies, whose unwitting imitations of each other attest to a common unreality. Thus Stephen Morley describes the Chartist Convention, with obvious narrative approval, as a parody of Parliament: "Our career will be a vulgar caricature of the bad passions and the low intrigues, the factions and the failures, of our oppressors" (251). At the same time Sir Vavasour Firebrace's fantasy that the baronets will march on Westminster to secure their class rights is a ludicrous parody of Chartist organization (49–51). While the ironies seem to cut both ways, the workers' seriousness gives them a higher status in the analogical process—a point that can be most fully shown through Disraeli's most detailed contrast between the young aristocrats at the Jockey Club (chap. 1) and the Mowbray youths at their gin palace (chap. 10).

Both the Jockey Club and the "Temple of the Muses" are edifices of some pretension. The Jockey Club is "a vast and

12. Gallagher also reads the scenes in parallel, arguing that the juxtapositions of aristocrats and workers ironically reveal their similarities, so that the two classes end up representing one another in their worst aspects (*Industrial Reformation*, pp. 203–205).

golden saloon, that in its decorations would have become, and in its splendour would not have disgraced, Versailles in the days of the grand monarch" (1). French paintings and exotic drinks made of foreign components and named for patrician creators suggest the dangerous and "un-English" decadence that hovers about the languid discussion of "the great question" of horse racing. Elegance is ennui: the young nobles "had exhausted life in their teens, and all that remained for them was to mourn, amid the ruins of their reminiscences, over the extinction of excitement" (2).

The tone of Dickensian facetiousness is replaced by one of Dickensian relish when Disraeli turns to the factory workers. "Putting on the class" is the rule here as well: the Cat and Fiddle has been elegantly renamed and advertised in green and gilt, much to the amazement of the factory girls, who imagine that it looks like the Queen's palace. The garrulous proprietor imitates the head butler of a London tavern, the entertainers put on the style, and Dandy Mick orders the waiter about. The hand-me-down quality of factory culture is wonderfully caught in Dandy Mick's line as he points out a picture of the Lady of the Lake: "I've seen her at the circus, with real water" (95–96). The Mowbray sense of social superiority extends to the girls' disdain and ignorance of agricultural workers, and to their feeling that the ideal conditions at Trafford's mill are dull and restrictive.

Yet for all its comic pretensions, the Temple of the Muses— like comparable settings of lower-middle-class joy in Dickens— floats on "real water." The paintings on the walls are English: scenes from Shakespeare, Byron, and Scott done by "a brush of no inconsiderable power" (91). One may not want to know the ingredients of the "bar mixture," but it is a distinctively local brew. The customers are civilized (compared with a barbaric American visitor) and have a wonderful time; their tawdry "elegance" is represented as a form of excited energy. Dandy Mick exudes joy in life, and his "great friend" Devilsdust represents the triumph of life over impossible conditions. It is difficult to read this scene without feeling that Dandy Mick, Devilsdust, and their girlfriends are more alive and more honest in their pretensions than the aristocracy. Although the Mowbray characters have a special claim on our attention, the feeling extends to the scenes in which the miners and their wives react to the tommy shop, and even to the brutalized characters of Wodgate when they are set up in dialogue.

These scenes convey a sense that the poor are more attractive, energetic, and public-minded than the aristocrats. Their social theories may be wrong, but they are valid attempts at an active membership in the social order. Far from being rendered as threats, their anticapitalist ideas appear less wrong than the blinkered party politics of Parliament and county.[13] Oddly enough, Disraeli's highly artificial working-class dialogues also have the effect of making the workers seem more real—that is, more equal in rhetorical status to the other sets of characters— than do the more carefully realistic dialects or sentimental portraits of other social novelists. Dandy Mick, Devilsdust, Tummas, and the rest are not "the People"; they are the variously debased or talented individuals who inhabit the contemporary world of politics. Yet they signal their potential as "People," as generous and energetic spirits waiting only for the reemergence of the leadership symbolized in the Crown.

Beginning with the shift in time that opens book IV, Disraeli puts all of his assembled social fragments into motion. The public plot is an account of Chartism from the first presentation of the Charter in 1839 to the Plug Plot risings in 1842, apparently designed to demonstrate that the movement must ultimately fall into the hands of the lowest form of life, signified by Bishop Hatton of Wodgate. Like the depiction of the workers themselves, however, this little history contains pockets of writing that lead our sympathies toward Chartism, even toward mass movement, in a way that, much like Carlyle's "Chartism," covertly argues for a view of Chartism as an assembly of People in search of their leader.[14] At the same time the private plot

13. Brantlinger claims that Disraeli's pictures of working-class life betray his commitment to the poor by representing them as villainous or mistaken (*Spirit of Reform*, pp. 99–100). I tend rather to agree with Schwarz's sense of the vitality and individuality in the working-class portraits (see *Disraeli's Fiction*, p. 118).

14. Carlyle presents Chartism as a symptom of a condition-of-England

follows the intensified search for the writ of right that will restore Gerard to his inheritance and his aristocratic status. Masterminded by Stephen Morley and Baptist Hatton, this plot represents the restoration of leadership that Disraeli's Chartism calls for. The moment of riot, disorder, and disruption toward which both plans move is actually used to effect an obliteration of recent history and a restoration of the mythic continuity that the novel proposes. Replete with action and melodrama, the end of the story presents images of feudal battle wherein Disraeli parts company with Carlyle's call for a "changed Aristocracy" appropriate for a changed era of history.[15]

The account of Chartism moves ostensibly toward demonstrating how parliamentary indifference and political factionalism in the working class leads to "physical force" Chartism, to repressed violence in Birmingham and Newport, and finally to the travesty of leadership represented by Bishop Hatton, who has no idea what Chartism is. The idealistic Walter Gerard, first drawn into violent intrigue and jailed for it, ends his career by attempting to deflect the violence of Bishop Hatton's marches on Trafford's mill and then on Mowbray Castle. During this process Sybil is "weaned" from her belief in Chartism through her direct experiences of mob action and through her love for Egremont, its aristocratic alternative.

Yet in a symbolic way Disraeli gestures toward a Chartism that is not the political, historical Chartism he buries in violence. Egremont's speech in support of the spirit of labour is not offered in the text, but it is characterized through the gossip of MPs: "'What does he mean by obtaining the results of the Charter without the intervention of its machinery?'" (282). "Intervention" is the salient word here, suggesting that the points of the Charter would effect one more usurpation or interruption of an ideal history that can go forward without political "machinery." When we consider the Charter's demand for working-class suffrage, the formulation is obviously absurd. Yet it articulates a way of think-

---

disease that requires a "real" aristocracy as its cure. See "Chartism" (1839), in *Critical and Miscellaneous Essays: Collected and Republished* (London, 1869), V, 325–423.

15. Ibid., p. 379.

ing about history which Disraeli has made so integral a part of his narrative that we know, in a way that measures his success as a novelist, just what Egremont "means."

Disraeli also uses Gerard's double status as aristocrat and Chartist leader to show what he means: that Chartism is an unconscious quest for a true, hence an aristocratic, leader. In three scenes, Gerard appears to address the Mowbray multitude; in each he appears as the high priest of a peaceful and highly ritualized assembly. The first "TORCH-LIGHT MEETING" (215–217) is set out of history, "amid these ruins of some ancient temple, or relics of some ancient world"; unlike every other fictional account of mass meeting, the description evokes the awe and religious fervor of an orderly populace. The second "monster meeting" takes place when Gerard has been released on bail from prison (337–339); Disraeli emphasizes the instant organization now easily effected by trade union lodges, the proud fanfare and excitement that union orders create, the religious ceremony that is merged with the social one. This is hardly a critique of Chartism; rather it uses Chartism in order to discover the "true" impulses of the workers: "how mankind, under the influence of high and earnest feelings, recur instantly to ceremony and form" (338). In both scenes the image of a leader in a high place addressing an adoring crowd is suffused with solemnity and grandeur. And that image is, perhaps, as close as the novel ever gets to a representation of The Crown and The People.

Even after the Plug Plot actions that occupy the narrative of book VI have been set in motion, Disraeli emphasizes the intrinsic orderliness and reverence of the people. Violence is isolated and confined to the Antichrist Bishop Hatton, who has already been firmly set beyond the pale of human society. The Lancashire populace, by contrast, is perfectly genteel. Disraeli tells the story of a completely disciplined "visit" of a striking crowd to the local squire's manor, where they peacefully gather food to feed the starving, walk admiringly through the gardens and hothouses, and cheer the lady of the house when they depart (375–376). When Bishop Hatton leads the strikers toward a violent assault on Trafford's mill, Gerard appears like a god on the mill roof, commands the love of the people, and manages to turn the mob in another direction (396–398). A competition for leadership is at issue here, and Gerard's "disinterestedness" and eloquence quench the force of violence temporarily. In the same vein, the Lancashire workers who have come to know Sybil and St. Lys split off from the brutal Wodgate contingent during the riot at Mowbray Castle, gathering around their "natural" religious leaders (408–410). All of this is quite blatantly designed to transform the Chartists into an ideal People.

Meanwhile, in the inheritance subplot, Disraeli makes Stephen Morley and Baptist Hatton act out in melodrama what he has been doing as a narrator. Together these morally ambiguous characters plan to use the occasion of Chartist uprising as a cover for a raid on the strongbox of Mowbray Castle, where Gerard's writ of right is held. For them, as for Disraeli the novelist, violent disruption creates a break in the course of fraudulent history and allows for the restoration of authentic continuity. Those who make the necessary break are nonetheless guilty of political agency in the corrupt world. Paired in this enterprise and as suitors of Sybil, Morley and Hatton are matched studies in the incompatibility of action and theory.

Stephen Morley makes little sense as a character unless he is understood as a portrait of the contradictions between political theory and political action. Believing that society is in its infancy, he wants to reground it on new principles: equality, community, association. Both aristocratic rule and domestic life are outworn social forms in his view: privacy goes along with private property. The purity of his reconstructive ideal is matched by the asceticism of his life: he abstains from meat, drink, colored clothing, and emotional fervor of any irrational sort.

Disraeli is less interested in investigating and opposing Stephen's social principles than in showing that they are contradicted by his actions.[16] From the beginning Stephen's indifference to the past is compromised by his special alacrity in tracking down clues to Gerard's writ of inheritance. Coiled within the

---

16. Arguments that Morley's social theory is discredited by his alienation from the past and by his self-interested actions have been made by Cazamian, *Social Novel in England*, p. 198, and by Schwarz, *Disraeli's Fiction*, pp. 120–121.

tight restraint of his asceticism is the violent jealousy and uncontrollable passion that burst out in his assault on Egremont and in his manipulative declaration of love for Sybil. Twice he becomes an actor in social movements of which he disapproves. In a very Disraeli-like way he finds the Charter "a coarse specific for our social evils. The spirit that would cure our ills must be of a deeper and finer mood." But when Sybil asks him why he has come to the Chartist Convention, he answers, "If I had refused to be a leader, I should not have prevented the movement; I should only have secured my own insignificance" (250). And when Baptist Hatton suggests his plan to use social violence as a means of getting at the writ of right in Mowbray Castle, the moral-force Chartist becomes the principal agent in the plot.

In Stephen's dying speech he calls attention to the misjudgment of the world which will inevitably follow (415). Apparently engaged in working-class violence against the landed gentry, he is in fact doing the dirty work that will restore Mowbray Castle to its true succession; the disjunction between his presence and his meaning recalls Disraeli's theory of history. As we are given to read him, however, Stephen's story is clotted by a multiplicity of meanings. He represents the impossibility of divorcing social theory from history, for he is compelled toward that writ of right if only through a need to substantiate his power. He is like Disraeli the politician in representing the tainting compromises of active politics, the uses of mass movements for his own ends. Finally he is himself used as another element in the novel's pattern of rereading history by discovering a search for authentic aristocracy in the very heart of working-class politics.

Baptist Hatton, opportunistic, worldly, and cultivated, is Stephen's opposite and counterpart. After Disraeli has satirized the false genealogies of his aristocrats, it is initially surprising that he presents the creator of those fictions with so much respect. But Hatton's life is a mirror of Morley's dilemma: the actions that have allowed and sustained his worldly success are antithetical to his social beliefs. Disraeli describes him as someone "who was free from all pretension, and who had aquired, from his severe habits of historical research, a respect only for what was authentic" (252). Society seems to him "at once dull and trifling," but he is deeply versed in art and music, and educates Sybil in those cultural traditions. He is himself shaped as a portrait of a Renaissance scholar, set in his velvet cap in the luxurious and tasteful furnishings of his study (237–238). Reverence for the past and cultivated taste link him with the novelist's values, yet Hatton has made his fortune as the instrument of usurpation, selling titles and genealogies to nobles he manipulates and despises.

If Stephen Morley contains a self-reflexive image of Disraeli the politician, Baptist Hatton is a figure for Disraeli the novelist. He creates and names characters and gives them fictional histories; he is talent coming from nowhere, who has made his name through worldly manipulation. Like the novelist, he reveres the past but uses it to create the fictions of the present. Removed from action himself, he is interested in making things happen. And, guilty of interrupting a true succession by selling Gerard's ancestral papers, he makes the gestures of the narrative itself: he turns back to the moment of usurpation and undoes it, coldly awaiting the occasion of working-class violence in order to put it to use in his inheritance plot. In this character, Disraeli understands himself. In the pairing of Morley and Hatton, he comments on the absolute gap between politics and history.

The two unsuccessful suitors of Sybil join talents in an enterprise that benefits Egremont without tainting him with his own set of contradictions. Morley dies pouring his last words into Egremont's ear, his life's work into its proper aristocratic container: "Your star has controlled mine; and now I feel I have sacrificed life and fame . . . for your profit and honour" (415). The battles at Marney Castle clear the field of all those characters who have entangled their lives in the wiles of politics: Gerard, Marney, Morley, Bishop Hatton. Egremont, who has been reserved for "history," has entered the world only in two acts of rescue, to remove Sybil from its frays. He is the link between past and future, the bearer of the ideal. For this it is necessary that he be allowed to remain innocent of the present.[17]

17. Gallagher stresses Disraeli's inability to represent Egremont's politics in the narrative as part of her argument about Disraeli's autonomous political realm (*Industrial Reformation*, p. 215).

Even as the narrative seems to call for a generation of Egremonts, its language strips them of the guilt of agency. Egremont himself is the spokesman for a mystical process of social transformation: "There is a change in them as in all other things, and I participate in that change" (276); "It is civilization that is effecting, that has effected, this change. It is that increased knowledge of themselves that teaches the educated their social duties" (276); "The mind of England is the mind ever of the rising race. Trust me, it is with the People" (293). Even the tenses of these formulations defy the reader to comprehend how and when change occurs. It has already happened, and it is in the future. So with the narrator's final summation: "it is the past alone that can explain the present, and it is youth that alone can mould the remedial future" (421). Between the parallel phrases is the unfillable gap, the actual history that constitutes the present.

Such phrasings mirror the novel's larger terms, making configurations that cannot account for the process of social change. Disraeli tests ordinary or "fictional" history against ideal succession in a way that hopes for the restoration of the usurped past but simultaneously bars the movement from present to future. Only in the violent disruption of the present generation can he imagine a historical moment in which the ideal may be inserted. Even that insertion is transitory; the last we hear of the regeneration symbolized by the marriage of Sybil and Egremont comes to us through the gossip of the London lady politicians. This event, like all the others, has been transformed into social discourse.[18]

Disraeli's narrative technique regularly exhibits the same propensity to leap from prospect to retrospect over an excised present. With the exception of the final sequence, "events" in *Sybil* occur most often between chapters. We hear characters talking about an anticipated event or moving toward an important encounter that is frozen at the end of the chapter. In the next chapter, which places us after the anticipated event, we

18. Gallagher points to this as a moment in which political gossip becomes, for once, true representation (ibid., p. 216).

hear a retrospective account of it in relation to the next phase of activity or anticipation. Over and over the reader "misses" the moments of decision, of encounter, of change, only to come in upon the accomplished effect in the next block of narrative.

The narrative motion is a theory of history in action; it asserts the insignificance of event in relation to what is made of it by the needs and imaginations of those who comment upon it and shape it to the exigencies of their power. And it simultaneously asserts the mystic significance of event, its transcendance of mere gossip, story, history, and other forms of negotiable human fiction. Disraeli describes his own sense of event early in the narrative, when he comments on the Derby races, which stand as a metaphor for all the political activity in the story:

> A few minutes, only a few minutes, and the event that for twelve months has been the pivot of so much calculation, of such subtle combinations, of such deep conspiracies, round which the thought and passion of the sporting world have hung like eagles, will be recorded in the fleeting tablets of the past. But what minutes! Count them by sensation, and not by calendars, and each moment is a day and the race a life. Hogarth, in a coarse and yet animated sketch, has painted 'Before' and 'After.' . . . and yet the 'Before' and 'After' of a first-rate English race, in the degree of its excitement, and sometimes in the tragic emotions of its close, may vie even with these. [7–8]

In this little satire, anticipation turns instantly into retrospect—a retrospect itself written on "fleeting tablets." The present is absent, indescribable except in the sense that it is infinitely expandable, uncontained within measures of time. Sensation belongs to the present; articulation, emotion, and every other human activity to anticipation and retrospect. As in Disraeli's larger narrative gestures, "After" works to join itself with "Before" in the wake of the present event, which is a disruption of time.

Thus the narrative of *Sybil* works in a number of interlocking ways to excise the present while asserting that it has been here all along. Disraeli's expansions of historical time are meant to suggest a seamless line running back through English history to Jehovah, while his double readings of contemporary events contrive to read those continuities as muffled within politics. Repeatedly the narrative imagines the act of connecting an ideal past with an ideal future over the head of a political present, but this act is linked with its necessary counterpart, a need for violent disruption that can stop the process of the present. And all the time we know that the narrative is ultimately controlled by the Baptist Hatton figure of Disraeli, who sees history as a fabrication separate from any human event, and as the sole arena of human ingenuity and survival.

As all of these complications suggest, Disraeli wrote novels for reasons more interesting than the wish to publicize his ideas in a popular and readable form. The form of fiction allows him to put characters that signify different levels of ideality and reality in action together, apparently occupying the same fictional universe of cause and effect. The opportunities provided by narrative description, summary, dialogue, and action make it possible for him to activate his idealism and his irony simultaneously, and about the same characters or ideas. The extended metaphorical resources of fiction make such symbols as Marney Abbey, or Sybil herself, possible. The self-conscious use of fictional narrative can both make a claim to be a "true history" and implicitly recognize that all politics, and all history, is the making of stories before and after. And, because a novel is not a political program or any other single-stranded kind of narrative, it can embody a tacit model of social change, however that model may consort with social theory.

What Disraeli reveals in *Sybil* is a model of change as a series of usurpations or violent disruptions within an endless continuity. It is a world in which it is impossible to get from the past to the future through the machinery of the present. Yet this is the only course Disraeli proposes in his plot, which figures a final disruption, a tear in the social fabric which admits the redemptive beings. The plot melodrama through which that is accomplished makes it tempting to write off Disraeli's fantasy as an opportunistic manipulation of working-class violence as deus ex machina, a familiar recourse in industrial novels less sophisticated than this one. But *Sybil* shares the peculiar blocking in its model of social action with novels by contemporaries of very different political persuasions. If their narratives imagine the clash of temporalities in more literary ways, they nonetheless attest to a common configuration in Victorian imaginations of social change.

The Interrupted Stories of *Hard Times*

In *Hard Times* (1854) Dickens sets two metaphors of time against one another: Time the "great manufacturer," "that greatest and longest-established Spinner of all," and the time of the "deadly statistical clock, which measured every second with a beat like a rap upon a coffin-lid."[19] As the great manufacturer, Time quietly and secretly weaves destinies whose mysteries can reveal themselves only "in time"; its "manufacture of the human fabric" (71) is associated with seasonality, nature, and the invention, or "manufacture," of stories. Appropriating the central activity of industrialism as a metaphor for history, Dickens also aligns himself with Time, who "made the only stand that ever *was* made in the place against its direful uniformity" (69): the narrator and Time share in the process of unfolding stories about their character creations.

The statistical clock, on the other hand, works by fragmentation: it seems to break every second off from its successor, only to leave a heap of dead moments lying on the floor. As a metaphor for the violation of temporality that Dickens associates with the utilitarian-industrial society of Coketown, the clock disrupts continuity, development, narrative, and history by measuring experience in social cross sections and "tabular statements" (18). The misreadings that result are the lies that Dickens refers to as "the fictions of Coketown" (84, 90)—fictions that support and sustain the exercise of middle-class power. Against them Dickens uses the narratives of *Hard Times* to define and recover the truths of story.[20]

Like Disraeli, Dickens juxtaposes two ways of thinking about time in order to delegitimize a ruling form of social government. He does so not by creating a historical ideal of continuity and

19. Charles Dickens, *Hard Times*, (New York, 1966), pp. 69, 73. Further references to this edition will appear in the text.
20. The fiction making of the "Fact" characters is particularly well specified by Janet Larson in "Identity's Fictions: Naming and Renaming in *Hard Times*," *Dickens Studies Newsletter* 10 (1979), 14–19. Larson stresses the abstraction from experience in the fictions of Coketown. Brantlinger notes the fiction making in Coketown, and sees Dickens offering only "more fictions" in response (*Spirit of Reform*, p. 217).

class identity but by showing how the categories in which the middle class thinks of the working class miss the truths of historical experience that are available only in narrative form. This investigation is set in a context of misunderstanding between classes, and means to attack the self-interested fictions through which the middle class imposes its power of social control; Dickens shares with Disraeli the strategy of associating political power with political fiction. But the truths that Dickens is interested in recovering are always truths of character as it reveals itself in the course of time; they are not—and they spurn the possibility of being—truths about class experience. *Hard Times* is, therefore, ultimately about forms of social knowledge, not about forms of social government.

Dickens is angry not at industrialization itself but at the production of social discourse about it. Of course he attacks the monotony and the formlessness of Coketown in his "keynote" passages, but the analysis goes little further. Factory work comes in for some rhetoric about mechanized monotony, but as employment it is really quite satisfactory; the problems of Stephen Blackpool and Rachael do not follow from its nature or conditions. Throughout the novel, in fact, the "keynote" addresses are quite different from the issues pursued in the stories, where Dickens's real target is the kind of social knowledge exemplified by blue books and perpetuated in all kinds of middle-class discourse, including the social novel itself. As Dickens dramatizes "Fact" in action, his emphasis falls on the way middle-class rhetoric misses the life experience of the poor or of its own children, even as it is used an instrument of domination. Following closely on Carlyle's procedure in *Past and Present* (1843), Dickens's rhetoric pounds ironically at the word "Fact" until it reveals its status as "semblance" rather than "substance"; and like Carlyle, he goes on to associate substantial fact both with inarticulate workers and with narratives of personal experience.[21]

21. Thomas Carlyle, *Past and Present* (London, 1912), pp. 13–45. Carlyle identifies the "Laws of Fact" with Nature, God, and inarticulate workers, setting them against "Laws of Sham and Semblance" which shape social speech and jargon. He offers the personal narrative of Jocelyn of Brakelond as "historical Fact" distinguished from "all Fiction whatsoever."

Even as he attacks the antihistorical nature of middle-class discourse, Dickens participates in the middle-class failure to understand the working class in political terms. His scornful treatment of unions and the unsatisfactorily sentimental portraits of Stephen Blackpool and Rachael have elicited their full share of critical complaint;[22] but I want to pause here before pursuing the main argument in order to clarify my separation of "keynote" from story in terms that locate the class discomfort in Dickens's homiletic appeals to his audience. The exhortations that call for "Fancy" to sweeten lives ruled by "Fact" have almost universally been read as the novel's organizing dichotomy, as its true and only social recommendation.[23] If we attend to their placement in the text, however, it becomes clear that they play a rather defensive role in the narrative as a whole.

Immediately after a rousing attack on tabular statistics which shows how they are used to bludgeon and defame the working class, Dickens retreats to the first of his paternalist appeals, calling for fancy as a "vent" for working-class monotony and comparing the troubles of workers to those of the Gradgrind children (19). The analogy breaks down immediately: fancy turns into "physical relief" from work, as though Dickens were deploring long factory hours rather than satirizing utilitarian concepts. Later, after the affecting farewell scene between Stephen and Rachael, the narrative moralizes on the parting, exhorting utilitarian governors to "cultivate" the graces of fancy and affection in the poor lest "Reality . . . take a wolfish turn, and make an end of you!" (125). This moment is particularly jarring because the characters' affections have been abundantly dramatized as indigenous to working-class morality; the conven-

22. The argument that Dickens failed to create a typical worker is a familiar one. However, see Stephen J. Spector, "Monsters of Metonymy: *Hard Times* and Knowing the Working Class," *ELH* 51 (1984), 365–384, for the view that *Hard Times* reveals Dickens's honest awareness of his own inability to know the working class.
23. Recent work on Dickens's attitudes toward industrialism and utilitarianism continues to stress the fact-fancy dichotomy. See Philip Collins, "Dickens and Industrialism," *Studies in English Literature* 20 (1980), 651–673; Patrick Brantlinger, "Dickens and the Factories," *Nineteenth-Century Fiction* 26 (1971), 270–285, and Brantlinger's account in *Spirit of Reform*, pp. 216–219.

tionally melodramatic rhetoric about preventing revolution is equally irrelevant and out of place. Both of these injunctions occur at moments when Dickens's writing begins to imply the existence of a distinct working-class culture that functions independently of the governing classes; that is, when he is confronted most fully with theoretical implications he does not wish to pursue.

Other, less obtrusive comments also display Dickens's dis-ease with the factory material he had taken up—belatedly, quickly, and for the first and last time in this novel.[24] In political terms he did not know how to feel about the industrial working class, and he seemed to feel the need to cover himself on all fronts, as he does in this sentence describing the workers reading the "wanted" poster for Stephen Blackpool: "These people, as they listened to the friendly voice that read aloud—there was always some such ready to help them—stared at the characters which meant so much with a vague awe and respect that would have been half ludicrous, if any aspect of public ignorance could ever be otherwise than threatening and full of evil" (187). The sentence twists itself around: from its original impulse to record working-class mutuality and respect for learning, it shifts to a mockery of its comic aspect, and then to the fortuitous scare language; its social content is practically unintelligible. But it is a miniature of the discontinuities in Dickens's mind when he moves from ideas of individual character to ideas of social class as a political entity. His strident depiction of the union exactly reduplicates that anxiety: he sees it as an evil mobilization of class and gives it only one action: its attack on the idiosyncratic position of Stephen Blackpool.

Dickens's complicities with the middle-class social observers he attacks show up in the heavy hand that erratically nails down the paternalist position in *Hard Times*. The dense weaving of the novel goes on around those moments, however; and even the presentation of Stephen Blackpool has still more to unravel for

24. Both Collins ("Dickens and Industrialism") and Brantlinger (*Spirit of Reform*, pp. 87–90) tell the story of Dickens's unfulfilled promise to write a novel about factory children in support of the Ten Hours Movement.

us if we attend, again, less to its failures of realism or social recommendation than to its status as story.

In the largely expository book I, Dickens's narrative shuttles back and forth between two modes. One, in which the book opens, imitates the fragmented atemporal thinking of the "Fact" characters in truncated, often verbless or present-tense sentences. The other, associated especially with Sissy Jupe and Stephen Blackpool, establishes a leisurely, interior, past-tense storytelling voice. Many of the scenes in book I dramatize the clashes between the two modes in dialogues that are contests between one way of apprehending reality and the other, in which the dominant characters attempt to interrupt or suppress the historical narratives of the working-class character. Through these juxtapositions Dickens reveals in one instance after another that the "Fact" characters, who call themselves realists, are engaged in the sinister occupation of fictionalizing or erasing the past. And, far from being in need of fancy or entertainment, Sissy Jupe and Stephen Blackpool are presented as characters who have stories, and *are* stories, that place them on a higher level of rhetorical reality than the "Fact" characters against whom they are pitted.

The contests begin in the schoolroom, where Sissy's answers contend against Gradgrind's attempts to erase her history of emotional connection with the circus. His public redefinitions outlaw Signor Jupe, the circus clown, by taking away the name Sissy's father calls her and by reclassifying his occupation: "He is a veterinary surgeon, a farrier, and horsebreaker" (3). The renamings cancel Sissy's language of relationship ("It's father as calls me Sissy, sir"; "He belongs to the horse-riding, if you please, sir"). And Bitzer's definition of a horse as an assemblage of unconnected teeth, hoofs, legs, and coat underlines the fragmenting separation of definition from experience.

When the visiting commissioner attempts to redefine taste as fact, Sissy scores some points for the opposition. In his eagerness to ban pictorial ornamentation, the commissioner only reveals his inability to distinguish between objects in nature and pictures of them; Sissy has to assure him that flowers on carpets would not be crushed by heavy boots. Her easy transition between representation and reality ridicules the fear of art displayed by the fact school, while the scene suggests that the commissioner's power lies precisely in his failure to distinguish between his own fictions and the ordinary human experience of decorative art.

Sissy is at the center of the first question of interpretation that arises in the plot: Why has her father abandoned her? In the Pegasus Arms scene (bk. I, chap. 6) Bounderby's conclusion, based on his pretense to personal knowledge of the working class, is simple: Jupe is a rogue and a vagabond. The truth of the matter lies in the "remarkable fact" asserted by Mr. Childers, that Jupe left in order not to shame his daughter with his failures as a performer. This "fact" is of course accessible only to those who know the history of love and suffering shared by father and daughter; but Bounderby and Gradgrind are uninterested in that story. Gradgrind explicitly suppresses it, forbidding Sissy to talk about her past: "From this time you begin your history" (36).

Gradgrind fails, of course, to erase Sissy's memory, which bursts forth illegally in a chapter that connects her immunity to statistics with her power as a narrator (bk. I, chap. 9). When Louisa questions her about her progress, Sissy defines statistics as "stutterings"—fragments of speech—and transforms the numbers into narratives of feeling in individual lives. Louisa then leads her into telling her past, question by question, and Sissy's answers grow gradually into a full-blown narrative, full of "when" and "then." In Dickens's characteristic way, the narrative contains an image of itself: Sissy tells how her father loved stories, and amused himself in wondering "whether the Sultan would let the lady go on with the story, or would have her head cut off before it was finished" (46). In just that way the two girls contrive to get to the end of the story before it is cut off; the scene dramatizes storytelling as a surreptitious activity amid Coketown's threats to narrative. Meanwhile Dickens insists on its healing potential: as she listens to the story, Louisa, who is usually indifferent to "what happens," finds herself experiencing suppressed powers of sympathy and engagement.[25]

25. Peter Brooks uses *The Thousand and One Nights* as a paradigm of the way

Sissy's life story sets an emotional history of parental abandonment against Bounderby's made-up and deceitful claim to
that same experience. The contrast defines the difference
between story, a history of feeling in time, and fiction, a lie
constructed out of social stereotypes of working-class behavior.
Stephen Blackpool is Dickens's second opportunity to retell "an
old story" in a way that defies categorization. His life history
contends against Bounderby's reductive way of hearing it, and
against middle-class ways of thinking about the working class
satirized by the narrator. None of the "tabular statements"
proving that the workers drink, don't drink, take opium, and
frequent "low haunts" (18) touches Stephen's experience of
marriage to a drunkard. And none of the charitable middle-class
"bodies" who imagine the workers as "grown-up babies" and
fight like children about the proper ways to reform them (38)
can touch the weight of experience that has gradually aged him
beyond his forty years. When Dickens brings "Old Stephen"
onstage, he is immediately associated with the power of Time
and history (49). And his is the first extended story that the
narrator tells.

The chapters of book I which tell this story of the
nineteen-year marriage, the wife's drunken and sporadic
returns, and the stalemated love between Stephen and Rachael
are the only ones in which the narrator intimately imagines the
private mind of a character. The passage recording Stephen's
thoughts as he walks about in the rain, hating to go home
(62–63), and the dream sequence in which he is haunted by
fantasies of remarriage and fears of public disgrace and
punishment (65–66) are the most extended examples of an
interiority that pervades the narrative of this section. It does not
return when Stephen returns in books II and III as a
spokesman for the working class; there his function has
changed, and he is placed at a distance. It is important to note,
however, that Stephen has two roles in the novel, and that the

---

storytelling cures derailed desire by narrativizing it. His notion of narrative as
lifegiving in the way it arouses and sustains desire seems peculiarly akin to
Dickens's own intuitions about it. See *Reading for the Plot*, pp. 60–61.

first one, exactly because it does not bear directly on class politics, allows Dickens to ally himself with Stephen as he does with no other character in *Hard Times*.

The story is about the burden of the past and Stephen's attempts to unshackle himself from it. Loyalty is its theme; Stephen and Rachael have aged in the service of their loyalty to the memory of what Stephen's wife had once been, and to one another. But that allegiance blocks the future, and Stephen experiments with ways of breaking the block when he goes to Bounderby to ask about remedies in law and again when he sits in paralyzed fascination while his wife puts a bottle of poison to her lips. Rachael's intervention reconciles Stephen to things as they are; this Victorian angel teaches him to endure his past. When Stephen tells his story to Bounderby (55–56), however, Dickens tests Stephen's faith that storytelling is a form of power.

Stephen begins his story in the narrative manner: "I were married on Eas'r Monday nineteen year sin, long and dree." But Bounderby quickly interrupts; to him it is an old story he has heard before, and he summarizes it impatiently: "She took to drinking, left off working, sold the furniture, pawned the clothes, and played old Gooseberry." When Stephen reaches the climax of the present—"There she IS!"—Bounderby says he knows it all already, "except the last clause." What Bounderby cannot hear is the weight of time and repetition in Stephen's narrative: "She coom back, she coom back, she coom back." Erasing the experience such language conveys, he can respond only by reprimanding Stephen for having gotten married at all; and his answer to Stephen's sense of injustice is to put him in the "gold spoon and turtle soup" category. His inability to hear the story is a corollary of the freedom to rewrite history which is a sustaining activity of his own power.

Stephen's tortured consciousness of the shape that cannot be made to disappear is the exact inversion of Bounderby's fictional extermination of his past. Both characters pay their pasts to stay away, but everyone knows Stephen's story, while Bounderby's invented life history goes unchallenged. Bounderby manages to wipe away both his parents and his failed marriage, while

Stephen's whole life is confined and distorted by the legal shell of a marriage. Throughout the novel these two characters are entwined in a contrast that sets the powerless endurance of history against the insubstantial fictions that Bounderby wields in order to subdue his adversaries in dialogue and his obstacles in life.

Dickens's satire of the social rhetoric generated by industrialization is nowhere more brilliantly or disturbingly conceived than in Bounderby's fictional autobiography, a tale that is less a parody than a literal rendering of the conventional story of the self-made man.[26] As it is told by his mother, Mrs. Pegler (198–199), the true story of Bounderby's life really is a rags-to-riches tale; in her version Bounderby has made his gradual progress to wealth and fame nurtured by loving, sacrificing parents and a kind master. Bounderby's version, a gratuitous substitution of hack melodrama for an ordinary success story, obliterates every trace of the energy and loyalty that gave his rise a social context and a consecutive history. It is a narrative equivalent of the ladder kicked over when the climber reaches the top; the story denies that there is a respectable working class or a chain of social interdependence that can nurture ambition. In this way Bounderby cleanses himself of the taint of his working-class origin. He does so, paradoxically, by constantly throwing it in his auditors' faces; and Dickens's wilder satire lies there, in the parodic treatment of the social rise stories that he puts in Bounderby's mouth.

At the moment when he uncovers Bounderby's lie, Dickens allows himself a paragraph of moralizing in which he compares the lie to "the mean claim (there is no meaner) to tack himself on to a pedigree" (200). Bounderby is made equivalent to Disraeli's false aristocrats; instead of tacking on a title, he has tacked on the stories of some fictional risers and claimed to be the hero of them. The invented details of his infancy parody accounts of

26. Dickens's parody of the myth of the self-made man is noted by Brantlinger in "Dickens and the Factories," pp. 279–280, and by Melada in *Captain of Industry*, pp. 110–115. Janet Larson goes further along the lines I pursue to suggest how Bounderby fabricates himself out of "popular clichés from the Victorian mythologies of *Self-Help*" ("Identity's Fictions," pp. 16–17).

underclass degradation in both fictional and nonfictional forms; Geraldine Jewsbury's tale of John Withers's childhood comes to mind, but Disraeli's Devilsdust may be the most immediate inspiration. Bounderby's pride in being born in a ditch and kept in an egg box is Dickens's comment on the "market value" of such details of deprivation, a critique of the way those stories have passed into negotiable social currency.

Bounderby's account of his rise asserts an absolute lack of support from any source, including fate. No person "threw me out a rope," he boasts; he pulled through "whether I was to do it or not." His history is merely a sequence of fragments, a list of job titles that are "antecedents" to his "culmination" as Josiah Bounderby of Coketown (13); even the connectives of cause and effect are eliminated in the description. "Josiah Bounderby of Coketown" is a class unto itself, depending on none of the advantages inherent in social position. All of this verbal play is quite wonderfully designed to literalize the phrase "self-made man" so that it means the man who makes himself up.

Bounderby's rhetorical repertoire is familiar to readers of industrial narratives; slight adaptations in it allow him to manipulate members of every other class through the power of social guilt. With Mrs. Sparsit he plays the game of "rich and poor," juxtaposing pictures of her at the opera with ones of him in the mud of the street (35). With Harthouse he plays the role of bluff manufacturer to Harthouse's gentleman of good family. With Gradgrind he sets his ignorance against the utilitarian system of education. When he goes the way of all fortunes and buys into a landed estate, he plays the man of humble origins against the flower gardens and expensive pictures of his social-climbing predecessor. Throughout it all, Dickens calls attention to these class stereotypes as rhetoric, and as rhetoric that is available for purposes of social manipulation quite other than those to which it pretends. It is a brilliant portrait of language on the loose, of a kind that Dickens invented in *Bleak House*, when he created in Harold Skimpole a character who plays on social controversy about charity and responsibility.

Bounderby is the novel's most blatant demonstration of its thesis that fact is really "false fiction" against which the narrator offers the historical truths of story. He and Stephen remain at the extremes of the argument: Bounderby continues to assert his fictions even after his unmasking, while Stephen dies as a martyr to working-class history in the Old Hell Shaft, itself an image of a forgotten and covered-over past. His power in the novel lies only in his subjection to the past and in the depth of feeling with which he confronts, endures, and expresses it. Within the industrial social order Dickens imagines no reconciliation, no significant intersection between powerful fictions and the experience they bury. As a counterimage to "the fictions of Coketown" (84, 90), he has rather to invent a realm that is free from all dangerous social rhetoric and social anger, one that will work like Disraeli's Marney Abbey to reconcile the novel's dichotomies in the image of a unified system that combines society and narrative. Dickens's version, the circus, manages a great deal of metaphorical compression in the picture of a credibly unideal world.

If we are to believe the "key-note" rhetoric, the circus is in *Hard Times* to represent the fancy and entertainment prescribed by the narrator for the amelioration of industrial and educational monotony. But fancy to the contrary, Sleary's troupe does not function as a source of entertainment in the plot; it makes no one laugh, and when its "acts" are described at all, they are made to seem preposterous.[27] Its actual status is of a different kind: it is there to represent a healthy vision of temporality, a model of social interdependence, and a correct apprehension of the relations between representation and life. What is advertised as fancy turns out to be the novel's definition of realism—not the realism of photographic representation, but the realism of life in historical time.

When Bounderby meets E. W. B. Childers in the Pegasus Arms, he describes the troupe as "the kind of people who don't know the value of time." Childers's retort aptly defines Bounderby's idea of value as money: "if you mean that you can

27. For a discussion of the seamy side of clown life in Dickens, see Joseph Butwin, "The Paradox of the Clown in Dickens," *Dickens Studies Annual* 5 (1976), 115–132. Butwin sees the circus in *Hard Times* as, finally, an "impossible" alternative.

make more money of your time than I can of mine . . . you are about right" (23). To the members of the circus, who eke out their livings on the margins of these "hard times," time is time: they confront it and respect its effects. For both the troupe and its individual members, survival through time is the keynote. Their work is entertainment, but the stress is on the work: on its risks, its physical dangers, its dependence on the age and strength of the performer. Jupe can no longer survive as a clown; Sleary introduces himself as a damaged survivor who has been "chilled and heated, heated and chilled, chilled and heated" in the ring since he was young (28). Yet as a group the circus, like Sleary's eyes both rolling and fixed, exemplifies a balance of continuity and change. When it reappears at the end of the novel, after years, Sleary gives Sissy a long account of all the deaths, marriages, and births that have occurred since her time; he is the living memory that connects past and present through the recordings of change. Members of the troupe have changed jobs because of their ages, and the young have replaced them. Despite its marginality, the circus is the only entity that allows for its own perpetuation in history.

It is also a repository of history, not a museum but a collection of living scraps. Myth and story survive in its costumes and acts. In a similarly blurred form, old names for social roles survive in Sleary's conversation: he calls Gradgrind "Thquire" and dresses Tom up as a "Jothkin." People and animals share work and intuition in the process of daily life. Preindustrial work patterns prevail: family life and business are the same enterprise, jobs are diversified according to the ages and talents of the children, or to accommodate the adults who happen to marry into the extended family. Yet the circus is less an image of a lost past than a dislocated realm of "culture" surviving on the edges of society, valuing the past but reshaping it into new forms.

As a social order the circus exemplifies the intense interdependence that Bounderby's autobiography erases. The pyramid of fathers is a direct metaphorical counter to Bounderby's myth of rise; in it "the father of one of the families was in the habit of balancing the father of another of the families on the top of a great pole; the father of a third family often made a pyramid of both these fathers, with Master Kidderminster for the apex, and himself for the base" (27). In this nonhierarchical hierarchy all the actors are equal and probably interchangeable; the one at the top balances only because of the work of those below. It is a structure composed of "fathers" who are simultaneously defined as parts of another familial structure; interdependency penetrates the identities of these characters in both realms, and the realms themselves are dependent on each other.

As it is practiced in the dramas of the novel, the art of the circus is not an entertaining show but the art of knowing and interpreting human behavior. Making its living by means of mediations between representation and ordinary life, the troupe knows the difference between fiction and social reality, between semblance and character. In the Pegasus Arms scene Bounderby is instantly seen through and dismissed, while Gradgrind's concealed kindness is discovered and made the subject of an appeal. The art of disguise is practiced as an art of revelation: when Tom is sheltered in the circus disguised as a black servant, he is so well hidden that he cannot be identified, yet the humiliating costume "shows," for the first time, what he really is. Getting at interior truth through an interpretation of outward show, the circus inverts Bounderby's art of misrepresentation, which relies on rhetorical show to deflect attention from the interior.[28]

As Sleary expounds his philosophy, interpretation must proceed inward from "what happens." In his final scene, he tells Gradgrind a story—the story of how Jupe's dog, Merrylegs, came back to Sleary, as though to inform him of his master's death. He can only make up scenes to guess at the chain of events that brought the dog back, as he can only guess at Jupe's original reason for leaving, though in both cases he has some good guesses based on his knowledge of their characters. But

28. The analogy between the circus's tawdry illusions and Bounderby's boastful bluster noted by Gallagher (*Industrial Reformation*, pp. 161–162) is there, as such intimately distinguished processes often are in Dickens, to indicate the profound differences of moral orientation which may underlie similarities in "show."

the truth of the story, as Sleary meditates on it, lies in the mysteriousness of the ways of dogs and men, ways that attest to bonds of loyalty that reveal themselves only in the course of time.

Sleary and his circus stand midway between the artless life stories of Sissy and Stephen and the fictional autobiography of Bounderby. They allow Dickens to make the crucial distinction between lying and art which his scheme requires and to solidify his central contrast between the rhetorics of fiction and story, the first characterized by fragmentation and categorization, the second by its linkage of temporality and emotion. With these distinctions in place, it is time to turn to the stories Dickens tells in the plots of *Hard Times*. What models of history and change do they trace out? How does he assess the effects of attitudes toward storytelling in the imagined fates of characters?

Read as a story in itself, *Hard Times* generates a sense of obstruction, of resistance to the unfolding of plot and action. Partly a consequence of unusually compressed writing, the sense of obstructed action is also central to the novel's moral design. Every plan except those initiated by circus characters ends in abortion and failure. Gradgrind's plans for his children, Bounderby's marriage, Harthouse's seduction, Mrs. Sparsit's plot to replace Louisa, Tom's plot to frame Stephen for the bank robbery, even Rachael's plan to bring Stephen back to clear his name—all these designs are stalemated. The successful plans are those unmotivated by self-interest, launched on someone's else's account: the troupe's appeal to Gradgrind on Sissy's behalf, Sissy's banishment of Harthouse, and Sleary's scheme to spirit Tom out of the country. The moral contrasts are simple enough; but the two kinds of plots are contrasted as well by the kind of knowledge that frames them.[29] The successes of the circus people are based on their knowledge or intuition of character and on their ability to adapt their strategies according to circumstances: Bitzer's intervention in the escape plot, for

29. Dickens's interest in talking about different kinds of human design is beautifully worked out in Robert Kiely's essay "Plotting and Scheming: The Design of Design in *Our Mutual Friend*," *Dickens Studies Annual* 12 (1983), 267–283.

example, only generates a revised plan. The failures of
Coketown plans result from fatal entanglements in fictions,
failures to distinguish between social stereotype and individual
character.

Thus Tom's plot is based on the hope that the "fictions of
Coketown" will be read as true, and that the conventional
description of workers as idle, degenerate, and criminal will
prevail in the town's interpretation of the robbery. The plan
works for a time, until someone who knows Stephen begins to
work against it. Similarly, in a comic vein, Mrs. Sparsit has cast
herself as the deserving woman in a conventional melodrama
featuring the sexual descent and fall of Louisa. She dashes about
the country in the rain in order to witness the climax of the story,
missing the concealed truth of Louisa's character which sends
her back to her father. In Harthouse, represented as a penetra-
tor of all conventional rhetorics, Dickens makes a subtler case.
Harthouse "sees the truth" that Louisa is moved only by her
brother and woos her by playing on the meaninglessness of
rhetoric; in this way he embodies the dangerous underside of
the impulse that generates *Hard Times*. Harthouse's only response to the world's array of social fictions is deliberately to
adopt one fictional role after another for amusement, in a dark
parody of the circus's—and the narrator's—talent. His theatri-
cality as a seducer is not saved from conventional melodrama by
his ability to play the role consciously; and he, too, is finally
vanquished by his inability to predict what Louisa will do and by
Sissy's plain command to leave Coketown.

The end of the novel condemns the Coketown characters
to something more than a local frustration of action, pointing
without fanfare to the extinction of their species. The circus
characters (including Sissy) reproduce themselves, adapt
themselves to changing circumstances, and perpetuate themselves in time. To the Bounderby-Gradgrind circle Dickens
metes out an unusual fate: even fall and redemption do
not guarantee continuity in time. Although Gradgrind and
Louisa are redeemed for their own lifetimes, neither Tom nor
Louisa has descendants; and Dickens makes of Bounderby's
sterility the extraordinary joke of his will, which legislates into

existence twenty-five duplicates of himself, all born as adults (225).

The novel's single story of change lies in the father-daughter drama of Gradgrind and Louisa. Its punishable error is Gradgrind's denial of development in time, its climax an act of storytelling that redeems the teller and reforms the listener. Gradgrind, like his capitalist predecessor Mr. Dombey, sees no value in childhood and educates Louisa so that she might be, while still in youth, "almost any age" (78). His defiance of nature and time is literalized in Louisa, who exhibits a premature extinction of the will to live. It is as though the second generation punishes the parent's desire by fulfilling it, in the eerie form of wishing to erase the future, to get quickly to the end of its time. Louisa reads the sparks that glow and fall in the fire as emblems of her single consolation: that "life is very short" (76). Yet her ability to intuit the explosive consequences of the repressions her father has imposed on her is expressed, on the verge of her unwilling engagement, in her enigmatically compressed reference to the Coketown chimneys: "When the night comes, Fire bursts out, father" (76).

Louisa puts herself back into time by breaking her long silence and "bursting" into story. At the moment when Harthouse expects her suppressed feeling to issue in an adulterous elopement, she returns home to tell her father the sad story of her childhood and marriage. Replacing the seduction and fall story that has already occurred in the craven fantasies of Mrs. Sparsit, Louisa's "true" story ends in a literal fall at Gradgrind's feet. "You have brought me to this," she asserts, and cries out against her father's attempts to hold her up as though to enact before his eyes the causal connection between his educational system and the corruption of nature more conventionally associated with a sexual fall (167).

The story works: it moves Gradgrind as Sissy's story had moved Louisa in childhood, forcing him to a confrontation with the incalculable powers of Time and history. As a blue-book-reading MP, he had presumed to settle the destinies both of his children and of the populace at large; he "had no need to cast an eye upon the teeming myriads of human beings around him, but could settle all their destinies on a slate, and wipe out all their tears with one dirty little bit of sponge" (73). But Gradgrind, who has only made the mistake of believing utilitarian rhetoric, is allowed to descend from his observatory into the realm of tears and history. Unlike Bounderby, he revises his account of things when he is confronted with "what really happened." His change, which ages him significantly, is an acquiescence to history and a corresponding acceptance of emotion as a force in its making. Out of the reconciliations with her father and Sissy Louisa's end too is mitigated by a retrieval of childhood as she grows "learned in childish lore" and in the love of Sissy's children (226).

Louisa's story is the only form in which her suppressed powers of feeling take shape or through which she is able to exert any influence over her father. Because he is moved to believe it, he is reformed; and because his reform constitutes an acceptance of his own family history, he is granted a story of his own, parallel in meaning with Louisa's and with all the other stories—Sissy's, Merrylegs', Sleary's—that trace out a circular shape of loyal return to a difficult past. Both Gradgrind and his daughter are tested for their loyalties to past connection, and both pass the test, Louisa when she returns to the father who hurt her and Gradgrind when he defies Bitzer and the law of the land he serves to help Tom escape from punishment. The ambiguity of Gradgrind's position in that action only emphasizes Dickens's point about personal loyalty: Gradgrind will publish the truth about the robbery, but he will also protect his son from the justified course of the law. He is both facing up to history and saving an individual life from public processing and punishment; the illegal and antisocial nature of the rescue is fully supported by the novel's concept of reform.

The nature of the changes recorded in these stories is so private that it hardly seems to bear on the question of social change. Gradgrind and Louisa (along with the circus characters whose values they adopt) embrace the values of memory, loyalty, and private adherence to a past connection that can be tested only in time. And they are reconciled to their own histories, facing what has happened and looking back from a revised point of view.

What they see, like what the circus characters see, is painful but
true; to be initiated into history brings no assurance of happiness
or harmony. Merely to acknowledge and countenance the world's
collection of sad stories is an achievement of character in *Hard
Times;* its plots press, one after another, toward such recognitions.
Reconciliations between a character and its history are the
"romances" of the novel, its only offers of solution. One ensures
a personal future by admitting to the past; one kills the future by
misrepresentation. But what one ensures or kills is simply lives.
The stories fight for the right to get from the beginning of a life
to the end without having it appropriated, distorted, or erased by
the social formulations of ruling theorists.[30]

Yet in the act of recovering the integrity of private lives, the
stories of *Hard Times* suggest an unexpectedly radical social
stance. They oppose every attempt at social reform that can be
imagined within a capitalist society that conceives of people in
classes and groups. They offer no shadow of hope that "masters
and men" might be reconciled, opening instead vistas of incommensurate realms of discourse. They accuse the ruling class of
basing its power on the rhetorical manipulation of fictional social
constructs. And they foretell the inherent sterility in its mecha-
nisms of control, showing how they engineer their own destruc-
tions. In sum, the stories of *Hard Times* offer a social critique so
bleak, a vision of society so fractured, that only Marx could have
accommodated it to mid-nineteenth-century ways of thinking. Is
it any wonder that Dickens falls back on the paternalist appeals,
evoking the image of a world in which rulers might touch the lives
of the ruled? Or that he deflects even his own attention from the
unmitigated sadness of the stories he tells by calling for amusement? And in spite of those inabilities to admit to what he is doing,
"it is a remarkable fact" that Dickens does not mitigate the sadness

30. Raymond Williams gives the best description I have seen of Dickens's way
of absorbing ideas in his narrative: "From a position in experience like his, it is
the consequence of an idea, and not its formal substance, that really tells. And he
works more finely than anyone in his time the tension—often the unbearable
tension—between orthodox ideas, the ratifying explanations of the world as it
was, and the tearing, dislocating, haunting experience which the ideas, in
majority, were meant to control" ("Dickens and Social Ideas," in *Dickens 1970*, ed.
Michael Slater [London, 1970], p. 87).

of his story by making it amusing, or by accommodating it to wishes for social harmony and reconciliation.

In these respects, Dickens's use of the "double" historical perspective sets him markedly apart from the paternalist fantasies of Disraeli. For both writers the recovery of suppressed material is the special province and the special justification of the novel in a political world. And both rely on the values of memory, loyalty, and continuity as the touchstones of reform. But for Dickens the limits of continuity are the limits of a single life span; where Disraeli expands his historical perspective to embrace a bloodline, Dickens contracts, insisting that history has no significance except as it is expressed in particular life experiences. Dickens's villains behave like Disraeli's: they interrupt histories and make up fictional ones to take their places; their political power is exercised in ignorance of its subjects. Disraeli, happy to embrace a new fiction if it is his own, would change the leaders; Dickens stubbornly asserts the intrinsic dependence of power on fiction.

The difference in scale also amounts to a difference in content when it comes to relations between the past and the future. In both novels the momentum for change is generated from a revision of the past. Where Disraeli perpetrates a myth of political futurity sprung full-blown from the forehead of a mythic past, Dickens also requires of his characters that they confront their pasts before he allows them to proceed into a limited future. But the private arena of his historical operations constitutes in itself a rebuke to historical justifications for political power. When his characters look back, they shed their public roles and become defined by the courses of their emotional lives—the only courses that Dickens allows as conduits of life. Disraeli wants to save the state; Dickens wants to save lives from the state. When *Hard Times* works at its best, it works as a fiction that liberates life stories from the rhetorical spells cast by antihistorical fictions of power.

"Toward a More Assured End": *Felix Holt*

In *Felix Holt the Radical* (1866), George Eliot works in both of the historical modes used by Disraeli and Dickens, fusing an

expanded perspective of historical process with the moral stories
of individual lives. The dense and peculiar narrative that results
has always been open to the charge that George Eliot rejects
politics and, in particular, that the rejection creates the unac-
ceptably underdetermined character of Felix Holt.[31] Catherine
Gallagher has importantly recast such assessments by describing
Felix Holt as a text in which Eliot simultaneously confronts
contemporary issues of political representation and her own
earlier belief in realistic representation, deliberately shaping in
Felix Holt a character who stands for an Arnoldian "best self"
that is also culture, a realm necessarily separate from social
conditions, and therefore also from the readable social signs of
realism.[32]

As Gallagher's analysis reveals, Felix's ability to remain undetermined by his social conditions is also a commitment to
"continuity," to a larger familial past. It is that paradox I want to
explore in the context of all the personal histories that are either
told or suppressed in *Felix Holt*. For, as Dickens does in *Hard
Times*, George Eliot builds her novel and its plots on a set of
carefully distinguished relationships with the past. Two intimately opposed patterns emerge from the contrast: the potential for changing the future is expressed as the ability to
construct continuity out of acknowledged breaks in a life, while
stasis is defined—through analogies linking politics, inheritance,
and personal suppressions of the past—as an attempt to appropriate the future in despite of past determinants. Insofar as this
novel offers terms for the solution of its paradoxes, they lie in
the moral powers of telling and hearing stories.

As a historian of politics, George Eliot may be compared with
Disraeli in the way she develops an ironical account of social
change by looking "before and after" and in her sketch of an
expanded historical perspective that points to "true history."
Her Introduction makes an elaborate presentation of the nar-

31. For essays on George Eliot's rejection or abandonment of politics in *Felix
Holt*, see chap. 2, n. 18.
32. Gallagher, *Industrial Reformation*, pp. 217–267; or see Gallagher, "The
Politics of Culture and the Debate over Representation," *Representations* 5 (1984),
115–147.

rator as historian; not a revisionary political analyst like Disraeli, but a living memory that subtly draws the political present of the mid-1860s together with the moment of the first Reform Bill. In her first paragraph, she lets us know both that there is a visible difference between coach-riding 1832 and train-riding 1866 and that the times are continuous in nothing so much as in the conventional belief that "times were finely changed."[33] Even in this familiar voice of social irony, Eliot sets out the issue that may fairly be called the obsession of this text: belief in change is blindness to continuity; things seem to change, but people stay the same. And the memorializing narrator, taking her reader on a coach ride through the midlands of 1832, mixes her nostalgic evocation of scenes with ironic summaries of the political and religious opinions of their inhabitants. Detail by detail the past appears before our eyes, each recorded observation attesting to a social matter that was still critically present at the time of writing, when politics hesitated on the verge of a second Reform Bill.

George Eliot locates her story in the months after the passage of the first Reform Bill in order to emphasize the ironic view of social change established in the Introduction. Things sound different but nothing has changed: the Sproxton miners have no idea what reform means; local politicians use new words to oil the wheels of old machinations. "The higher pains of a dim political consciousness" (44) which have developed in Treby Magna are represented only as increased sensitivities to differences of political label which set one person against another. The narrative perspective on the fate of the Reform Bill offers a view of political change as anticlimax:

> At that time, when faith in the efficacy of political change was at fever-heat in ardent Reformers, many measures which men are still discussing with little confidence on either side, were then talked about and disposed of like property in near reversion. Crying abuses—"bloated paupers," "bloated pluralists," and other corruptions hindering men from being wise and happy— had to be fought against and slain. Such a time is a time of hope.

33. George Eliot, *Felix Holt the Radical* (Oxford, 1980), p. 5. Further references to this edition will appear in the text.

Afterward, when the corpses of these monsters have been held up to the public wonder and abhorrence, and yet wisdom and happiness do not follow, but rather a more abundant breeding of the foolish and unhappy, comes a time of doubt and despondency. [157]

The perspective is akin to Disraeli's in its placement of political activity in anticipation and retrospect; but Eliot is far more sure that politics makes nothing happen, or worse, that the heroic story anticipated in the image of monster slaying necessarily ensures more of the same: "a more abundant breeding" of monsters is the heritage of the promise to reform an era. The simile connecting the promise of political reform with "property in near reversion," quietly introducing the link between politics and the inheritance plot, also manages to suggest both that the illusion of going forward is equivalent to going back and that the motion of politics, like that of property, is determined by laws independent of what is said or claimed by interested parties. Politics sins both against the past and against the future through its falsely heroic stories and its willed ignorance of the laws that govern its own activity.

A brief general formulation of an alternative, genuinely heroic relation to history issues when Eliot expands the time frame within which her idealists are judged. Of Rufus Lyon (and implicitly of Felix Holt) she says:

For what we call illusions are often, in truth, a wider vision of past and present realities—a willing movement of a man's soul with the larger sweep of the world's forces—a movement toward a more assured end than the chances of a single life. . . . We see human heroism broken into units and say, this unit did little— might as well not have been. But in this way we might break up a great army into units; in this way we might break the sunlight into fragments. . . . Let us rather raise . . . a monument to the faithful who were not famous, and who are precious as the continuity of sunbeams is precious, though some of them fall unseen and on barrenness. [161]

The heroic language is released by the invocation of a time zone within which meanings unreadable within a political life span may be conferred. What looks like failure is heroism; heroism depends on a belief that there is another story, one with "a movement toward a more assured end than the chances of a single life." This larger history displays the signs of evolutionary theory: the sunbeams to which heroes are compared both guarantee the existence of life on earth and act like the random fall of seeds that may or may not alter the species in the course of a longer adaptive process. The image suggests that both the continuities and the changes in the human race depend on, even if they arc not cxprcssed within, the life of an individual.[34] For Eliot the transcending "illusions" she celebrates here are forged in the histories of character. It is in that context that she most fully explores their meanings, while, for the most part, her narrative sticks to its view of political change as anticlimax.[35]

The stories in *Felix Holt* reproduce the view of action as anticlimax, revealing a perpetual frustration of anticipated relationships between thought, action, and consequence. The election campaign ends in the riot that shifts all the terms of debate and suspense; Mr. Lyon's religious debate peters out into nothing when his opponent turns tail and runs away; Felix's pardon is an afterthought that turns into a scene of another kind, the melodramatic exposure of Harold's paternity. Throughout the novel one story turns up to blunt the outlines

34. This image complicates the Spencerian model of adjusting internal relations with external ones, an idea attributed to Eliot by Brantlinger (*Spirit of Reform*, pp. 128–131) and by Shuttleworth (*George Eliot and Nineteenth-Century Science*, pp. 120–121). Shuttleworth's discussions of earlier novels, which stress the multiple and changing meanings of organicism in George Eliot's ideas of society and show contradictory models of history working within a single text, could also be developed in *Felix Holt*. In "The Natural History of German Life" (1856), for example, Eliot's more entirely organic metaphor for development nevertheless suggests a point of discontinuity as a moment of change: "The nature of European man has its roots intertwined with the past, and can only be developed by allowing those roots to remain undisturbed while the process of development is going on, until that perfect ripeness of the seed which carries with it a life independent of the root" (*Essays of George Eliot*, ed. Thomas Pinney [London, 1963], p. 288). The strange image of sunlight in *Felix Holt* pushes the notion of the seed's independence further, suggesting a line of individuals descending as a kind of moral reseeding.

35. William Myers gives a strong analysis of George Eliot's distrust of politics as it is related to Comtean positivism in "George Eliot: Politics and Personality," in *Literature and Politics in the Nineteenth Century*, ed. John Lucas (London, 1971), pp. 105–121. Because the development of political theory in the individual is in itself a political event, Myers shows, "Personality is thus the central political fact in both Positivist theory and George Eliot's novels" (p. 111).

of another; what seem to be major scenes end inconclusively; foreseen consequences are displaced by others; apparently major actions end up as curiously muffled events.[36]

Yet there is another discernible meaning within the pattern of anticlimax: public occasions create opportunities for connections that fuel the private plot. The campaign puts Harold in relation to his father and uncovers rumors about the Bycliffe claim; the aborted religious debate allows Christian to identify Esther with Annette and Bycliffe; Felix's speech on nomination day puts Christian in touch with Johnson; the electoral riot kills Tommy Trounsem; the meeting to pardon Felix is the occasion for Jermyn's revelation of paternity. This narrative movement from outward to inward event links the activity of political reform with the necessity for confronting the past. Public business makes nothing happen except for unanticipated airings of private secrets: the past obtrudes itself, demanding to be settled. As in *Hard Times*, the task of reform or change is redefined by the plot structure so that it lies in the difficult activity of facing what has happened in personal histories.

Felix Holt offers individual life stories as forms that give specific shape to questions of history and social change, and develops its thesis through a dichotomy between those who conceal and those who acknowledge their pasts. The historian-narrator we meet in the Introduction moves, like her plots, from an ironic recording of social change to an explication of the inner life; she takes her audience on a trip through the midlands which ends in a vision of private history. The landscapes observable from the outside of the coach produce social generalizations appropriate to the vantage point of the traveler, but these observations dissolve into the coachman's local gossip about the families of landed proprietors and come to rest on the

---

36. In *Plot, Story, and the Novel* (Princeton, 1979), Robert L. Caserio offers a suggestive discussion of George Eliot's devaluation of action and her resistance to plotted action, using *Felix Holt* as an example of actions that are subordinated to other actions or to mental relations. He also notes Eliot's "vigilant skepticism towards the self's plots" (p. 123), an observation that is highly relevant to Eliot's ironic treatment of the stories her characters tell themselves. Caserio's project does not include speculation about what Eliot's patterns of anticlimax might signify about politics and history.

rumors that linger about the Transome estate. Finally the essay ends in a "parable," the narrator having transformed herself into a recoverer of hidden histories, with access to a vision of the passions that secretly feed the life of memory (11). The inward movement brings us to the threshold of Mrs. Transome's story. It also traces a moral direction: like Dickens, Eliot will move from politics to character in her search for a ground of social virtue. Thus she builds her novel on a distinction between two moral relationships with history, dividing her characters into groups linked by their uses of the past.

The characters in the Transome-Jermyn group, along with the servant Christian and the agent Johnson, attempt to manipulate their destinies without regard for history. For them the past is a suppressed arsenal of secrets to be drawn out one by one as required for the manipulation of others, the future an arena of calculated prediction based on the formula "If I do x, y will do z." Figured in metaphor either as chess players or as gamblers in a lottery, these characters depend on the interplay of calculation and chance to determine what they will define as good and evil. As Eliot shapes their stories, their attempts to determine futures guarantee only that they will be determined by a past: the internal experience of Mrs. Transome and her son's election campaign are equally imprisoned by this pragmatic view of history.

The second model requires that its practitioners see themselves both as determined by their histories and as authors of their own stories; in this paradox lies Eliot's version of "true history." It is what Felix Holt calls vision; practiced by himself and Rufus Lyon, it is taught to Esther through the medium of love. Visionaries imagine the consequences of actions as they affect the moral continuities of the self and others. Fusing passionate feeling with a strict code of responsibility, vision is tested in acts of choice, acts that portray continuity as the moral incorporation of gap and that present chances as opportunities to be used rather than as fates to be risked.

Felix Holt investigates its characters' understandings of their own histories through the pairing of two triangles: Mr. Lyon, Esther, and Felix Holt make one family; Mrs. Transome,

Harold, and Jermyn the other. The two parents with concealed histories of love and the two young men who call themselves radicals make the central contrasts, but the triangulations are important in the development of relationships between generations which ensure or fracture continuity. The stories of Mrs. Transome and Mr. Lyon conceal information about the paternity of their children; how each of them imagines the meaning of that break in life, how and when each tells the story, and how it is received are the focal points of the comparison. Harold Transome and Felix Holt both lay claim to independence from their personal histories; the differences in their conceptions of that freedom make the differences in their fates.

The stories of the older generation, Mrs. Transome and Mr. Lyon, are plotted around the question of how and when their pasts will be told. Both withhold their secrets for fear of losing the affection of a child, while the plots demonstrate that the telling is a condition of that affection. The two pasts emerge very differently from the narrative: Lyon's is fully and transparently recounted, while Mrs. Transome's is revealed in rather heavily weighted hints that convey the melodramatic quality of her interior experience. In the complexity of her story lies some of the tragic quality that Eliot promises in her Introduction; "pity and terror" are the responses that she elicits from "some hard entail of suffering, some quickly-satiated desire that survives, with the life in death of old paralytic vice, to see itself cursed by its woeful progeny" (11); and in Esther's response to Mrs. Transome the reader is meant to see and share in that pity and terror. But Mrs. Transome is not in herself of tragic stature; her experience is shaped in a language of miscalculation and melodrama, suggesting failures of imagination that have made her past a prison.[37]

37. Mrs. Transome's story has long been read as the "tragic" part of the novel, the part in which the complications left out of the political plot come into play. Even a critic so acute about Eliot's divided ideas of history as Sally Shuttleworth returns to that split, to see Mrs. Transome's suffering as a challenge to the simple ideals of continuity expounded by Felix and enacted by Esther (*George Eliot and Nineteenth-Century Science*, pp. 134–141). The language of mirrors and melodrama should also alert us to Eliot's emphasis on the failures of Mrs. Transome's own imagination.

Mrs. Transome is a pragmatist of domestic life; she has gambled on adultery and illegitimacy to ensure her future happiness. Just as Jermyn tries to ensure her continued possession of the estate by misrepresenting the identity of Bycliffe, the legitimate heir, she has attempted to "give unity to her life, and make some gladness through the changing years" (22) by having Jermyn's child and passing it off as legitimate. In both cases an actual gap in hereditary succession is covered over because of a wish to create unity in a single life. Like all the gamblers in the book, Mrs. Transome fails to control the future because she miscalculates character: Jermyn's, Harold's, and her own. Jermyn's courtship turns into blackmail; he uses their secret as a power to silence her while he makes his fortune in shady dealings with the estate. Harold soon grows into an independent life indifferent to his mother's. And she suffers from the very power of her desires; her wish that her eldest son would die, her fear that Harold will learn of his illegitimacy, all "make life a hideous lottery, where every day may turn up a blank" (22).

Her gamble for a proud and happy future results in a life arrested at a moment in the past. Not unlike the more highly stylized Miss Havisham of Dickens's *Great Expectations,* Mrs. Transome has trapped herself in her mansion, proudly fixated on a past event that controls every present response, living in the hope that the next generation will be a weapon and a consoling stay against that all-determining historical moment. Her pride and terror of exposure freeze her relation with Jermyn. She carries herself like a young woman; the portraits and mirrors with which she is surrounded continually emphasize the simultaneous presence of her past and her present self. The estate has not changed, only faded, in the years that Harold has been away; she resists the changes that he brings. The shape of her story is that of outburst and collapse: she moves from the rigid suppression of the early scenes to her long-delayed outburst at Jermyn, and then to the disintegration of the final episodes. When Harold confronts her with his knowledge of the truth, "she seemed as if age were striking her with a sudden wand—as if her trembling face were getting haggard before him" (384).

The significance of this shape lies in its distortion of the life cycle, in the absence of gradual aging and change, or of affection sustained over time. Attempting to write her own future by suppressing her past, Mrs. Transome succeeds only in making herself a victim of time and chance.

Her own conceptions of change take the melodramatic forms of salvation or damnation—fantasies that are consistently subjected to the rule of anticlimax associated with politics. The first chapter opens brilliantly on her anticipation of Harold's return; although it has come almost too late, it is nevertheless an event that may change everything, a final reward for her years of privation. Within two pages of Harold's entrance "she had a sickening feeling that it was all of no use that the long-delayed good fortune had come at last" (18). Harold does, ironically, bring about household changes with the "magical quickness" of fairy tale (99), but Mrs. Transome's life is only diminished, robbed of its last traces of power. Harold fails to take up the role her imagination has assigned him as salvation and consolation:

> Nothing was as she had once expected it would be. If Harold had shown the least care to have her stay in the room with him—if he had really cared for her opinion—if he had been what she had dreamed he would be in the eyes of those people who had made her world—if all the past could be dissolved, and leave no solid trace of itself—mighty *ifs* that were all impossible—she would have tasted some joy. . . . [99]

Her imagination can move only in the direction of wishing to undo the past, dissolving Harold along with it; her miscalculations have arrested her ability to move forward into a continuous future.

In the later chapters, she has switched from the dream of a past made good to its equivalent and opposite, a tale of helpless subjection to retribution and punishment. When Harold tells her about Esther's claim on the estate, she "saw these things through the medium of certain dominant emotions that made them seem like a long-ripening retribution" (293), and she puts herself bitterly in the hands of fate: "I must put up with all things as they are determined for me" (294). In her last great flare of youthful passion she throws a revenge scene for Jermyn, refusing to save him from Harold's lawsuit by telling Harold the truth about his paternity. It is the only card left in her pack, and she uses it melodramatically, telling Jermyn how she has dreaded the relationship between father and son as one that might breed murder (337–338). When Harold comes home with his new knowledge written on his face, she imagines it as a death: "It was as if a long-expected letter, with a black seal, had come at last" (384).

What happens to Mrs. Transome is very unlike the sensationalist drama that her fantasy produces. She does not die. She loses neither Harold nor the estate. Through Esther's intervention she belatedly gets at least a minimal reconciliation with her son. What she loses is her role, "that of the clever sinner" (17), which has sustained her sense of importance in life. Now her mask of imperial majesty disintegrates, and she becomes the image of her fearful inner life. Although she has not dared to tell her story, it has been told for her, and she is finally purged, of her meaning as well as her past. Her imagination is to the end inadequate to the task of seeing without the aids of conventional story forms; in her last words she imagines that Esther will become Harold's compensation, as Harold was supposed to be her own.

Mrs. Transome is condemned to be a prisoner of her history because she is incapable of seeing the greater forces that lie, for good or evil, beyond her. Eliot's judgment upon her grants her only the pathos of suffering: "Here she moved to and fro amongst the rose-coloured satin of chairs and curtains—the great story of this world reduced for her to the little tale of her own existence—dull obscurity everywhere, except where the keen light fell on the narrow track of her own lot, wide only for a woman's anguish" (280). The track has been narrowed for her as well as by her; "woman's lot," with the special torments of the guilty adulteress, has been her portion with a vengeance. And yet Eliot condemns her not for what she has done but for her inability to see around her own failures, for imprisoning her life in conventional social forms and her imagination in conventional forms of story. The vision offered as an alternative to this "dull obscurity" takes as its basis a view of history that is larger than the scope of an individual life.

Rufus Lyon sees, and is seen, in such a light. He is made to articulate "that larger rule whereby we are stewards of the eternal dealings, and not contrivers of our own success" (301). His history is told early in the novel (chap. 6) in the form of straightforward narrative.[38] The manner of telling evokes the manner of living: the strategy of foreboding hints in which Mrs. Transome's story is told suggests her inability to face and name what has happened, while Mr. Lyon sees exactly what he is doing when he falls in love with Annette. Knowing the union to be irreconcilable with his calling, he resigns his ministry, and supports himself and Annette as a printer's reader until her death ends "that four years' break in his life" (80). To him, the passion remains a fall to which he has humbly bent; Mrs. Transome, always turning away from the past, relies on her hopes for Harold to justify her adultery.

Lyon's passion, like hers, produces only anticlimax. It begins as an improbably romantic rescue: a moonlit night, a chance halt along the way, the beseeching voice of a woman with an infant. No romance ensues: Lyon's "wild visions of an impossible future" (73) move only toward a marriage made belatedly, as a muted effect of the illness accompanying the collapse of Lyon's deferred hopes. Thereafter his passion is transformed into "a period of such self-suppression and life in another as few men know" (79). Released from this period, Lyon returns to his calling, his career diminished and his sympathies widened. Esther is "the one visible sign" of the break (80), which he continues to describe as "his own miserable weakness and error" (216).

Telling Esther the story proves, however, to be the act that ensures the continuity of vision for which Lyon lives. He faces up to the task the moment he hears that Christian knows her identity, not relying on chance to determine the event. And he

38. In her journal (15–24 November 1865) George Eliot noted, "Writing Mr. Lyon's story, which I have determined to insert as a narrative" (quoted in *The George Eliot Letters*, ed. Gordon S. Haight, 9 vols. [New Haven, 1955], IV, 209.

is rewarded not only with an increase of affection but with Esther's eventual conversion to the visionary. In essence, his narrative makes Lyon her real father, a predecessor whose history empowers her to shape the direction of her own life. When she imagines living at Transome Court, she is suddenly possessed with "a vision, showing, as by a flash of lightning, the incongruity of that past which had created the sanctities and affections of her life with that future which was coming to her. . . ." Seeing her father with "the grandeur of his past sorrow and his long struggling labors" (307), she understands the vulgarity of Transome Court. Thus she is helped to realize the power of a choice "which gives unity to life" and makes "an unbroken history sanctified by one religion" (360), while Eliot connects unity with break: the break in Lyon's career which allows him to choose his own history; the break in Esther's which reverses and cuts her ties to Transome Court. Allowing her to add other life spans to her own, Mr. Lyon's life becomes a link in the chain of sunbeams that figures as Eliot's version of true history, moving "toward a more assured end than the chances of a single life." A created and narratable history thus displaces genealogy—the discovery of Esther's blood parent—as the force that creates the "most assured end."

Harold Transome's story is a negative image of Esther's. A told past is precisely the opportunity he is not given, either by his mother or by his own trust in the chances of a single life. His story is told in the ironic mode that befits a character ignorant of himself and of the crucial conditions of his existence. The overriding irony lies in his notion of reform, which he defines as "rooting out abuses" (39); for his claims to eliminate abuses in the country and on the estate only serve to root out the ugly and unavoidable fact that Jermyn is his father. In narrative summary, this state of mind is defined as "the sadder illusion [that] lay with Harold Transome, who was trusting in his own skill to shape the success of his own morrows, ignorant of what many yesterdays had determined for him beforehand" (161–162). In the drama, it is represented as a belief in self-determination which is continually undercut by the similarities between Harold and his father.

Harold sweeps into Transome Court and immediately begins to rearrange it according to his desires, without inquiring about what he is displacing. His mind moves quickly and without reference to others; he wants no wife to "interfere with a man's life" (20); the fact that his mother has managed the estate for years means nothing to him. Had he not come into the Transome estate, he would have bought one for himself; he sees no difference between these modes of acquisition (19). His own history is concealed, but it has conveniently produced an heir without the trouble of a real marriage. In all of these beliefs he denies the existence of a determining history while helplessly reproducing versions of his father's character. He inherits not only his father's looks but his tendency to put others into bondage: Eliot's metaphors for relations of sex and power at Transome Court characterize them as genteel sadism, literalized when Mrs. Transome's grandson, carrying on the family tradition in a childish form, bites her in public. Esther senses that "Harold had a padded yoke ready for the neck of every man, woman, and child who depended on him" (351); and Harold's opportunistic courtship of her promises to replicate Jermyn's use of his mother.

Although Harold is not responsible for his ignorance of well-kept secrets, he is punished for his disregard of history by having a heavy dose of it applied to him. His single passion, hatred of Jermyn, leads him down the path to the revelation that forces him to confront the past. Harold's suit against Jermyn is gratuitous; although Jermyn is guilty of illegal transactions on the estate, Harold's persistence in the suit is fed by a passion that goes beyond the call of his usually impeccable calculation. As in the other life histories, passion proves to be the key to revelation, the break in the continuity of a life that may generate either vision or suppression.

The major anticlimax in Harold's story lies in what does not follow from the melodramatic revelation of paternity in the White Hart. Everything is hushed up, Harold's "radicalism" is wiped off the slate, he is taken under the Tory wing and reabsorbed into the family. Harold has fitted yokes; now he has fitted to him "the yoke of that mighty resistless destiny laid upon

us by the acts of other men as well as our own" (386). Yet he
continues to respond with pride, hope, and calculation. Only in
the last brief scene between Harold and Esther does George
Eliot allow for the possibility of internal reform. When Esther
tells him of his mother's suffering, there is "a pale rapid flash"
of "painful thrill" in his face (394); his first recognition of her
pain leads to an undramatized reconciliation. But there is little
depth in this language of feeling, and we are left to assume that
for Harold, as for his mother, the confrontation with destiny
takes the form of a diminishment that leads nowhere.

Felix Holt's history is the inverse of Harold's. Because he is
sensitive to historical process and consequence, he is personally
absolved of its effects. This is true not only in the way the plot
frees him from the consequences of his actions in the riot but in
the matter of heredity as well. Harold pretends to disregard the
traditions of his family, but his body and mind are determined
by the person of Jermyn. Felix, the son of a narrow-minded
Baptist and a disreputable quack, sets those determinants aside
and becomes the novel's chief spokesman for visionary history.

George Eliot goes to great lengths to complicate this gap in
her argument. The close contrast with Harold shows, for
example, that Felix has looked at his father's fraud, refused
himself the chance to rise on the fortunes of those patent
medicines, and publicly accepted a fall in social status, while
Harold has not cared to know anything of his antecedents and
wishes to ruin Jermyn only because he is afraid of a stain on his
public reputation. Felix's freedom from his parents depends,
then, on his ability to see what they are, and to take the
consequences of his shift in direction—consequences that include the cheerful support of a mother he despairs of. His
mental freedom lies in the acceptance of those determining
conditions; out of them he invents a new way of life.

But where did that initial vision come from? Eliot covers her
difficulty by making Felix argue that his choices are determined;
she must have him acknowledge the forces of destiny that
Harold ignores to his peril.[39] The argument lands us more or

39. As Gallagher puts it, "Felix's ability to determine his determinants must

less where we began. Felix says that "it all depends on what a man gets into his consciousness—what life thrusts into his mind, so that it becomes present to him as remorse is present to the guilty, or a mechanical problem to an inventive genius" (222). While this exemplifies the correct response to "chance," the analogies tell us that the mind is determined by the special powers of the individual mind. Felix remains a primary catalyst in the plot, a character who makes his consciousness out of itself.

Why must the gap be there? Because Felix is required to perform two different tasks in the narrative: he must give social meaning to personal choices and personal meanings to symbolic social actions. He must simultaneously be a character who has effected true reform in his own history and stand for a different zone of values and wishes comparable to those that shape Disraeli's abbey and Dickens's circus. He must, in other words, be both a character with an exemplary relation to his own past and an alternative social order in himself. And the latter meaning requires that he be in some way disconnected from the chain of social cause and effect which determines the histories of his fellow characters. Much like Disraeli's plot, Felix's career posits a disruption of continuity which restores an ideal history.

Felix enacts in person the model of change that he espouses in theory. As the spokesman for George Eliot, he articulates the creed implicit in the narrator's stance. Political reorganization effects little. Genuine change occurs in the understandings of individual persons, which can only then shape new social orderings. Felix assumes the priority of character in society, likening the process of social change to the invention of the steam engine, which depends on knowing how water will act. Political machinery will work only if men power it with good feelings, "and if we have false expectations about men's characters, we are very much like the idiot who thinks he'll carry milk in a pail without a bottom" (249). Reform means the reform of public opinion so that it can penetrate the manipulative language of politics with a

itself remain undetermined, beyond the reach of social and historical, indeed of narrative explanation." Yet to say that *"Felix Holt is simply unconcerned about those issues in the life of Felix himself"* is to miss Eliot's attempts to create explanations in Felix's voice. See *Industrial Reformation,* pp. 244–245.

moral vision of its own. Thus Felix's "politics" is perfectly clear: it simply implies that every person must learn to divest himself of self-interest, think around social and rhetorical convention, and act for the greater good. He comes into the narrative as a character who has reformed himself in just that way and is capable of effecting similar changes in others.

As an embodiment of general social values, Felix stands for ideas similar to those in Dickens and Disraeli. Disraeli invents the society of Marney Abbey and its "child," Egremont, who appears to embody its meaning in the modern world. Dickens gives us the circus, another image of a whole social order, and its child, Sissy, who infuses Coketown with her values. Both *Sybil* and *Hard Times* posit a separated society that produces an individual with the power to affect the fraudulent politics of the dominant social order; they imagine change as the fertilization of one culture by another. George Eliot imagines no other culture; the point of Felix is that he makes himself, that there is no society to which he refers. Thus Eliot divests her argument of any suggestion that societies or cultures can shape individuals to the good and shows change flowing only in the other direction, from the self-reformed individual to others—one at a time.[40]

Since Felix is not a society, the contradictory aspects of Eliot's social ideals cannot be contained or authorized by a descriptive narrative rhetoric evoking a benevolently functioning social order. Nevertheless, he represents paradoxes of ahistorical continuity that link him directly with the earlier novels. He sees his chosen life as a restoration of continuity, a return to a heritage: "I have my heritage—an order I belong to. I have the blood of a line of handicraftsmen in my veins, and I want to stand up for the lot of the handicraftsman as a good lot . . ." (224).

The deliberate recovery of the artisan culture is elaborated in the picture of Felix running his household on principles of

40. Again the later novel seems to revise the theory that person and medium are organically interdependent, as Eliot expressed it in "The Natural History of German Life": "the internal condition and the external are related to each other as the organism and its medium, and development can take place only by the gradual constantaneous development of both" (*Essays of George Eliot*, p. 287).

domestic economy which recall Dickens's circus: he simultaneously repairs watches, teaches children, and brings out his mother's best self by giving her an adopted child to care for. And, rather like Disraeli's monks and Dickens's extended family, he aspires to an ideal of continuity that is not based on family lineality or inheritance. He is "a man of this generation" who will work for a universal family, a few he will "make life less bitter for"; and he contrasts that ambition with the conventional channeling of work and wealth into the fortunes of a family that may turn to imbecility in the third generation (225). Lateral rather than lineal inheritance characterizes the ideal of continuity in all three novels; laying no personal claim to the future is their common guarantee of perpetuation.

George Eliot relies on Felix's character both to represent and to act; in the latter role he becomes a special problem in the text. His self-reform occurs before he appears on stage to tell it as a story to Lyon and Esther. The plots that move him into action suggest that there is somewhere to go from there—perhaps that he will be a study of a character with a vision of himself as a moral hero, who comes to modify that view through collisions with love and politics. (In just that form George Eliot rewrote Felix's story as Lydgate's in *Middlemarch*). In broad outline, the differences between romance and politics sketch the novel's view of reform: through the linkage of one life story with another, Felix can change Esther, but his political actions effect nothing. Written into scene and story, the matter is not so simple. Felix's actions—his renunciation of Esther and his intervention in the election riot—are both attempts to brake courses of passions that are irrevocably in motion; they are, or should be, tests of Felix's pretensions to shape his life. In each case he fails to achieve his purposes, creating instead consequences that he had not intended. While the plot silently argues that his interventions are well-intentioned failures, the narrative unfailingly promotes his character. The disjunction underlines a gap between the free mind and the social body: Felix is determined by social conditions when he acts, but not when he thinks.

On the day of the election, Felix does two things that muddle passion and principle, with results that entirely escape his control. He goes to Esther to inform her that it has cost him something to renounce her, imagining that he does so for her sake, to show "that he set a high value on her feelings" (263). Throughout the scene he casts himself in a rather self-important role, and then goes away feeling that he may have made things harder rather than easier for her. The scene cries out for some narrative irony, some sign that Felix's solemn sense of superiority conceals an uncontrollable wish to name his love. But the narrator only declares his motives "thoroughly generous" and praises his ability to feel for Esther's pain (263). Although the scene uncovers a basis for irony, George Eliot must rely on all the values of Felix's character even when they contradict one another. Again in the riot scene she endorses his own sense of worthy motive at the same time that she shows a passionate impulse working within the principled stance. Although Felix is fueled by anger, he is depicted as fully conscious of the "tangled business" in which he is involved. "We hardly allow enough in common life," the narrator comments, "for the results of that enkindled enthusiasm which, under other conditions, makes world-famous deeds" (269). Thus she reinforces the "meaning" of the scenes: that actions taken for the most selfless motives may have unforeseen and even destructive ends, but that the key to judgment lies in the private motives of the actor. Felix's motives are never complicated, lest George Eliot lose the single ground of heroic consciousness on which her argument rests.

As a result, the question of whether Felix learns from the collision of vision and action is raised and then muffled.[41] Ultimately Felix in action means the same thing as does his original conversion: a refusal to allow social and material conditions to imprison his consciousness. Events in the riot go against him, but he resists defining them as failure; his mind transcends the conditions that condemn and imprison him. His four-year prison sentence recalls the four-year break in Mr. Lyon's life: both men are prepared to take full and public

41. David R. Carroll has rather unconvincingly argued that Felix does change in the course of his plot, see "*Felix Holt:* Society as Protagonist," in *George Eliot: A Collection of Critical Essays,* ed. George R. Creeger (Englewood Cliffs, N.J., 1970), pp. 124–140.

consequences of their passionate actions and then to resume their callings. Like Mr. Lyon, Felix is associated with the heroic continuity that transcends the chances of a single life—and both are rewarded in the same way. When Esther shapes her own life in the image of theirs, continuity is ensured through the process of conversion, in which one life history forms a model for another.

Esther's choice is a choice of histories, plotted so as to set her rejection of a legal lineage against her adoption of a place in a moral history authorized only by personal belief. She is offered the political continuity of family lineage only to realize that her real history has been shaped by her stepfather and by her own feeling. Eliot's use of the inheritance plot—that much-abused part of the novel—is in this way a crucial part of her definition of history, a conventional move used to overturn its own conventions of meaning. In an ordinary inheritance plot, as in *Sybil*, the discovery of a legal claim to social status is used both to explain and to reward character: gentility of mind and manner is justified by its blood lineage and restored to a corresponding social sphere. Eliot raises just this possibility for Esther in order to reject it as a historical ground for character. First, she constructs the legal history of the Transome estate so as to undermine the myth of authentic recovery; the endless contingencies of the claim are essential to that purpose, because they make it clear that the line of inheritance based on land and law is nothing more than a messy web of politics, based on chance and circumstance. Second, she constructs Esther's choice in a way that rejects family lineage as the key to continuity or character. Esther sees that she should not disrupt either the Transome family or her historical connections with Rufus and Felix. Her story asserts that character is forged in the choices of each person and that continuity lies in the integrity of life stories as they are experienced and transmitted to other consciousnesses.[42]

Eliot's system of rewards and punishments endows her

42. For a discussion of Eliot's devaluation of inheritance in terms of her necessary separation between concepts of culture and society, see Gallagher, *Industrial Reformation*, pp. 256–263.

visionaries with the power to choose and portrays her pragmatists in lives locked in by past determinants. The characters who attempt to shape a destiny without regard for the past face the absolute impediments of inheritance; as in *Hard Times,* the past revenges itself by undoing their carefully calculated futures. The act of choosing a past allows the visionary a determining history that enables personal movement into the future. Together the stories of Felix and Esther present the thesis that character makes its own history out of its sense of a larger vision of time. Thus Eliot's plots make a familiar case: it is only by looking for—perhaps by writing—an authentic past that one opens the way to a future. In her work, that authenticity lies nowhere but in the powers of a consciousness to embrace a past both given and chosen, and to imagine a consonant future.

When we look at *Felix Holt* as a political novel among others, it becomes clear that its retreat from politics is a critique of an attitude toward history and change rather than a rejection of political activity as such. Electoral politics appears as one of many forms of gambling for the future; all of those forms are under attack because they are inadequately imagined responses to the persistence of the past. Much like Dickens, George Eliot proposes that the alternative to political thinking about change lies in the truth of individual histories; her novel, too, offers itself as a retrieval of story and a vindication of the reforming power of personal narrative. But her idea of life history altogether removes the governing state as a source of authority. Dickens's stories happen to his characters; requiring an audience of governors, they plead with the power of pathos for comprehension from above. Eliot's stories are made by her characters; their audiences are peers; they have the power, in singular cases, to help in the redefinition and reimagination of other lives. Her histories are shaped not from above but from within; she dissolves and internalizes the idea of government.

Perhaps because of that dissolution, George Eliot also appeals to an idea of suprahistorical continuity which is akin to Disraeli's. Both novelists expand historical perspectives in order to focus their judgments of contemporary politics and to sketch out alternative, legitimate lines of succession. Disraeli grounds his true history in systems of continuity created by the state: the lineage of landownership or the succession of great statesmen who might make history from above. Eliot explicitly rejects both ideas in *Felix Holt;* for her all legitimate forms of continuity are located in consciousness alone. Nevertheless, she depends on a fantasy of historical change that acts rather like Disraeli's mystical emergence of the future from the past. Felix Holt, like Charles Egremont, is the vessel for the fantasy. Both characters are rendered personally ahistorical in order that they may be identified with a more generally past-laden future; both are put into motion only as interveners and rescuers, in attempts to stop or amend destructive political actions in progress; both are made innocent of politics. These characters represent wishes for breaks in the chain of political consequence; coming out of the ideal, they create interventions that are meant to slow history down long enough to insert a new element, a new conception of how history is made.

Since the actions of such characters can only be imagined as forms of local resistance, they must be justified through large historical motions that are separate from political events and their consequences. So we have heard Egremont appeal to "the mind of England" as "the mind of the rising race"; and so George Eliot defines the consciousness of her heros as "a wider vision of past and present realities—a willing movement of a man's soul with the larger sweep of the world's forces." The rhetoric gestures in both cases toward a similar political end: the transformation of the populace. But its main import lies in the language of motion. It asserts that there is another history above and beyond the one in which we are immersed; that it is a history that knows where it is going, and that actions in politics mean something different when they are taken in its light.

Disraeli and Eliot differ in the matter of how and why they mean; their transcending time zones point in opposite directions. Disraeli extends his perspective backward, in search of a prior ground for the relegitimation of politics in the present. Although he actually creates an endlessly expanding quest for origins, he works within the hypothesis that the past is a powerful ground of appeal. The life of the individual is significant to him as a conduit for extending the past into the future, either through blood lineage—a nonevolutionary idea—or through the aristocracy of talent, which is accorded a lineage of its own. George Eliot's image of transcendant temporality is perhaps an expanded version of Disraeli's aristocracy of talent, one that pointedly substitutes the self-generated consciousness for the legally constructed lineage of blood and land. For her, continuity is locatable only in narration; the ability of a consciousness to tell its own history simultaneously lifts it above its determinants and seems to credit their full power of being. If Rufus Lyon and Felix Holt are heroes "precious as the continuity of sunbeams is precious" (216), that elusive comparison comes finally to suggest the intangible flow of a story that may find its germinating soil in another soul. The novel, a public act of storytelling, is offered as Eliot's vehicle for a social reform that reaches hopefully into the sunbeamed future for its fertile ground of appeal.

The nature of Dickens's imagination shows up with a special clarity in the context set by *Sybil* and *Felix Holt.* In his work there are, so to speak, no ideas but in metaphor. His invention of the circus is a triumph of metaphor; the circus itself is a scrap bag of images of the past, newly forged into a believably concrete account of a social order. Unlike the higher continuities that Disraeli and Eliot appeal to, it occupies the same temporal zone with political life, rolling along on its edges, dependent on it as art is dependent on the social order for its images and for its support. The function of the circus is to penetrate what is there in society, and to unravel its pretensions to meaning; it is not a zone that confers new meaning, but a mode of interpretation.

So, too, the image of movement in time which Dickens sets against the calculators of Coketown is one that asserts mystery and unknowability. Louisa, trying to fathom her future, "tried to discover what kind of woof Old Time, that greatest and longest-established spinner of all, would weave from the threads he had already spun into a woman. But his factory is a secret place, his work is noiseless, and his Hands are mutes" (73). Dickens mixes the factory labor metaphor with the traditional image of fates spinning destinies to reinforce his distinction between the human arrogation of power to settle destinies and the essentially mysterious story of human lives. The mute spinner that emerges from the metaphor is as far as Dickens will allow us to think, or as far as his thought goes. Similarly Sleary, musing on the meaning of Merrylegs's return, stops short of articulation, pointing only to "thomething very different . . . hard to give a name to" (222). The exercise of language itself seems in these moments to be a violation of a great silence in which things happen; human storytelling fills that silence with feeling, but has no power to shape or articulate its own direction. In that absence of a separate, meaning-conferring history, Dickens is forced to ground his argument in an appeal to the power of emotional response in the ruling class. It is, perhaps, his version of the wish implicit in the structures and perspectives of all three novels, a call to a vision higher than politics which might infuse the forms of political change with the matter of temporal experience.

Afterword

The patterns of plot and narrative with which this study is concerned did not end with *Felix Holt*. The romance of the female paternalist turns up again in Mrs. Humphry Ward's *Marcella* (1894), embodied in a latter-day Shirley whose fervent feminist socialism is modulated through her experience of direct social action into an uneasy embrace of late-Victorian paternalism. *Howards End* (1910), E. M. Forster's version of the condition-of-England novel, draws on several of the narrative conventions established by its nineteenth-century predecessors: Forster's doubled heroines pursue in their different ways an increasingly threatened quest of mediation between classes and genders, business and gentility, politics and memory. These are only examples of texts that loosen the boundaries within which the social-problem subgenre has so far been discussed; while, of course, the creation of alternative histories through pastoral writing or storytelling might readily be studied in a wider range of Victorian fictions.

Nevertheless, *Hard Times* and *Felix Holt* are meaningful end points for a discussion of social-problem novels, because their narratives reflect directly on fictions of political life between 1832 and 1867, commenting on their constructions and their consequences. As a group, the social-problem novels take on a common task of confronting and negotiating the rift between

231

public languages that theorize social relations and the temporal, formative experience of individual life histories. Dickens and Eliot participate in that project while also creating plots that resist and make visible the assumptions on which their colleagues rely. The special positions they assume may be clarified by a brief sketch of the major shifts in orientation that emerge when we look back on the social-problem subgenre as a whole.

The earlier novels in the group—in particular the texts I discuss in Part One—are shaped as stories of mediation: parts of society that are represented as broken apart are reintegrated. Whether the reintegration fuses paternalist with worker, gentleman with engineer, female with male, or child with parent, the story wishes something imagined as divided to be reunited in social harmony. Yet even as this pattern depends on a model of social order as parts that fit to make a whole, the narratives themselves uncover splits between idea and social structure, producing images of paternalism separated from power, or gentility separated from class.

That narrative of reunion, itself undermined in the telling, is increasingly abandoned. The mediating act of rescue and reintegration becomes the act of narration itself, "saving" the past and the future from the present. The temporality of narrative becomes a metaphor for revised histories; storytelling gives characters a place within temporal continuity which social identity violates, or fails to confer. Reform changes its meaning: if in the earlier novels it means an effort to merge incompatible models of social order, it comes in the more sophisticated ones to mean re-forming social history itself through the invention and telling of stories.

The shift from narratives of reunion to narratives of narrative overlaps with a second change in the way continuity is guaranteed. *Oliver Twist, Sybil,* and the pastoral part of *Ruth* appeal to a "natural" continuity grounded in genealogy. Nature is fused with history as an antagonist to politics or to conventional social judgments; the physical world is endowed with an essential power of integrity. The appeal is not uncomplicated; particularly in Disraeli we also find "true history" as another kind of fiction. *Alton Locke* represents an impasse where the appeal to nature is continually called into question, through a text that poses alternative readings of socially constructed natures without being able to choose among them. In *Hard Times* and *Felix Holt* the authorization by blood or nature gives way to narrative activity alone: continuity is guaranteed only in a character's ability to tell its story, apart from either social or inherited definitions of identity. Dickens's single career is itself a model of these changes, for Oliver Twist's natural history of gentility is superseded by the metaphor of manufacture which controls the whole range of storytelling in *Hard Times*. George Eliot takes the process a step further, attempting not only to oppose politics with storytelling but to reabsorb politics into narrative act. The stories her characters tell themselves are both the agents of reform in the novel and the locus of politics itself; in *Felix Holt* politics resides in choices of narrative consequentiality made by individual wills.

Taken together, these shifts in the ground of social-problem tales pull away from unitary views of society and naturalized accounts of history, toward the recognition that social history is an arena of competing narratives. The increasingly self-conscious recourse to "alternative histories" need not, however, be read as a formal indicator of an irrevocable split between politics and culture, or as a self-reflexive withdrawal of narrative into itself. In fact, the more reflexive novels tend rather to make politics and narrative into commensurate terms: while the earlier works position economic or political theory as a plot determinant—the system that controls what happens on a large scale—the more self-conscious novels present politics as one of many constructed fictions about society. Thus the brief unfolding of the Victorian social-problem novel may be characterized by its emergent understanding of politics as one kind of narrative fabrication among others.

In that view *Hard Times* and *Felix Holt* occupy, in their different ways, special positions as metafictions of industrialism. They look directly at acts of social storytelling in order to meditate not only on the merits of opposing narratives but on the sources that produce them and the futures they generate. Both Dickens and Eliot reject systemic or natural explanations of what happens, revealing through the construction of their own fictions that all stories are made, and thus chosen. Public and private histories are presented as willed human fabrications that are available for judgment as stories with consequences. If, finally, these texts despair of politics, it is because they define the political story as a narrative of necessity that issues only in despair.

Bibliography

PRIMARY WORKS

Brontë, Charlotte. *Shirley.* 1849. Harmondsworth: Penguin, 1974.
Carlyle, Thomas. "Chartism." 1839. In *Critical and Miscellaneous Essays: Collected and Republished.* London: Chapman & Hall, 1869.
——. *Past and Present.* 1843. London: J. M. Dent, 1912.
——. "Signs of the Times." 1829. In *Critical and Miscellaneous Essays: Collected and Republished.* Boston: Houghton, Osgood, 1879.
Cooke-Taylor, William. *Notes of a Tour in the Manufacturing Districts of Lancashire: In a Series of Letters to His Grace the Archbishop of Dublin.* 2d ed. London: Duncan & Malcolm, 1842.
Craik, Dinah Mulock. *John Halifax, Gentleman.* London: J. M. Dent, 1961.
Dickens, Charles. *Hard Times.* 1854. Ed. George Ford and Sylvère Monod. New York: Norton, 1966.
——. *Oliver Twist.* 1837. Harmondsworth: Penguin, 1966.
——. "Preface to the First Cheap Edition." In *Oliver Twist.* 1850. New York: New American Library, 1961.
Disraeli, Benjamin. *Coningsby, or The New Generation.* 1844. New York: Signet, 1962.
——. *Sybil, or The Two Nations.* 1845. Ed. Sheila M. Smith. Oxford: Oxford University Press, 1981.
Eliot, George. *Felix Holt the Radical.* 1866. Ed. Fred C. Thompson. Oxford: Clarendon, 1980.
——. *The George Eliot Letters.* Ed. Gordon S. Haight. 9 vols. New Haven: Yale University Press, 1955.
——. "The Natural History of German Life." 1856. In *Essays of George Eliot,* ed. Thomas Pinney. London: Routledge & Kegan Paul, 1963.

235

Engels, Friedrich. *The Condition of the Working-Class in England in 1844.* 1845. Trans. and ed. W. O. Henderson and W. H. Chaloner. Stanford: Stanford University Press, 1958.

Forster, E. M. *Howards End.* New York: Random House, 1921.

Gaskell, Elizabeth. *The Letters of Mrs. Gaskell.* Ed. J. A. V. Chapple and A. Pollard. Cambridge: Harvard University Press, 1967.

———. *The Life of Charlotte Brontë.* 1857. Harmondsworth: Penguin, 1975.

———. "Lizzie Leigh." 1854. In *Four Short Stories.* London: Pandora, 1983.

———. *Mary Barton: A Tale of Manchester Life.* 1848. Harmondsworth: Penguin. 1970.

———. *North and South.* 1855. Harmondsworth: Penguin, 1970.

———. *Ruth.* 1853. London: J. M. Dent, 1967.

Gaskell, Peter. *The Manufacturing Population of England.* London: Baldwin & Cradock, 1833.

Jewsbury, Geraldine E. *Marian Withers.* 3 vols. London: Colburn, 1851.

———. *Selections from the Letters of Geraldine Endsor Jewsbury to Jane Welsh Carlyle.* Ed. Mrs. Alexander Ireland. London: Longmans, Green, 1892.

Kay-Shuttleworth, J. P. *The Moral and Physical Condition of the Working Classes Employed in the Cotton Manufacture in Manchester.* 1832. Rpt. Shannon: Irish University Press, 1971.

Kingsley, Charles. *Alton Locke: Tailor and Poet.* 1850. Ed. Elizabeth A. Cripps. Oxford: Oxford University Press, 1983.

———. *Charles Kingsley: His Letters and Memories of His Life.* 1876. Ed. Fanny Kingsley. New York: Scribner, Armstrong, 1877.

Martineau, Harriet. *Illustrations of Political Economy.* London: Charles Fox, 1834.

Mayhew, Henry. *London Labour and the London Poor.* 1851. New York: Dover, 1968.

Stone, Elizabeth. *William Langshawe, the Cotton Lord.* 2 vols. London: Richard Bentley, 1842.

Tonna, Charlotte Elizabeth. *Helen Fleetwood.* 1840. 4th American ed. New York: Baker & Scribner, 1848.

———. *Personal Recollections.* 1840. New York: American Tract Society, 1851.

———. *The Wrongs of Woman.* New York: John S. Taylor, 1844.

Trollope, Frances. *Jessie Phillips: A Tale of the Present Day.* London: Henry Colburn, 1844.

———. *Life and Adventures of Michael Armstrong, the Factory Boy.* 3 vols. London: Henry Colburn, 1840.

Ward, Mrs. Humphry. *Marcella.* Harmondsworth: Virago Press, 1984.

Wordsworth, William. *The Poetical Works of Wordsworth.* Ed. Thomas Hutchinson. New York: Oxford University Press, 1933.

Secondary Works

Literary Studies

Auerbach, Nina. *Communities of Women.* Cambridge: Harvard University Press, 1978.

——. *Woman and the Demon.* Cambridge: Harvard University Press, 1982.

Bamber, Linda. "Self-Defeating Politics in George Eliot's *Felix Holt.*" *Victorian Studies* 18 (1975), 419–435.

Bayley, John. "*Oliver Twist:* Things as They Really Are." 1962. In *Dickens: A Collection of Critical Essays,* ed. Martin Price, pp. 83–96. Englewood Cliffs: N.J.: Prentice-Hall, 1967.

Bayne, Peter. "Charles Kingsley." In *Essays in Biography and Criticism,* 2d ser. Boston, 1860.

Beer, Gillian. *Darwin's Plots: Evolutionary Narrative in Darwin, George Eliot, and Nineteenth-Century Fiction.* London: Routledge & Kegan Paul, 1983.

Bergmann, Helena. *Between Obedience and Freedom: Woman's Role in the Mid-Nineteenth-Century Industrial Novel.* Gothenburg Studies in English 45. Gothenburg, 1979.

Blom, J. M. "The English 'Social-Problem' Novel: Fruitful Concept or Critical Evasion?" *English Studies* 62 (1981), 120–127.

Bodenheimer, Rosemarie. "Dickens and the Art of Pastoral." *Centennial Review* 23 (1979), 452–467.

——. "*North and South:* A Permanent State of Change." *Nineteenth-Century Fiction* (1979), 281–301.

——. "Private Griefs and Public Acts in *Mary Barton.*" *Dickens Studies Annual* 9 (1981), 195–216.

Brantlinger, Patrick. "The Case against Trade Unions in Early Victorian Fiction." *Victorian Studies* 13 (1969), 37–52.

——. "Dickens and the Factories." *Nineteenth-Century Fiction* 26 (1971), 270–285.

——. *The Spirit of Reform British Literature and Politics,* 1832–1867. Cambridge: Harvard University Press, 1977.

Braun, Thom. *Disraeli the Novelist.* London: George Allen & Unwin, 1981.

Briggs, Asa. "Private and Social Themes in *Shirley.*" *Brontë Society Transactions* 13 (1958), 203–214.

Brooks, Peter. *Reading for the Plot: Design and Intention in Narrative.* New York: Knopf, 1984.

Butwin, Joseph. "*Hard Times:* The News and the Novel." *Nineteenth-Century Fiction* 32 (1977), 166–187.

——. "The Pacification of the Crowd: From 'Janet's Repentance' to *Felix Holt.*" *Nineteenth-Century Fiction* 35 (1980), 349–371.

———. "The Paradox of the Clown in Dickens." *Dickens Studies Annual* 5 (1976), 115–132.

Carroll, David R. "*Felix Holt:* Society as Protagonist." In *George Eliot: A Collection of Critical Essays,* ed. George R. Creeger, pp. 124–140. Englewood Cliffs, N.J.: Prentice-Hall, 1970.

Caserio, Robert L. *Plot, Story, and the Novel.* Princeton: Princeton University Press, 1979.

Cazamian, Louis. *The Social Novel in England.* 1903. Trans. Martin Fido. London: Routledge & Kegan Paul, 1973.

Chaloner, W. H. "Mrs. Trollope and the Early Factory System." *Victorian Studies* 4 (1960), 159–166.

Chitty, Susan. *The Beast and the Monk: A Life of Charles Kingsley.* London: Hodder & Stoughton, 1974.

Collin, Dorothy W. "The Composition of Mrs. Gaskell's *North and South.*" *Bulletin of the John Rylands Library* 54 (1971).

Collins, Philip. "Dickens and Industrialism." *Studies in English Literature* 20 (1980), 651–673.

Craig, David. *The Real Foundations: Literature and Social Change.* London: Chatto & Windus, 1973.

Craik, W. A. *Elizabeth Gaskell and the English Provincial Novel.* London: Methuen, 1975.

David, Deirdre. *Fictions of Resolution in Three Victorian Novels.* New York: Columbia University Press, 1981.

Dawson, Carl. *Victorian Noon: English Literature in 1850.* Baltimore: Johns Hopkins University Press, 1979.

Duffy, Joseph M., Jr. "Another Version of Pastoral: *Oliver Twist.*" *ELH* 35 (1968), 403–421.

Eagleton, Terry. *Myths of Power: A Marxist Study of the Brontës.* London: Macmillan, 1975.

Easson, Angus. *Elizabeth Gaskell.* London: Routledge & Kegan Paul, 1979.

Empson, William. *Some Versions of Pastoral.* 1935. New York: New Directions, 1974.

Faber, Richard. *Proper Stations: Class in Victorian Fiction.* London: Faber & Faber, 1971.

Feltes, N. N. "To Saunter, to Hurry: Dickens, Time, and Industrial Capitalism." *Victorian Studies* 20 (1977), 245–267.

Fryckstedt, Monica Correa. "The Early Industrial Novel: *Mary Barton* and Its Predecessors." *Bulletin of the John Rylands University Library of Manchester* 63 (1980), 11–30.

———. *Elizabeth Gaskell's "Mary Barton" and "Ruth": A Challenge to Christian England.* Uppsala: Uppsala Universitet, 1982.

Gallagher, Catherine. *The Industrial Reformation of English Fiction: Social Discourse and Narrative Form, 1832–1867.* Chicago: University of Chicago Press, 1985.

_____. "The Politics of Culture and the Debate over Representation." *Representations* 5 (1984), 115–147.

Ganz, Margaret. *Elizabeth Gaskell: The Artist in Conflict.* New York: Twayne, 1969.

Garrett, Peter K. *The Victorian Multiplot Novel: Studies in Dialogical Form.* New Haven: Yale University Press, 1980.

Gérin, Winifred. *Elizabeth Gaskell.* Oxford: Oxford University Press, 1980.

Gilbert, Sandra M., and Susan Gubar. *The Madwoman in the Attic: The Woman Writer and the Nineteenth-Century Literary Imagination.* New Haven: Yale University Press, 1979.

Goodin, George. *The Poetics of Protest: Literary Form and Political Implication in the Victim-of-Society Novel.* Carbondale: Southern Illinois University Press, 1985.

Hardy, Barbara. "The Complexity of Dickens." In *Dickens 1970,* ed. Michael Slater, pp. 29–51. London: Chapman & Hall, 1970.

Heinemann, Helen. *Mrs. Trollope: The Triumphant Feminine in the Nineteenth Century.* Athens: Ohio University Press, 1979.

Holloway, John. "*Hard Times:* A History and a Criticism." In *Dickens and the Twentieth Century,* ed. John Gross and Gabriel Pearson, pp. 159–174. Toronto: University of Toronto Press, 1962.

Hopkins, A. B. *Elizabeth Gaskell: Her Life and Work.* London: John Lehmann, 1952.

Howe, Susanne. *Geraldine Jewsbury: Her Life and Errors.* London: George Allen & Unwin, 1935.

Jameson, Fredric. *The Political Unconscious: Narrative as a Socially Symbolic Act.* Ithaca: Cornell University Press, 1981.

Keating, P. J. *The Working Classes in Victorian Fiction.* London: Routledge & Kegan Paul, 1971.

Kestner, Joseph. *Protest and Reform: The British Social Narrative by Women, 1827–1867.* Madison: University of Wisconsin Press, 1985.

Kettle, Arnold. "The Early Victorian Social-Problem Novel." 1958. In *From Dickens to Hardy,* ed. Boris Ford. London: Cassell, 1963.

_____. "*Felix Holt the Radical.*" In *Critical Essays on George Eliot,* ed. Barbara Hardy, pp. 99–115. London: Routledge & Kegan Paul, 1970.

_____. *An Introduction to the English Novel.* 1951. 2 vols. New York: Harper & Row, 1968.

Kiely, Robert. "Plotting and Scheming: The Design of Design in *Our Mutual Friend.*" *Dickens Studies Annual* 12 (1983), 267–283.

Kincaid, James R. *Dickens and the Rhetoric of Laughter.* Oxford: Clarendon, 1971.

Knoeflmacher, U. C., and G. B. Tennyson, eds. *Nature and the Victorian Imagination.* Berkeley: University of California Press, 1977.

Korg, Jacob. "The Problem of Unity in *Shirley*." *Nineteenth-Century Fiction* 12 (1957), 125–136.
Kovačević, Ivanka. *Fact into Fiction: English Literature and the Industrial Scene, 1750–1850*. Leicester: Leicester University Press, 1975.
_____ and S. Barbara Kanner. "Blue Book into Novel: The Forgotten Industrial Fiction of Charlotte Elizabeth Tonna." *Nineteenth-Century Fiction* 25 (1970), 152–173.
Kucich, John. *Excess and Restraint in the Novels of Charles Dickens*. Athens: University of Georgia Press, 1981.
Lankford, William T. "'The Parish Boy's Progress': The Evolving Form of *Oliver Twist*." *PMLA* 93 (1978), 20–32.
Lansbury, Coral. *Elizabeth Gaskell*. Boston: Twayne, 1984.
_____. *Elizabeth Gaskell: The Novel of Social Crisis*. New York: Barnes & Noble, 1975.
Larson, Janet. "The Arts in These Latter Days: Carlylean Prophecy in *Little Dorrit*." *Dickens Studies Annual* 8 (1980), 139–196.
_____. "Identity's Fictions: Naming and Renaming in *Hard Times*." *Dickens Studies Newsletter* 10 (1979), 14–19.
Levine, George. *The Realistic Imagination*. Chicago: University of Chicago Press, 1981.
Lucas, John. *The Literature of Change*. New York: Barnes & Noble, 1977.
_____. *The Melancholy Man: A Study of Dickens's Novels*. London: Methuen, 1970.
_____. "Mrs. Gaskell and Brotherhood." In *Tradition and Tolerance in Nineteenth-Century Fiction*, ed. David Howard, John Lucas, and John Goode, pp. 141–205. London: Routledge & Kegan Paul, 1966.
_____, ed. *Literature and Politics in the Nineteenth Century*. London: Methuen, 1971.
McGann, Jerome. *The Romantic Ideology*. Chicago: University of Chicago Press, 1983.
Marcus, Steven. *Dickens from Pickwick to Dombey*. New York: Simon & Schuster, 1965.
_____. *Engels, Manchester, and the Working Class*. New York: Random House, 1974.
Martin, Graham. "*Daniel Deronda*: George Eliot and Political Change." In *Critical Essays on George Eliot*, ed. Barbara Hardy, pp. 133–150. London: Routledge & Kegan Paul, 1970.
Martin, Robert Bernard. *The Accents of Persuasion*. London: Faber & Faber, 1966.
_____. *The Dust of Combat: A Life of Charles Kingsley*. London: Faber & Faber, 1959.
Melada, Ivan. *The Captain of Industry in English Fiction, 1821–1871*. Albuquerque: University of New Mexico Press, 1970.

Miller, J. Hillis. "Nature and the Linguistic Moment." In *Nature and the Victorian Imagination*," ed. U. C. Knoeflmacher and G. B. Tennyson, pp. 440–451. Berkeley: University of California Press, 1977.

Mitchell, Sally. *The Fallen Angel: Chastity, Class, and Women's Reading, 1835–1880*. Bowling Green, O.: Bowling Green State University Popular Press, 1981.

Moers, Ellen. *Literary Women*. New York: Doubleday, 1976.

Moglen, Helene. *Charlotte Brontë: The Self Conceived*. New York: Norton, 1976.

Myers, William. "George Eliot: Politics and Personality." In *Literature and Politics in the Nineteenth Century*, ed. John Lucas, pp. 105–129. London: Methuen, 1971.

Newton, Judith Lowder. *Women, Power, and Subversion: Social Strategies in British Fiction, 1778–1860*. Athens: University of Georgia Press, 1981.

Pikoulis, John. "*North and South:* Varieties of Love and Power." *The Yearbook of English Studies* 6 (1976), 176–193.

Pinney, Thomas. "The Authority of the Past in George Eliot's Novels." In *George Eliot: A Collection of Critical Essays*, ed. George R. Creeger, pp. 37–54. Englewood Cliffs, N.J.: Prentice-Hall, 1970.

Poovey, Mary. *The Proper Lady and the Woman Writer*. Chicago: University of Chicago Press, 1984.

Sale, Roger. *English Literature in History, 1780–1830: Pastoral and Politics*. New York: St. Martin's Press, 1983.

Schwarz, Daniel R. *Disraeli's Fiction*. New York: Barnes & Noble, 1979.

Shapiro, Arnold. "Public Themes and Private Lives: Social Criticism in *Shirley*." *Papers on Language and Literature* 4 (1968), 74–84.

Showalter, Elaine. *A Literature of Their Own: British Women Novelists from Brontë to Lessing*. Princeton: Princeton University Press, 1977.

Shuttleworth, Sally. *George Eliot and Nineteenth-Century Science: The Make-Believe of a Beginning*. Cambridge: Cambridge University Press, 1984.

Smith, David. "*Mary Barton* and *Hard Times:* Their Social Insights." *Mosaic* 2 (1971), 97–112.

Smith, Frank Edmund. "Perverted Balance: Expressive Form in *Hard Times*." *Dickens Studies Annual* 6 (1977), 102–118.

Smith, Sheila M. *The Other Nation: The Poor in English Novels of the 1840's and 1850's*. Oxford: Clarendon, 1980.

Speare, Morris. *The Political Novel*. New York: Oxford University Press, 1924.

Spector, Stephen J. "Masters of Metonymy: *Hard Times* and Knowing the Working Class." *ELH* 51 (1984), 365–384.

Stewart, Garrett. *Dickens and the Trials of Imagination*. Cambridge: Harvard University Press, 1974.

Stone, Donald D. *The Romantic Impulse in Victorian Fiction.* Cambridge: Harvard University Press, 1980.

Sussman, Herbert L. *Victorians and the Machine: The Literary Response to Technology.* Cambridge: Harvard University Press, 1968.

Thompson, Fred C. "Politics and Society in *Felix Holt.*" In *The Classic British Novel,* ed. Howard M. Harper, Jr., and Charles Edge, pp. 103–120. Athens: University of Georgia Press, 1972.

Tillotson, Kathleen. *Novels of the Eighteen-Forties.* Oxford: Clarendon, 1954.

Uffelman, Larry K. *Charles Kingsley.* Boston: Twayne, 1979.

Vance, Norman. "Law, Religion, and the Unity of *Felix Holt.*" In *George Eliot: Centenary Essays,* ed. Anne Smith, pp. 103–121. New York: Barnes & Noble, 1980.

Vicinus, Martha. *The Industrial Muse: A Study of Nineteenth-Century British Working-Class Literature.* New York: Barnes & Noble, 1974.

Wallins, Roger P. "Mrs. Trollope's Artistic Dilemma in *Michael Armstrong.*" *Ariel* 8 (1977), 5–15.

Webb, Igor. *From Custom to Capital; The English Novel and the Industrial Revolution.* Ithaca: Cornell University Press, 1981.

Welsh, Alexander. *The City of Dickens.* Oxford: Clarendon, 1971.

Wheeler, Michael D. "The Writer as Reader in *Mary Barton.*" *Durham University Journal* 67 (1974), 92–102.

Williams, Raymond. *The Country and the City.* New York: Oxford University Press, 1973.

———. *Culture and Society, 1780–1950.* New York: Harper & Rows, 1958.

———. "Dickens and Social Ideas." In *Dickens 1970,* ed. Michael Slater, pp. 77–98. London: Chapman & Hall, 1970.

Yeazell, Ruth Bernard. "Why Political Novels Have Heroines: *Sybil, Mary Barton,* and *Felix Holt.*" *Novel* 18 (1985), 126–144.

Zimmerman, Bonnie. "*Felix Holt* and the True Power of Womanhood." *ELH* 46 (1979), 432–451.

Historical Studies

Ashby, M. K. *Joseph Ashby of Tysoe, 1859–1919: A Study of English Village Life.* 1961. London: Merlin Press, 1974.

Briggs, Asa. *The Age of Improvement, 1783–1867.* 1959. New York: Harper & Row, 1965.

———. *Victorian Cities.* New York: Harper & Row, 1963.

———. *Victorian People.* Chicago: University of Chicago Press, 1955.

———, ed. *Chartist Studies.* London: Macmillan, 1959.

——— and John Saville. *Essays in Labour History.* London: Macmillan, 1967.

Brown, Brian R. "Lancashire Chartism and the Mass Strike of 1842: The Political Economy of Working-Class Contention." Working paper no. 203. Center for Research on Social Organization, University of Michigan.

Cole, G. D. H. *British Working-Class Politics, 1832–1914.* London: George Routledge, 1941.

Hammond, J. L., and Barbara Hammond. *The Bleak Age.* 1934. Baltimore: Penguin, 1947.

———— and ————, *The Town Labourer, 1760–1832.* London: Longmans, Green, 1918.

Himmelfarb, Gertrude. *The Idea of Poverty: England in the Early Industrial Age.* New York: Knopf, 1984.

Hobsbawm, E. J. *Labouring Men: Studies in the History of Labour.* 1964. New York: Doubleday, 1967.

Jones, Gareth Stedman. "Class Struggle and the Industrial Revolution." *New Left Review* 90 (1975), 35–69.

————. *Outcast London: A Study in the Relationships between Classes in Victorian Society.* Oxford: Oxford University Press, 1971.

Joyce, Patrick. *Work, Society, and Politics: The Culture of the Factory in Later Victorian England.* New Brunswick, N. J.: Rutgers University Press, 1980.

Longmate, Norman. *The Hungry Mills.* London: Temple Smith, 1978.

————. *The Workhouse.* London: Temple Smith, 1974.

Murray, Janet. *Strong-Minded Women and Other Lost Voices from Nineteenth-Century England.* New York: Pantheon, 1982.

Neff, Wanda Fraiken. *Victorian Working Women.* New York: AMS Press, 1966.

Polanyi, Karl. *The Great Transformation.* 1944. Boston: Beacon, 1957.

Roberts, David. *Paternalism in Early Victorian England.* New Brunswick, N.J.: Rutgers University Press, 1979.

Rose, Michael E. "The Anti-Poor Law Movement in the North of England." *Northern History* 1 (1966), 70–91.

Rudé, George. *The Crowd in History, 1730–1848.* New York: Wiley, 1964.

Thompson, Dorothy. *The Chartists: Popular Politics in the Industrial Revolution.* New York: Pantheon, 1984.

————. "Women and Nineteenth-Century Radical Politics: A Lost Dimension." In *The Rights and Wrongs of Women,* ed. Juliet Mitchell and Ann Oakley. Harmondsworth: Penguin, 1976.

Thompson, E. P. *The Making of the English Working Class.* New York: Vintage, 1963.

————. "Patrician Society: Plebeian Culture." *Journal of Social History* 7 (1973–74), 382–405.

————. "The Peculiarities of the English." *Socialist Register* 1965, 311–362.

————. "Time, Work-Discipline, and Industrial Capitalism." *Past and Present* 38 (1967), 56–97.

Toynbee, Arnold. *The Industrial Revolution.* 1884. Boston: Beacon, 1956.

Walkowitz, Judith R. *Prostitution and Victorian Society: Women, Class, and the State.* Cambridge: Cambridge University Press, 1980.

Ward, J. T. *The Factory Movement, 1830–1855.* London: Macmillan, 1962.

_____. *The Factory System.* 2 vols. New York: Barnes & Noble, 1970.

Wiener, Martin J. *English Culture and the Decline of the Industrial Spirit, 1850–1980.* Cambridge: Cambridge University Press, 1981.

Yeo, Eileen, and E. P. Thompson. *The Unknown Mayhew.* New York: Random House, 1971.

Index

Library of Congress Cataloging-in-Publication Data

Bodenheimer, Rosemarie, 1946—
    The politics of story in Victorian social fiction / Rosemarie
Bodenheimer.
       p. cm.
    Bibliography: p.
    Includes index.
    ISBN 0-8014-2099-7 (alk. paper)
     1. English fiction—19th century—History and criticism.
2. Social problems in literature.   3. Politics in literature.
4. Labor and laboring classes in literature. 5. Women in
literature. 6. Women and literature—Great Britain. I. Title.
PR878. S62B63 1988
823'.8'09355—dc19   87-17313
                                                CIP